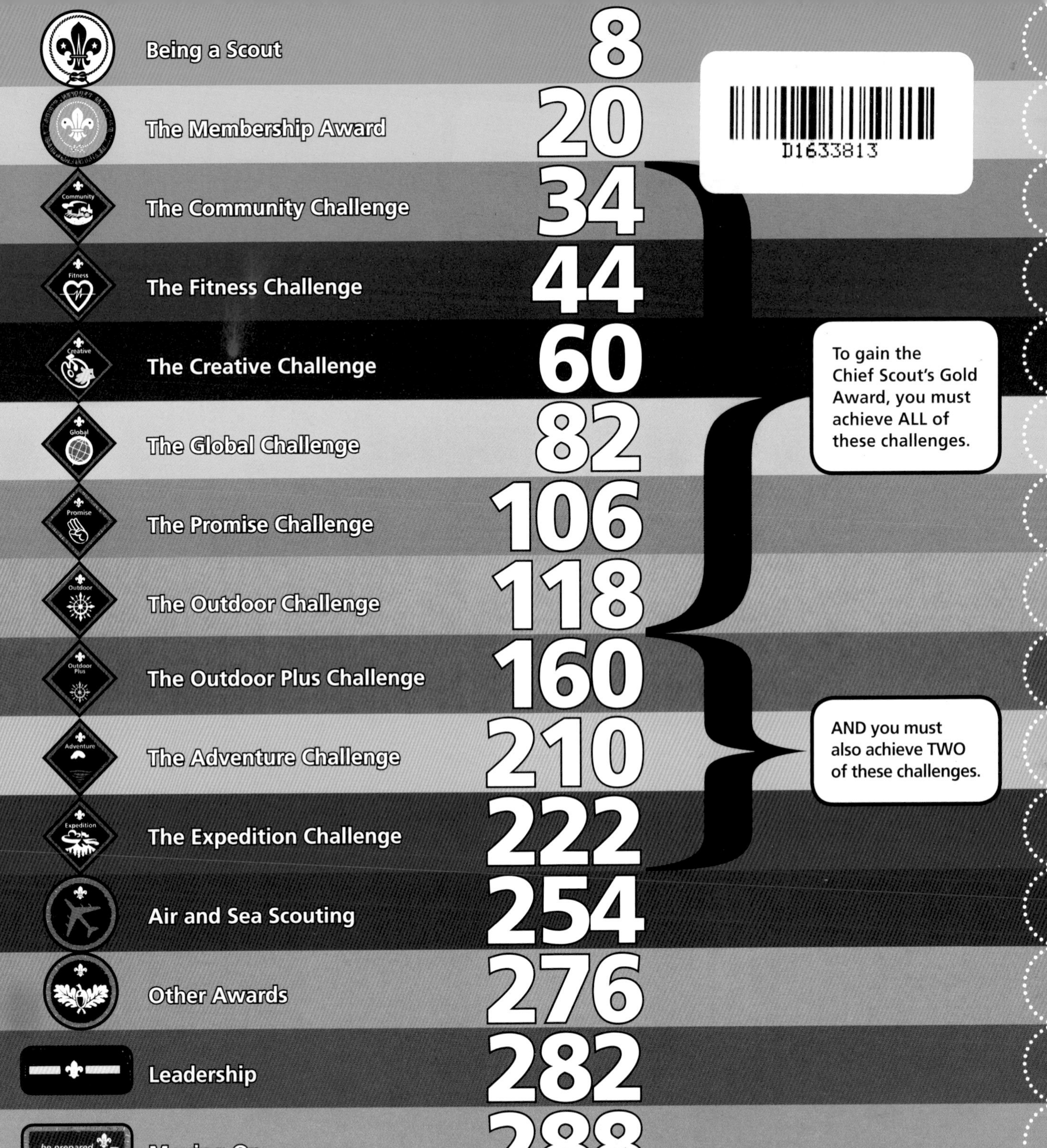
Being a Scout 8
The Membership Award 20
The Community Challenge 34
The Fitness Challenge 44
The Creative Challenge 60
The Global Challenge 82
The Promise Challenge 106
The Outdoor Challenge 118
The Outdoor Plus Challenge 160
The Adventure Challenge 210
The Expedition Challenge 222
Air and Sea Scouting 254
Other Awards 276
Leadership 282
Moving-On 288
To gain the Chief Scout's Gold Award, you must achieve ALL of these challenges.
AND you must also achieve TWO of these challenges.
D1633813
be prepared...

INTRODUCTION

Hi, and welcome to the *Scout Handbook*. I'm Hannah, and I'm the Patrol Leader of the Eagles. We're a Patrol made up of Scouts from around the UK, and we'll be popping up in this handbook telling you about our experiences at Scouts.

This book has been designed to help you achieve the Chief Scout's Gold Award, which is the highest award in the Scout section. To get it, you need to complete several challenges, and each challenge has a chapter in the handbook.

There's also information on the other badges available in Scouts, a chapter on water and air activities and a section on leadership. Finally, there's a bit about moving on to the next section, Explorer Scouts.

Even if you're not a Scout, there's plenty of tips and advice to help you with a variety of skills that will be useful in life, so get reading! If you enjoy Scouting half as much as we do, you'll be alright.

Yours in Scouting,

Hannah

GOING FOR GOLD
SO WHAT ARE YOU WAITING FOR?
START READING NOW!

INTRODUCING THE UK PATROL

Name: Ben
Age: 13
Claim to fame: Shares a birthday with David Beckham

Name: Darren
Age: 13
Favourite activity: Camping

Name: Hannah
Age: 10¾
Best adventure: Travelling to Switzerland with Scout Group

Name: Charlotte
Age: 11
Claim to fame: Has two Blue Peter badges

THE CHIEF SCOUT'S GOLD AWARD.

This is the highest award in the Scout section.
This book will help you know what you need to do to get there.

THIS CHAPTER IS A BACKGROUND TO SCOUTING:
HOW IT STARTED, HOW IT'S ORGANISED AND HOW YOU BELONG.
'I'm quite new to Scouts. Cubs do stuff, but at Scouts you do even more. Some of my friends spend half their time sat in their room playing on a games console, but at Scouts we're outside trying new things.'
Hannah

1 BEING A SCOUT

'Being a Scout is about doing loads of activities - camping, rafting, night hikes, pioneering. But it's also about the friendships that you make along the way. Thanks to Scouting I have friends in Malta and Portugal, plus plenty in my Troop.'
Cameron

THE SCOUT TROOP

When you join Scouts, you become a member of a Scout Troop. It is likely that there will be a weekly meeting for you to go to, but this is not the only way Scouts meet. You will get to do activities with your Troop at weekends, and there may be other events that happen with other sections and groups. You might also meet to discuss the way you do things at Scouts, and this is called the Troop Forum. This is a chance for all Scouts to have their say in the life of the Troop (see page 114 for more detail).

Most Troops have a Scout Leader, who is responsible for organising and planning the programme. However, you have an important say in what you do, and can plan and sometimes lead parts of the programme through the Troop Forum. Other leaders, assistant leaders and Troop assistants make up the leadership team and your Troop may also have Young Leaders.

Young Leaders are Explorer Scouts (aged 14-18) who learn leadership skills through the Young Leaders' Scheme, which they put into practice in the younger sections.

Every Troop is different, and people carry out different roles based on their skills, time and experience. As you get to know the Scouts in the Troop, you will also get familiar with who does what, and what skills they have.

Your Troop will probably be divided into Patrols – small groups of Scouts with a range of abilities and experiences, and a variety of names. You will do a lot of your Scouting in your Patrol, and this will have some of your best friends in it. Patrol Leaders and Assistant Patrol Leaders take the lead in the activity of the Patrol.

A typical Scout Troop on a typical day

Hilary * District Commissioner

In charge of Scouting in the District

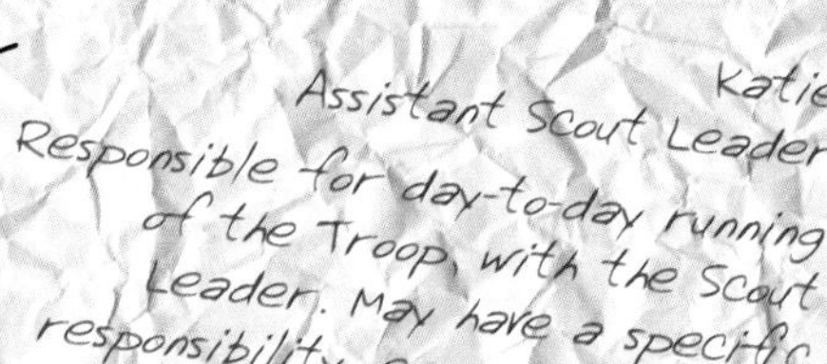

Katie

Assistant Scout Leader

Responsible for day-to-day running of the Troop, with the Scout Leader. May have a specific responsibility, eg Quartermaster

hris * Scout Leader

Responsible for the ay-to-day running of the Scout Troop

Adam

Young Leader (YL)

Explorer Scout who helps with the running of the Troop. Particularly useful at camps and renowned for building campfires

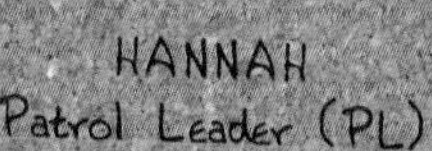

HANNAH

Patrol Leader (PL)

Organises the Patrol, plans the camp menu, helps plan the Troop's programme.

Gordon * Activity Instructor

Qualified to train Scouts in an adventurous activity (eg paddlesports) and may not necessarily attend every meeting

RUSHIL

Assistant Patrol Leader (APL)

Responsible for certain areas at camp and in team games

BEING A SCOUT

Scouts is not just something you do once a week; it's something you are. That's why this chapter is called Being a Scout. Unlike other clubs, Scouts are people who want to live a certain way and display values like caring for others, looking after the planet and having a positive outlook on life.

These values are best summed up in the Scout Promise and Scout Law, which every Scout makes when they get invested into the Scout Troop. In other countries the words of the Promise and Law vary, but all Scouts worldwide make a Promise, which means you belong to a global family of Scouts, starting in your Troop and extending to over 200 countries and territories from Albania to Zimbabwe.

PROMISE AND LAW

The Scout Promise

On my honour,
I promise that I will do my best,
To do my duty to God and to the Queen,
To help other people and to keep the Scout Law.

The Scout Law

1. **A Scout is to be trusted**
2. **A Scout is loyal**
3. **A Scout is friendly and considerate**
4. **A Scout belongs to the worldwide family of Scouts**
5. **A Scout has courage in all difficulties**
6. **A Scout makes good use of time and is careful of possessions and property**
7. **A Scout has self-respect and respect for others.**

The Promise and Law are explored in more detail in the next chapter.

HISTORY OF SCOUTING

Milestones in Scouting and in History

- 1901 > Death of Queen Victoria
- 1907 > Brownsea Island experimental camp; beginning of Scouting
- 1914 > Scouts enrol for war service
- 1920 > Baden-Powell acclaimed Chief Scout of the World at the first World Scout Jamboree
- 1939 > Germany invades Poland, starting World War II
- 1941 > Death of Baden-Powell (8 January); Air Scouts formed
- 1953 > Edmund Hillary and Tenzing Norgay summit Mount Everest
- 1966-67 > Major changes in Scouting: uniform, promise and law, age ranges
- 1969 > Apollo 11 moon landing
- 1982 > Start of Beaver Scouts
- 1984 > Daley Thompson wins second Olympic Gold for Great Britain in the decathlon
- 1992 > National Woggle Day
- 1997 > First Harry Potter book released
- 2007 > Centenary of Scouting celebrations

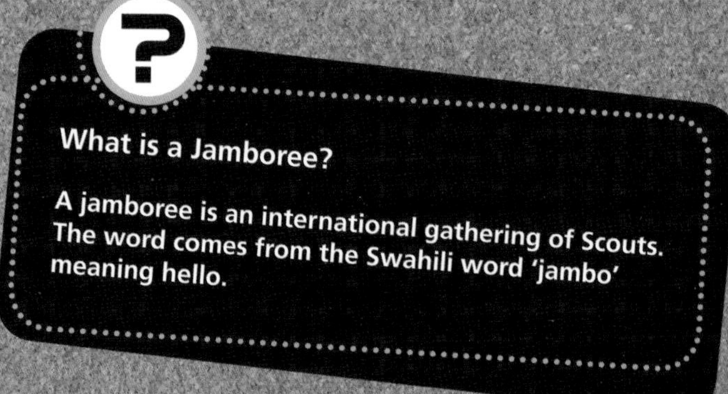

What is a Jamboree?
A jamboree is an international gathering of Scouts. The word comes from the Swahili word 'jambo' meaning hello.

1920 – London, UK

The only indoor Jamboree, held at Olympia arena.

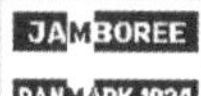

1924 – Copenhagen, Denmark

Attended by the King and Queen of Denmark.

1929 – Birkenhead, UK

Scouting's 21st anniversary, known as the 'coming of age' Jamboree.

1933 – Godollo, Hungary

B-P made rounds on a magnificent brown charger.

1937 – Vogelezang, The Netherlands

Last Jamboree attended by B-P before his death in 1941.

1947 – Moisson, France

Called Jamboree of Peace. Held just two years after the end of the Second World War.

1951 – Bad Ischl, Austria

Jamboree held while Austria was still under military occupation.

1955 – Niagara-on-the-Lake, Canada

First Jamboree held in the 'new world'.

1957 – Sutton Coldfield, UK

Golden Jubilee. Weather ranged from heat wave to storm.

1959 – Laguna, Philippines

First World Scout Jamboree in Asia

1963 – Marathon, Greece

Nearly 1500 UK Scouts chartered 20 aeroplanes to travel to this Jamboree.

1967 – Idaho, USA

Activities included a visit to a real wild west rodeo.

1971 – Asagiri Heights, Japan

Typhoon Olive struck the Jamboree site.

1975 – Lillehammer, Norway

Opened by Olav V, the King of Norway.

1983 – Kananaskis Country, Canada

Campers had to deal with the intrusion of bears, moose and other wildlife from time to time!

1987 – Sydney, Australia

First World Scout Jamboree to be held in the southern hemisphere.

1991 – Soraksan National Park, South Korea

The UK contingent took a replica of the Brownsea Island camp with them.

1995 – Dronten, The Netherlands

Theme was 'The future starts today' – Scouts learnt more about other people's ways of life.

1999 – Picarquin, Chile

First Jamboree to take place in Latin America.

2003 – Sattahip, Thailand

Around 35,000 participants attended from almost every country in the world.

2007 – Chelmsford, UK

Marked the Centenary of Scouting with a sunrise ceremony on the 1st August on Brownsea Island.

THE WIDER MOVEMENT

Scouts is the middle section in Scouting, and the oldest section in the Scout Group. You belong to a Group, which may include a Cub Scout Pack, a Beaver Colony, as well as other Troops.

Your Group may take part in events organised by the Scout District, the name for the grouping of several Groups in your local area. The Scouts in your Troop will wear a District badge to identify them.

A number of Districts make up a Scout County, Area or Region. These may also organise events and activities, in which you can take part.

On top of this there are also national events, like the Winter Camp at Gilwell Park and the Dino Pedal Car Championships (!)

Of course, it doesn't stop there! Many Scouts will have the opportunity to apply to attend a World Scout Jamboree. These take place about every four years, and are usually for Explorer Scouts aged 14-18. It's just one more reason to keep Scouting.

'For me, it's the range of activities that makes Scouting great. At an international camp at Blair Atholl I did gorge walking, hill walking and stilt walking, all in one day. There was barely time to breathe!'

Darren

OTHER SCOUT RESOURCES

Aside from this handbook, there are other resources that will help you during your time in Scouts. Here's a quick run down:

Scout Record Book – This is essentially for keeping a record of what you have achieved in Scouts and setting you in the right direction for your next challenge or activity badge. You can also record what camps and adventures you have been on and check how close you are to getting your Chief Scout's Gold Award.

Scout Badge Book – This is actually what it sounds like! You can find out all the requirements of all the badges available in the Scout section. Use it to plot your progress towards a badge, or to get ideas for a future activity.

Scout Skills Cards – These handy cards are useful in different types of situation you will find yourself in as a Scout. From reminding you how to light a fire, to teaching the phonetic alphabet, these cards are designed to be used when you're out and about, so keep them in your pocket with your *Badge Book*.

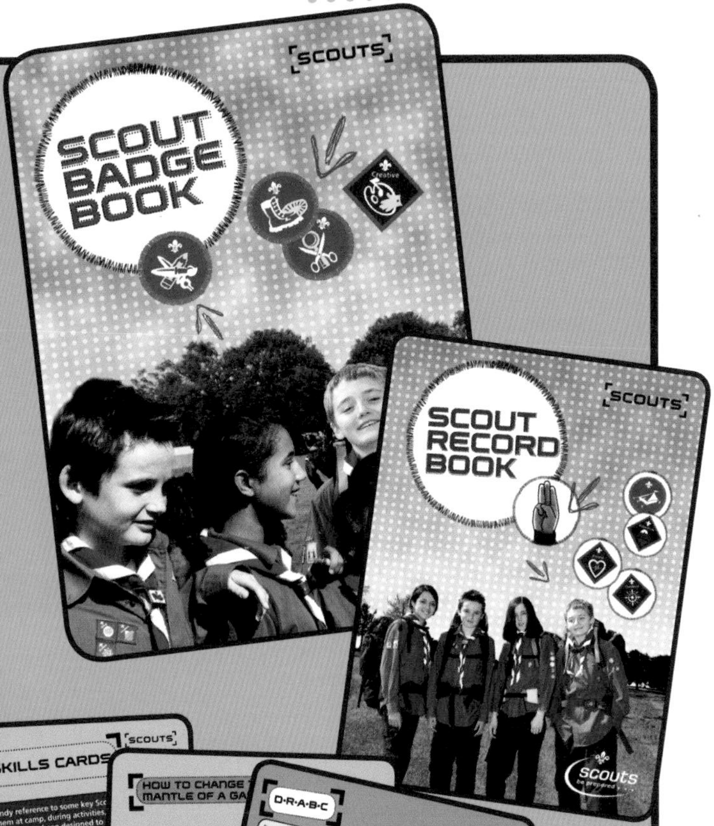

BADGES

Scouts are well known for doing a number of activities. To recognise achievement and participation, there are many badges to choose from, some of which you've already heard about. Here are a sample of other badges and awards you can gain:

> Activity badges
> Activity PLUS badges
> Activity Instructor badges
> Participation awards
> Partnership awards

Activity badges are listed at the end of each chapter as they usually involve activities which can be linked to a challenge. Details of the other badges and awards can be found in chapter 12, and also in the *Scout Badge Book*.

WWW.SCOUTS.ORG.UK/SCOUTS

Another place that you can find out lots of useful information is the Scout section's website www.scouts.org.uk/scouts.

There are the most up-to-date badge requirements and ideas that you can do in your Scout Troop.

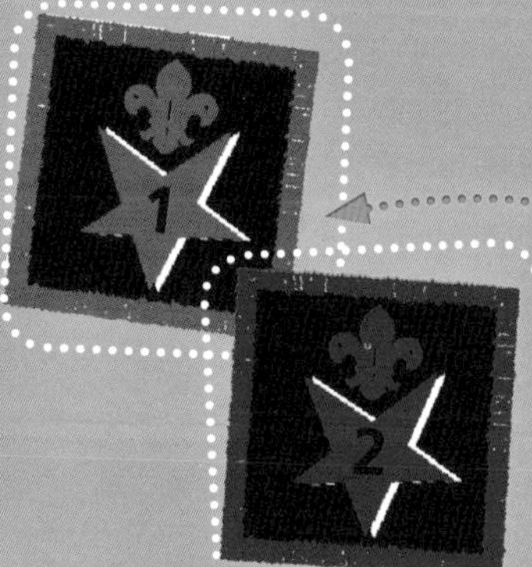

Participation badges 1 – 12

Activity badges

Activity PLUS badge

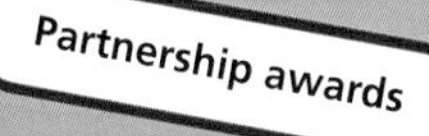

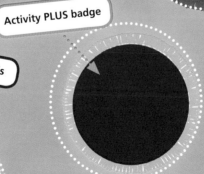

Instructor badge

'When I got invested
I knew I was joining something big
- with 28 million members across
the world, Scouts are making a big
difference everywhere and I want
to do my bit too.'
Charlotte

THE MEMBERSHIP AWARD

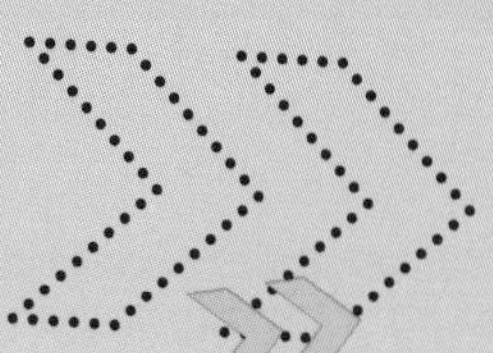

CHECK IT OUT!

AND LEARN HOW TO GET THE MEMBERSHIP AWARD!

REQUIREMENTS

Complete all of the following:

> Get to know the other members of the Troop and meet the Leaders, both in your Patrol and your Troop

> Find out about the ceremonies and traditions in your Troop

> Find out about the activities that your Patrol and your Troop does

> Know and understand the Scout Promise and Law and the rules of your Troop

> Know and understand the Scout Motto, Scout Sign, Scout Salute and Scout Handshake

> Show a general knowledge of the history and family of Scouts and of worldwide Scouting, eg by showing an understanding of the badges you will receive at your Investiture

> Know what to do at your Investiture.

KNOW ABOUT THE TROOP

The Scout Troop is the third section after Beavers and Cubs and is the oldest section in the Scout Group. You will be in Scouts roughly from the age of 10½ to 14, before moving on to Explorer Scouts.

The Scout Troop is led by a Scout Leader and a team of assistant Leaders and section assistants. Scout Troops are often divided into Patrols and each of these is led by a Patrol Leader and an Assistant Patrol Leader. Some Scout Troops also have Senior Patrol Leaders: their role varies from Troop to Troop.

Whilst in the Scout Troop you will take part in a wide range of exciting activities and camps whilst working towards your Chief Scout's Gold Award.

GET TO KNOW THE TROOP

You should get to know other members of your Patrol quite quickly as many of the activities you do will be with them. You should also make sure that you have full contact details of your Scout Leader, because it is likely that you or your parents will need to get in touch with them if you need information, to let them know if you are going to be absent from a meeting or an activity. Write their details in your *Scout Record Book*.

FIND OUT ABOUT THE CEREMONIES AND TRADITIONS IN THE TROOP

Ceremonies

Promises are often marked by a special ceremony such as the Christian Confirmation Service or the Sikh Amrit Ceremony (see page 108). Ceremonies are important as they are usually witnessed by other people who are able to remind us of the promises we made when we are finding them hard to keep.

In Scouting we have simple ceremonies when we make the Scout Promise.

When Scouts are being invested as members of the Scout Troop they make the Scout sign and say the Scout Promise. Many Investiture ceremonies take place in the Scout meeting place as part of the Troop meeting but some Troops are more adventurous about their Investiture ceremonies and they have taken place at the top of mountains or underwater in swimming pools!

Ceremonies are an important and a traditional part of Scouting. In the Scout section, they include the Investiture, Flag break and Flag down, Moving-On ceremony and inspections. You may have already witnessed or taken part in them. Many Troops have evolved their own particular way of doing things but there is no reason why you can't update your Troop's ceremonies after a discussion in your Troop Forum to check that they are still relevant.

In Scouting, whilst many ceremonies may have a tradition, they still play an important part today. They provide the opportunity to welcome people into Scouting, into another section, to recognise someone's achievements, and at the same time encourage self-discipline and mark a clear beginning or end to events.

Moving-On ceremony

The Moving-On ceremony for a Cub Scout moving on to Scouts often takes place at a convenient time for Cubs and Scouts to allow everyone to celebrate what you have achieved in your previous section and for you to look forward to the adventures that lie ahead in your new section.

Parade services

Many Scout Troops take part in parade services with their Scout Group or District when they attend a celebratory service, which may be part of a regular act of worship or might be for a particular Scouting occasion such as Founders' Day on 22 February or the Patron Saint of Scouting, St George's Day on 23 April.

Flag break

The ceremony of 'breaking' (that is to unfold a flag and hang it from a flagpole) the Union flag at the beginning of a meeting, event or camp is a sign of respect and serves to remind you of your duty to the Queen and our country.

Flags

The Union flag, as well as being the flag which is flown at the beginning of Troop meetings, is the flag that is often waved at national occasions such as The Last Night of the Proms or along processional routes. The flag is waved or flown from flagpoles by anyone wanting to celebrate a national event. It is a combination of the red and white cross of St. George (England), the blue and white saltire of St. Andrew (Scotland) and the red and white cross of St Patrick. This form of the flag comes from the union of England and Scotland in 1603. The red and white cross of St Patrick was incorporated in 1801 following the union with Ireland. When the flag was designed, Wales was already part of the Union, and this is why no dragon appears in the design.

In this picture, the flagpole would be to the left to ensure that the Union flag is flown the right way up.

The British flag is sometimes referred to as the Union Jack. Strictly speaking the term 'Union Jack' is a naval name for the Union flag used aboard ship. The Union flag takes precedence over all other flags and must always be flown from the 'senior' flagstaff, ie the highest of a group, or the flagpole to the left.

Flying one flag beneath another means that the lower flag has been defeated in battle.

A flag flown upside indicates 'I am in distress' and is primarily a naval signal. Other vessels in the area would then offer assistance if they were in a position to do so. In order to ensure that the flag is flown correctly, the broader diagonal white stripe should be to the left, at the top, nearest the flagpole.

Union flag (United Kingdom)

White background, red cross of St George

Blue background, white cross of St Andrew

White background, red cross of St Patrick

'It took me a little bit of time to realise I was flying the Union flag upside down - now I think I've got the hang of it!'

Hannah

On flag days the Union flag is flown from public buildings and government establishments.

Flag days in the UK

Month	Date	Occasion
January	20	Birthday of The Countess of Wessex
February	6	Her Majesty's Accession Day
	19	Birthday of the Duke of York
March	2nd Monday	Commonwealth Day
	10	Birthday of the Earl of Wessex
April	21	Birthday of Her Majesty the Queen
June	2	Coronation Day
	Variable	Official celebration of Her Majesty's birthday
	10	Birthday of Duke of Edinburgh
	17	Birthday of the Duchess of Cornwall
August	15	Birthday of The Princess Royal
November	2nd Sunday	Remembrance Day
	14	Birthday of Prince of Wales
	20	Her Majesty's wedding anniversary

Saints' Days

The Union Flag can also be flown on the days of the individual nations' patron saints' days, which are:

March 1 - St David's Day (Wales)

March 17 - St Patrick's Day (Northern Ireland)

April 23 - St George's Day (England)

November 30 - St Andrew's Day (Scotland)

This only applies to the relevant country

Folding flags

Flag down

Flag down is at the end of a meeting or event and marks the occasion as such. The flag is lowered at this time. A prayer or an opportunity for quiet reflection may be used either at the beginning or end of a meeting.

Flag break and flag down

These are part of most Troop meetings and you will find it valuable to have practised folding and hoisting the flag and breaking it, so that no embarrassing situations arise when it is your turn to break the flag.

Did you know that the Union flag is a constituent part of the national flags of four other Commonwealth countries:

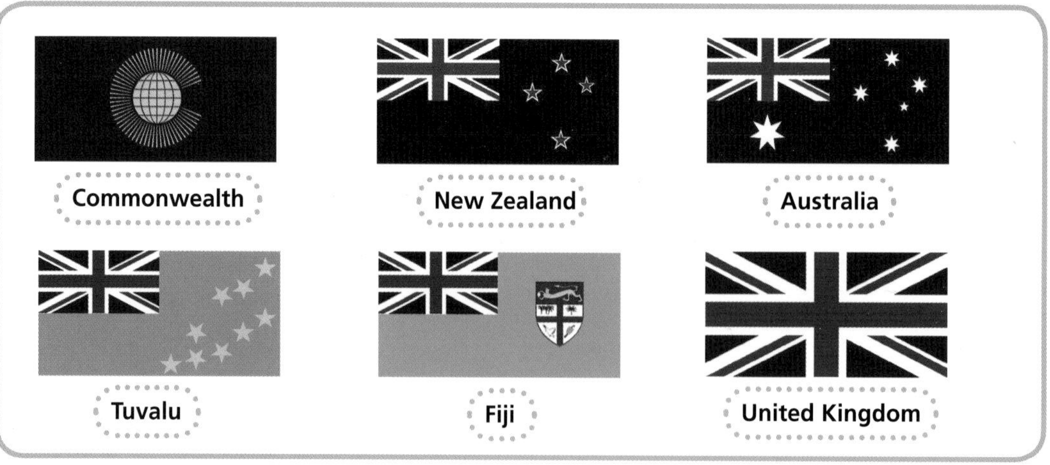

HOW TO PREPARE THE FLAG

Flag break:

> The Troop members fall in and traditionally form a horseshoe facing the flag standing 'at ease' (any leaders present stand on either side of the flagpole).

> The Troop is brought to the 'alert' and instructed to face the flag.

> The duty Patrol Leader walks up to the flag and pulls on the halyard or 'breaking rope' to break the flag.

> Once it has unfolded, the duty PL takes one pace back and leads the Troop in saluting the flag.

> The Scout then returns to their place in the Patrol. The Troop stand at ease.

Flag down:

> The Troop is assembled again in the horseshoe shape and brought to the alert. The Troop turns to face the flag.

> The duty Patrol Leader walks to the flag, unties the rope holding it in position and lowers the flag slowly and smoothly, ensuring it does not touch the ground, as this is considered disrespectful.

> The duty PL then takes on pace back, still facing the flag, and stands at the alert for a few seconds. No salute is given this time. Once the PL is back with his/her Patrol, the Troop is dismissed. Sometimes a short prayer or reflection is said before this.

> The flag is then folded and prepared for the next meeting.

Sea Scouts have a different ceremony for the beginning and end of meetings. It is called 'colours' and you can read more about this in chapter 12.

At camp, the procedure is much the same with Flag break at the start of the day's activities. It is carried out in the same manner as for an indoor meeting. It is quite appropriate for everyone to be dressed in camp kit at this time rather than have to change into uniform – although some Troops like to break the flag in uniform.

For flag down, which should be at a fixed time before sunset, the duty Patrol Leader goes to the flagpole. Scouts can either assemble, as for flag break, or a long blast on a whistle is sounded and everyone stops where they are and what they are doing, and stands to the alert facing the flag. The flag is then lowered. Then another signal is given to 'carry on'. The Scouts then attend to the flag by folding it and preparing it for the next day.

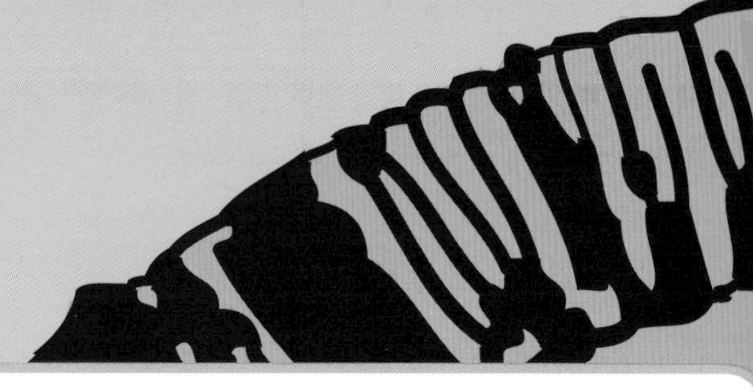

THE SCOUT PROMISE

On my honour,

I promise that I will do my best,

To do my duty to God and to the Queen,

To help other people and to keep the Scout Law.

UNDERSTANDING THE PROMISE AND LAW

Before you can make the Scout Promise you have to understand what it means, why you are making it and who you are making it to.

Scout Promise and Law

Scouting is distinctive as it has its own set of values – a Promise, a Law and a Motto.

The Scout Promise explained:

'ON MY HONOUR' means that this is a promise that you really mean to keep. This is why you wait a while before being invested, so that you can be sure about what you are promising to do.

Everyone tries to 'DO THEIR BEST.' As Scouts we include it in the Promise as a commitment to try our best in everything we do, at school, when playing games and, of course, at Scouts.

What about 'DUTY TO GOD'? Well, have you ever thought about what your God wants of you? God wants you to grow and learn and to be fully alive. In Scouts we grow and learn through the games we play and the activities we do together.

Duty 'TO THE QUEEN' is to show respect for our country. As Scouts in the United Kingdom, we do our duty to the Queen because she is the Head of State. We show this by saluting the Union flag and also by obeying the laws of the United Kingdom.

Scouts are always keen to 'HELP OTHER PEOPLE'. We can do this by working as a team to get jobs done and by using the skills that we have learnt so that we can help others to learn how to do things by themselves.

And finally 'TO KEEP THE SCOUT LAW'. On the next page, we have a look at what the Scout Law means.

Variations of the Promise

There are Scouts of all faiths and from all countries. Therefore people of other nationalities, who become Scouts in the United Kingdom may owe allegiance to their own country. To meet these circumstances, different forms of the Scout Promise can be made, which allow for the individual's obligations while upholding the essential spirit of the Promise. Similarly 'duty to God' can be adapted to more closely suit the faith and beliefs of Scouts making their Promise.

THE MEMBERSHIP AWARD 2

THE SCOUT LAW

A Scout is to be trusted.

A Scout is loyal.

A Scout is friendly and considerate.

A Scout belongs to the worldwide family of Scouts.

A Scout has courage in all difficulties.

A Scout makes good use of time and is careful of possessions and property.

A Scout has self-respect and respect for others.

... is to be trusted

When Scouts say they will do something, they will. When people know they can trust you, they will start to ask you to do more important and interesting things.

... is loyal

Loyalty means sticking to the side you have chosen. Lots of people are loyal to sports teams. In the same way, Scouts are loyal to their Troop and friends.

... is friendly and considerate

We can make lots of friends by sharing and thinking about other people rather than ourselves.

... belongs to the worldwide family of Scouts

No matter where you go in the world, you will find other Scouts who share something in common with you. They too will have made a Scout Promise.

... has courage in all difficulties

We have already talked about doing our best. By showing courage in all difficulties we are demonstrating that we will do our best, no matter what the situation.

... makes good use of time and is careful of possessions and property

By making good use of our time, we often find that there is more time for fun and to be useful in our communities. Scouts are also careful of possessions. If we take care of things, they will last longer and we can get more enjoyment out of them.

... has self-respect and respect for others

Scouts show self-respect by keeping fit and healthy and keeping smart. We show respect for others by respecting their property and opinions, even if we don't agree with them. Respect is important so that we can get along and work together.

SCOUT MOTTO, SIGN, SALUTE AND HANDSHAKE

The Scout Motto

The Scout Motto is:

BE PREPARED

It is based on Baden-Powell's initials, and is used and translated by Scouts all over the world.

The Scout Sign

The Scout Sign is made by Scouts when making or reaffirming the Scout Promise and at no other time. To make the Scout Sign, hold your little finger of your right hand with your thumb and extend the middle three fingers. Hold your hand level with you shoulder beside you.

The three fingers remind you of three important elements of the Scout Promise:

1. **Duty to God and to the Queen.**
2. **To help other people.**
3. **To keep the Scout Law.**

The Scout Salute

The Scout Salute is made only by members of the Movement in uniform on formal Scout occasions. Beaver Scouts do not use the salute. Make the Scout Sign with your right hand down by your waist. Then bring the hand up in a salute, hold by the temple (with palm facing out) and then bring down to your side. The correct way of doing the Scout Salute can be remembered by 'long way up, short way down.'

The Scout Handshake

Scouts traditionally shake hands with their left hand as opposed to their right.

The original reason for Scouts adopting a left hand shake is disputed, and perhaps we will never know the whole truth. One popular story says that B-P got the idea from chiefs of the Ashanti tribe during a military campaign. Because warriors would hold their shield in the left hand, they would lower it to shake with, leaving them unprotected. Therefore, the left handshake is a mark of trust, which links nicely to the first Scout Law.

True or not, Scouts certainly have a distinctive way of greeting each other, and much delight can be derived from giving the Scout Sign or Scout Handshake to a Scout from another country, to see them return it with gusto!

ACTIVITIES

As well as meeting weekly your Troop is likely to have a programme of other activities, camps and expeditions. Your Scout Leader may have published a programme of these activities which they will be able to give you. Your Troop may also have a website and you may be able to find out from that what the Troop has been doing recently and what planned activities there are to come. You could also ask Scouts what camps they have been on recently and where the next camp is going to be.

'When doing the salute, remember: 'Long way up, short way down.'
Ben

A BRIEF HISTORY OF SCOUTING

The young Baden-Powell

Scouting was started by a man called Robert Baden-Powell (or B-P for short). As a boy, B-P enjoyed the outdoors and spent many hours pretending to be a hunter or an Indian scout. He also went on expeditions with his brothers, often exploring the coast by boat. When they were not on the water, they were hiking in the countryside, carrying everything they needed on their backs.

The siege of Mafeking

When B-P left school he joined the British Army. He travelled all over the world, serving in India and South Africa. While he was in South Africa during the Boer War, B-P led the defence of a small town called Mafeking against the Boers. The Boers, who were Dutch farmers that had settled in South Africa, outnumbered his men nine to one.

The boys of Mafeking

B-P defended Mafeking for seven months. As there were so few soldiers, he asked local boys to be messengers. When help finally came, B-P became a national hero in Britain for his great achievement.

The returning hero

On returning to Britain from South Africa, B-P saw that, apart from sport, young people in Britain had very little to do. B-P remembered what he had learnt in Africa and decided to teach boys in Britain those skills.

Brownsea Island

To test his new methods B-P organised a camp for 20 boys on Brownsea Island, Dorset during the summer of 1907. Over the course of a week, B-P taught the boys exploring, camping, boating, life-saving and lots more activities, all of which Scouts still do today.

Scouting for Boys

After the camp, B-P wrote a book based on his experience in the Army and at Brownsea Island. It was called *Scouting for Boys*.

Thousands of boys all over the country bought the book and formed themselves into Patrols, taking part in the activities they had read about.

The Patrols asked adults to become their Leaders and so the Patrols formed Troops.

Scouting for girls?

Following the release of Scouting for Boys, Scout Troops began forming all over the country, with boys taking the initiative and trying out the adventures described in B-P's handbook. From the outset, girls were as attracted to the idea as much as boys, and did not want to be left out. Baden-Powell believed Scouting could be as much benefit for girls as boys. The attitude of society at the time was not so sure, and so the Founder set about devising a scheme that would adapt Scouting for girls. In 1910 a programme was launched for Girl Guides, with their own handbook and B-P's sister as President. Later, Baden-Powell's wife, Lady Olave, would become World Chief Guide, as Girlguiding grew alongside Scouting. Since then times have changed and girls can now join Scouting in any section.

First World Scout Jamboree

In 1920, the first World Scout Jamboree was held at Olympia in London. At the Jamboree, Scouts attended from many different countries and camped for eight nights. At this Jamboree, B-P was declared the first and only Chief Scout of the World.

A home for Scouting

In 1919, The Scout Association was given a large estate in Epping Forest called Gilwell Park. Since then, it has been used as a campsite for young people and a training centre for leaders. To this day, Gilwell Park is known to Scouts all over the world as the home of Scouting. When B-P was made a Baron in 1929, he chose to be known as Lord Baden-Powell of Gilwell.

World Scouting

Scouting spread quickly all over the world, and there are now over 28 million Scouts in more than 200 countries. It is estimated that over 250 million people all over the world have been Scouts at one time or another. Most Scouts have a Promise and many receive the same Membership Badge that you have or are about to receive.

The death of Baden-Powell

B-P died in 1941 in Kenya. On his death, Lord Somers became the Chief Scout. Since then, the title of Chief Scout of the United Kingdom has been held by Lord Rowallan, Lord Maclean, Sir William Gladstone, Major-General Michael Walsh, Sir Garth Morrison, George Purdy and Peter Duncan.

KNOW WHAT TO DO AT INVESTITURE

The Investiture, or joining ceremony, is one of the most important events in a Scout's life and is treated with respect. You may like to invite your family along to the occasion.

In addition to making your promise, investitures vary from Troop to Troop and you should make sure that you are well prepared and fully aware of the Investiture ceremony procedure used in your Troop before you are invested. You should ask your Patrol Leader or your Scout Leader if you are unsure about anything.

'Helping other people may be part of the Scout Promise, but it's more than that. At Scouts we learn about the local community, so that we can be an active part of it and get the most out of the local area.'
Cameron
Community
Global
Adventure

GET TO KNOW YOUR LOCAL COMMUNITY...

REQUIREMENTS

Complete the activities in the two following areas. Examples are provided below but other activities can also be undertaken.

Area 1 – Exploring the local community

> **Explore one aspect of how the local community works and is organised to the benefit of its members. The project should include some fact-finding, a visit to or from a community facility or group and some form of report back.**

For example: visits to see the workings of a theatre, tourist attraction, railway station, airport, local industry; chances to meet people involved in local government, charities, faith groups, interest groups; opportunities to hear about/take part in community traditions/customs, local clubs and interest groups.

Area 2 – Community service

> **Take an active part in some form of local community service totalling at least six hours. The time may be spent doing a number of different projects or by showing commitment to a single project over a longer period of time.**

For example: running a fund-raising stall or game; delivering leaflets, clearing an area, gardening, collecting materials for recycling, helping with activities for younger children; moving furniture, clearing debris, painting fences, environmental projects. Where possible the service should link in with the visit in Area 1.

EXPLORING THE LOCAL COMMUNITY

Introduction

One day in 1909, just two years after Baden-Powell had founded Scouting in the UK, a very wealthy American newspaper publisher, William D Boyce, was visiting London. Popular legend has it that he became lost in a London fog and that a young Scout emerged from the gloom and helped him find his hotel. What impressed Boyce was that the Scout refused a tip, saying that Scouts do not accept rewards for doing good turns. The following day, the American visited the offices of the Boy Scouts to find out more about this new organisation and the following year he founded the Boy Scouts of America at a meeting in Chicago.

During the Second World War, Scouts helped the emergency services, especially when our big cities were under attack; carrying messages when the telephones were destroyed and watching out for buildings on fire. Sea Scouts watched the shore for enemy invasion and Air Scouts were helping identify enemy aircraft.

Today all over the world Scouts are involved in helping others where they live often, in times of trouble, but also just lending a hand to make things better for everyone.

VISITS AND VISITORS

There are many places in your local area that would make the perfect venue for a visit. Communities are unique, and there are far too many places to list in this book, but it's up to you to find a place that will prove interesting to you and other Scouts in your Troop.

Here are some ideas of places to visit:

Police station

The police exists to reduce crime and disorder and make communities feel safer. Your local police station will be different to that of other Scouts based on where you live in the UK. For example, not all police stations have cells, and not all stations are open 24 hours a day.

You may go through your whole life never having to go to a police station, so a visit for the Community Challenge could be a real eye-opener!

Could your visit include a look inside an empty cell, a look at police cars or a demonstration of police dog units or interrogations in the interview room? Knowing the local police officers can help you get the most out of your community, as you never know when you might need their help.

Conservation project

Conservation happens in every community in a multitude of ways. It could be related to a country park, forest, coastal path, waterway, tourist attraction or area of natural beauty. Conservation is sometimes carried out by the local authority, or it may be a special organisation with a particular interest or expertise. Therefore there are many options open to you for deciding where to visit.

On your visit, try to find out what is needed to do the conservation work. Where does the funding come from? How many people are involved? You may discover that there are barriers to conservation, caused by people in the community. Sometimes the reckless actions of young people damage the heritage of an area, eg graffiti on public buildings or structures. Human erosion caused by large numbers of people can wear away coastal paths.

Visiting a conservation project may stimulate your interest in preserving your local heritage, and could lead on to service with a local conservation project.

Clearing a pond as part of a forest conservation project

Hospital or doctor's surgery

It is highly unusual that anyone goes through life never going to hospital, but 40 years ago 25% of people in the UK were born at home – now 97% are born in hospital!

You may be able to visit a hospital ward, health centre or surgery out of hours, and see what goes on behind the scenes. Discover what equipment is needed and what doctors do with the information they get on a patient. You may have a particular interest, like the blood service or prosthetics. See if you can find out about this during your visit.

In the UK, the National Health Service is available to all citizens, and employs more than 1.5 million people. What about other countries? By visiting a local health service, you might appreciate the benefits of having local, accessible, largely free healthcare on offer.

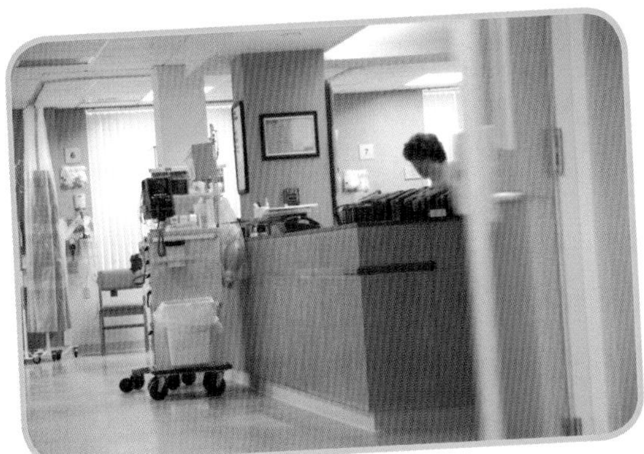

Fire Station

Even if your nearest fire station is many miles from your meeting place, the fire and rescue service is a great place to visit – after all, if you have the misfortune to suffer a fire, it's them that will be coming to your aid!

The fire station serves the community in more ways than you may think – much of the service's work with young people will concentrate on preventing fires through education rather than dealing with putting them out. Sadly, there are people who deliberately set fires without a full understanding of the consequences.

Getting to know the fire station and members of the local service will help you appreciate the men and women who put their lives on the line to protect the community.

Transport network

You could visit a transport provider vital to your locality. If you live near an airport, see if you can visit the control tower or air traffic controllers. A railway station could be the base to learn about what the signalman does, or how the tracks are repaired without causing huge delays.

If you live near a port you could ask a ferry service to show you what it takes to get large numbers from one side to the other. Similarly a bus depot could introduce you to the range of buses that service an area, what ages the vehicles are and how often they are cleaned.

This could lead to your patrol doing a bus wash for your community service, or doing a survey of passengers that you can feed back to the company.

Waste disposal and recycling

The UK produces about 330 million tonnes of waste a year, which amounts to around 517kg per person! All this needs to be disposed of, and there are facilities in your local area for disposing of waste and recycling as much as possible.

Your Troop could visit a recycling centre and learn from a recycling officer about what your local authority does with your rubbish. Could they do more? What are the biggest challenges? Seeing the journey of an aluminium can might make you think more carefully about where you dispose of it.

Learning what can and can't be recycled will make you better at managing your household's waste. It will also help you to campaign for better recycling facilities in your neighbourhood.

HOW AN ASPECT OF THE COMMUNITY IS ORGANISED

As part of the Community Challenge, you will find out about an aspect of your local community. This could be about a range of things or could be focused on:

- a local historical figure and how they made an impact locally, nationally or internationally
- the transport system. How the system meets the needs of different groups of your community; how they link up with each other or serve particular facilities, such as shops
- local emergency services
- an historical landmark and its importance
- the work of a farm
- wildlife and the environment: for example a badger set or the introduction of a species like red kites to your area
- a project researching a local harbour, shoreline or waterway; its history, particular currents and navigational aspects, the bridges, trade, craft, etc in the area you choose. You might focus on wildlife or the effects of pollution
- an airfield (used or disused), showing a plan of the runways, use of various buildings, flight paths, navigation beacons etc. This could include a history of its use and types of aircraft that might have flown from, and possibly crashed, there.

PREPARATORY FACT FINDING

Now you have looked in to aspects of the community you should pick one aspect to research. Start by doing some preparatory fact finding. Bear in mind that you will need to give a 'report back' on this, so you may like to think of some questions to ask on your visit.

ORGANISE A VISIT

Having decided where you are going, find out who to contact, either through the internet or telephone directory. If necessary, you should then write to them to ask whether you can visit, telling them the number of Scouts attending and what you would like to gain from your visit. Below is a sample letter:

1st Littleton Scouts
c/o 101 Little Street
Littleton
Wessex
LW21 4DJ

Dear Sgt Smallman,

I am writing on behalf of the 1st Littleton Scout Troop. We are currently undertaking our Community Challenge, and need to visit a community facility to find out about how it works. I was wondering if the Troop would be able to visit the police station on Wednesday 14th October? There would be about 12 Scouts aged 10-14, and we would be accompanied by our Leaders. We are keen to see what goes on inside the station, and possibly visit a cell!

Please let me know if this is possible, or if an alternative Wednesday can be arranged at your convenience.

Yours Sincerely,

William

Patrol Leader, 1st Littleton Scouts

Make sure you keep your Scout Leader informed about the visit. You should also write a letter to Scouts and their parents about the visit, if the whole Troop is to attend.

FEEDBACK

Make a report of your findings.

You could:

> make a static display, with maps, models and photos

> present it live, sharing the talk between you

> add a computer presentation of photographs and graphics

> create a blog

> present your findings to a Troop meeting, Parents' Evening, District event or AGM

> present the results to your school or college.

Don't wait to be invited. Ask your Scout Leader, Group Scout Leader or District Commissioner if you can have time and space to present the results of your work.

COMMUNITY SERVICE

To gain the Community Challenge, you need to take an active part helping people in your community for six hours as a volunteer. This may be in one day, a weekend or spread over a number of weeks. Your community service could be done as an individual, small group or with the whole Troop. It could entail:

> joining 'working parties' at your local campsite

> assisting with a youth group for younger children

> helping children learn to ride at a stables or horse riding club

> making and serving tea at a pensioners' club

> helping with worship at your place of worship

> visiting an elderly or housebound person with a friend

> becoming a regular helper at a city farm, dance class or play centre.

One Scout Troop carries out a DIY day at their District Scout Headquarters each year to help with the maintenance.

Another Troop did a 'community audit' and identified three problems: people sleeping rough, notices stopping children playing ball games and high rates of truancy in schools. As a result they baked and sold cakes to raise money for a local centre for the homeless, they produced new signs telling children where they could play ball games and they wrote their concerns about schools to the local Education Committee.

You might choose to become involved in shore line or river clear-ups, canal restorations, surveys on erosion and shore sea life. Some Scouts helped with fundraising for the RNLI by packing customers' bags at local supermarkets. Another Troop annually cleans up the local river by removing shopping trolleys and rubbish to make it safer and more accessible for the local community, and their own activities.

You may choose to help with marshalling at air displays, helping as guides or as ground crew with gliding, parascending and flying clubs. Scouts annually help at the UK microlight fair, stewarding and marshalling under supervision at air displays.

THE WIDE WORLD OUTSIDE OF SCOUTING IS CALLING YOU!

Don't stop at Scouting! You may choose to join the committee or group who plan the running of a club or society you belong to. Your church council, village hall committee, community centre or youth club may need young people to help with decision making, or you could put yourself up for election for your school, or faith group council. You may learn to 'chair' or take minutes ... but don't sit there moaning at other people... Get involved and change things for the better!

Cleaning up a public area

Sorting waste for recycling

Cooking a meal for the community

ASSOCIATED ACTIVITY BADGES

Administrator

Heritage

Emergency Aid (Staged)

Librarian

Fire Safety

Naturalist

Guide

Public Relations

'I like to keep fit anyway, so Scouts provides many opportunities to play games and sports with my friends. More than this, Scouting promotes a healthy lifestyle, getting lot of fresh air, eating wisely and staying away from harmful substances.'

Michael

Fitness

GET ACTIVE!

REQUIREMENTS

Complete the activities from one of the following two areas, demonstrating a noticeable improvement in the chosen discipline.

Area 1 - Physical Challenge

Choose a physical challenge which is new or which builds on an earlier achievement. The challenge could be an athletic event, a charity swim, a long distance cycle ride, a pool life-saving test or a long distance challenge hike. Indeed, it could be any event that requires the need to physically train in order to succeed. Consider a variety of activities/interests in choosing this challenge, and agree your choice with a leader.

To complete the challenge:

a. Spend between four and six weeks preparing for the event, through an agreed programme of activity/training.

b. Show an understanding of the importance of a sensible and appropriate diet and the need for sufficient sleep.

c. Be able to explain the dangers and harmful effects of smoking, alcohol and drugs.

d. Successfully take part in the chosen physical challenge.

Area 2 - Physical Development

Choose a physical activity, which you wish to develop.

For example: circuit training, football skill training, aerobics routine, light weight training.

To complete the challenge:

a. Exercise regularly over a period of four to six weeks and keep a record that shows improvement over this period.

b. Show an understanding of the importance of a sensible and appropriate diet, and the need for sufficient sleep.

c. Be able to explain the dangers and harmful effects of smoking, alcohol and drugs.

SENSIBLE AND APPROPRIATE DIET

My body – How does it work?

Your body is made up of billions of cells. These cells are the basic structural units of the body. Each one has a specific function. Cells depend on the blood to bring them the oxygen they need to survive, and to carry away the waste carbon dioxide.

For this process to work, you need a fit and healthy body, and a healthy heart.

Keeping fit helps you to stay positive, healthy and prepared for any challenge.

The heart

The heart is the powerhouse that drives the blood around the body, taking with it vital oxygen and nutrients. It is the most important muscle in the body. To keep your heart fit and strong it needs exercise. However, you cannot exercise your heart directly; you can only do it by exercising other muscles. You should aim to exercise at least two to three times a week for at least 20 minutes at a time.

If you are a keen sportsman or athlete, you probably do more than this already. If you are not keen on sport, you should still look for ways to exercise two or three times a week. You might consider:

- walking to and from school each day
- joining a swimming club
- cycling regularly.

Human development

Almost all of the body's development takes place in the first 18 years or so of life – after that it is simply a matter of maintenance and the replacement of worn-out parts. You have obviously grown a lot since you were born, and you probably have some more growing to do before you reach your full adult size.

Adolescence

Between the ages of 10-15 – earlier for some girls – come the changes that turn you from a child into an adult. These do not happen all at once, but gradually. With the onset of puberty, boys will start to grow hair on their face and body, and their voices deepen or 'break'. Sexual organs develop in readiness for parenthood. Girls will begin to have periods. Many teenagers experience a growth spurt. With these changes come changes in your feelings: you start producing more hormones, and this can cause sexual thoughts, which you may find disturbing or even exciting – perhaps both.

There is nothing unnatural or wrong in such feelings. They are a necessary part of growing up, and all young people go through this process of development at about your age. It may help you to understand what is happening to you if you can talk to a parent or another adult with whom you feel at ease. Or, if you would find such a discussion a bit embarrassing, you could ask a teacher or another adult to recommend a book or leaflet you could read.

Useful web link: www.ruthinking.co.uk

A healthy diet

Can you describe the most sophisticated machine on the planet? What does it look like? What can it do? How does it work? Believe or not you can see the most sophisticated machine on the planet in most bedrooms and bathrooms around the world – just look in a mirror!

The human body is complex and performs hundreds of tasks without you telling it to. Not only that, it can heal and repair itself, grow, regulate temperature, learn and respond to new information.

It is said that 25 minutes after a pregnant woman contracts a cold, the body has already made the antibodies to fight the disease and protect the baby in the womb. Do you realise how amazing you are?

Despite all this, your body needs to be given the right foods and nutrients to function to the best of its ability.

Carbohydrates – Your body burns most of what you eat for energy. The energy that goes out through exercise needs to be matched by the energy you put in through a healthy diet. Energy mainly comes from carbohydrates. Carbohydrates are found in foods such as bread, potatoes, pasta, cereals as well as sugary products. When you eat more carbohydrate than you need, it is stored in the muscles and liver as glycogen.

Fats – Fats are foods that are greasy and will not dissolve in water. Your body stores such fats for burning in the future. Fats are found in the fat of meat, cheese and butter as well as in oil.

Proteins

Proteins build up, maintains, and repair the tissue in your body. They are found in meat, dairy products, pulses and nuts.

5-a-day

Eating five or more servings of fruits and vegetables a day is part of an important plan for healthier living. That's because fruits and vegetables provide the wide range of vitamins, minerals, fibre, and natural chemicals your body needs to maintain good health and energy levels, protect against the effects of ageing, and reduce the risk of cancer and heart disease.

Salt content

Too much salt is bad for your heart and can raise your blood pressure. Young people and adults aged over 10 should eat no more than 6g of salt a day.

Staying hydrated

It is important you stay hydrated to stay healthy, especially if you are enjoying an activity which is causing you to sweat, or on warm, muggy days. Thirst is a good indicator that you need to drink, but by the time you feel thirsty you are already dehydrated.

One of the best tests for dehydration is your urine. If it is light yellow or colourless and odour free you are hydrated; if it is dark coloured and smelly, you are definitely dehydrated.

To stay hydrated remember to:

1. Drink in the morning either a full glass of fruit juice or milk
2. Drink during the day (Take a water bottle to school or camp)
3. Drink in the evening; have a tall glass of drink with your meal
4. Drink more during activities (Take a water bottle when playing football)
5. Drink after activity, eg water or sports drink
6. Drink some more (Get in to the habit of drinking water)

A good guideline is drinking 2.5 litres per day.

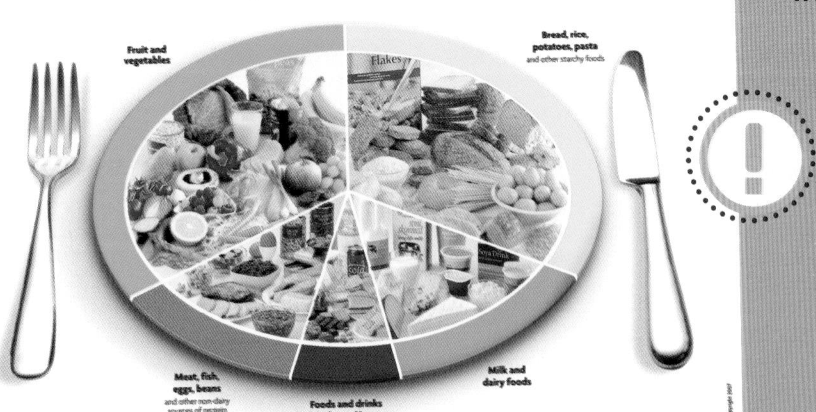

Useful web links:

www.5aday.co.uk
www.eatwell.gov.uk
www.bbc.co.uk/health

NEED FOR SUFFICIENT SLEEP

Sleep may seem a fairly pointless state, but it is actually really important. We need sleep as much as we need oxygen. Sleep increases our efficiency, extends lifespan and cures illnesses; we shouldn't deprive ourselves of sleep.

Regular sleep patterns

You should be getting between seven and nine hours of sleep per night, it is important to get in to a good pattern of sleep to improve your mood and efficiency during the day.

SMOKING

Even the smoothest running machine will grind to a halt if you pour sand into its works. In the same way, drugs like nicotine and alcohol can seriously damage the human body.

Smoke free

Britain is now smokefree and it is illegal to smoke in any enclosed public space. Tobacco is a widely used legal drug. Smoking has been directly linked to lung cancer and heart disease. It is very dangerous for a mother to smoke during pregnancy as it can adversely affect her unborn child.

Tobacco is a stimulant that gives smoker a 'lift' and helps them to cope with stress. Unfortunately, nicotine, the main drug in tobacco, together with the other gases in cigarette smoke, damage not only the lungs and the heart but can lead to a whole series of health problems from tooth decay to cataracts and hearing loss.

Despite all the dangers, one in five 15-year-old boys still smoke, and as many as one in three teenage girls.

While you are still young, your body can recover from the effects of smoking once you stop. However, it can be difficult to quit and requires more than a little perseverance. Modern research suggests that those that start smoking in their teens and continue into their thirties may well have shortened their life by 20 years.

For help and advice on quitting – www.quitbecause.org.uk

Effects of smoking:

- bad breath / smell
- antisocial behaviour
- yellow finger nails
- unpleasant for others
- addiction
- affects mood and self control
- respiratory problems, eg poor stamina, sport performance

Dangers

- lung cancer
- heart disease
- breathing difficulty

4

What the law says

> You must be 18 or over to purchase cigarettes in the UK.

'Smoking is just a ticket to death. You can get cancer, you'll die younger. Sometimes it's hard to say no because people might think you're a wimp and they won't be friends with you anymore, but that's no way to be friends with someone. A friend wants what's best for you, and smoking isn't.'

Charlotte

'I think alcohol's over-rated. People think it's the only way to have fun. I think sometimes people are more addicted to the idea of alcohol than the drink itself. There's loads of other ways to have fun ... if they joined a Scout Group they'd see.'

Rushil

ALCOHOL

In the UK there are strict laws on the sale and consumption of alcohol, but it is still freely available and is linked to more deaths each year than all illegal drugs put together.

Drinking in moderation is not usually a problem. Indeed for those in their middle age and beyond, moderate drinking can lower the risk of coronary heart disease. Drinking alcohol becomes a problem when heavy drinking and drunkenness become frequent. Many young people experience their first regular drinking in their mid teens. Moderate drinking for men is regarded as three or four units of alcohol per day. For women this would be two to three units.

Useful web link – www.truthaboutbooze.com

What is a unit of alcohol?

Alcohol content is measured in units. One unit contains 8g of pure alcohol. Different drinks contain different amounts of alcohol, depending on their strength and the quantity served. A 440ml can of beer, cider or lager at 4% (alcohol by volume) is equal to 1.8 units. A 125ml glass of wine at 12% ABV is 1.5 units. You can find out more about alcohol units at www.units.nhs.uk.

Binge drinking

To drink double or more than the recommended amount is referred to as 'binge drinking.' Regular heavy drinking puts a huge strain on the liver and can lead to cirrhosis (liver damage). However, alcohol is associated with between 15,000-22,000 deaths per year in the UK – many through accidents that might otherwise not have happened or through violence brought on by alcohol.

At any hospital A&E department, as many as 70% of admissions between midnight and 5 am can be alcohol-related. Half the victims of violent crime have said that their attacker was under the influence of drink.

Effects of alcohol:

- addiction
- loss of self control
- memory loss
- affects mood/judgement

Dangers:

- diseases (eg alcohol poisoning)
- liver damage
- poor judgement can lead to injury

Law:

- it is illegal to sell alcohol to under 18s
- under 18s should never consume alcohol during any Scouting event.

DRUGS

Statistics show that 25 per cent of young people aged 16-24 have tried illicit drugs in the past year. Many more than this will have been offered illegal drugs or seen them used socially or at home. The pressure to 'fit in' and take drugs is a reality, but it is important that you know the facts about drugs and consequences of abusing them before making a decision.

The largest consequence of taking drugs is addiction. Most illegal drugs have an addictive quality: some addiction is physical and some is psychological. If a drug is physically addictive, the user will experience a change in body chemistry, so if they stop taking the drug, they will have withdrawal symptoms, eg sweating, shaking, sickness. Psychological addiction is more common and isn't restricted to drug use. People who are psychologically dependent on drugs feel like they need to take drugs to carry on, even if they don't get the withdrawal symptoms above.

Taking drugs is a risky business. The pure fact that the drug is illegal means that you don't know what you're taking, as it does not come with the information you get with legally sold products. Often, the seller will have as little an idea about the content as you do, and this is very dangerous for your health and wellbeing.

Some drugs are depressants (alcohol, heroin, methadone, solvents, tranquilisers) and others are stimulants (amphetamines, cocaine, crack, ecstasy). Hallucinogens (cannabis, magic mushrooms, LSD) cause the mind to change the way it perceives things, and can lead to dangerous behaviour based on a false sense of invincibility. Long-term use of any illegal drug can lead to aggressive behaviour, depression, and psychotic episodes.

Useful links:

FRANK – www.talktofrank.com
The Site – www.thesite.org

'You don't have to try cannabis or heroin just to see what it is like. You have probably never tried drinking sulphuric acid either, because you know it wouldn't do you any good. It is much smarter to just say NO.'

Ben

Effects of drugs:

> addiction
> loss of self-control
> passing out
> change of heart-rate and body temperature
> paranoia

Dangers:

> mental illness
> panic attacks
> depression
> criminal prosecution and imprisonment

Law:

> it is illegal to buy, sell or grow illicit drugs, regardless of age
> drugs are classified under The Misuse of Drugs Act, 1971. Possessing drugs is treated as follows:

  > Class A - 7 years in prison + fine
  > Class B – 5 years in prison + fine
  > Class C – 2 years in prison + fine

> driving under the influence of drugs is a serious offence, and the maximum sentence for causing death by driving on drugs is 14 years.

KEEPING FIT

Warm up exercises

It is important that we warm up before exercising. This is because our muscles are like chewing gum. If you take cold chewing gum and stretch it, it snaps. If it is warmed up, it stretches. This is the same with our muscles. You should spend about 10-15 minutes warming up before strenuous exercise to get your muscles warmed up and improve blood flow. This will prevent injury and muscle stiffness.

You should begin your warm up slowly, building up gradually. The warm up should focus on the muscles you will be using during your activity. For example if you are playing football, you should concentrate on your leg muscles.

A good warm up has three stages:

1. Gentle aerobic exercise such as jogging or skipping, involving the whole body.
2. Gentle stretching, starting at the top of the body and moving down.
3. Cardiovascular exercise such as jogging or skipping.

Once you have warmed up, you should move straight into your activity.

Warm down

It is easy to forget to 'warm down' after exercise, but this is equally important. The warm down helps to return the body to its normal state. It helps to effectively break down the build up of waste products from activity such as lactic acid.

A good warm down should repeat the first two stages of the warm up.

1. Gentle aerobic exercise such as jogging or skipping, involving the whole body.
2. Gentle stretching, starting at the top of the body and moving down.

Useful web links:

Need 2 know - www.need2know.co.uk

NHS LiveWell - www.nhs.uk/livewell

FIVE SIMPLE EXERCISES

1 Shoulder stretch
2 Neck stretch
3 Quadriceps stretch
4 Hamstrings stretch
5 Back stretch

FITNESS ACTIVITIES

A – athletics
B – basketball
C – cycling
D – dance
E – equestrianism
F – fencing
G – golf
H – hockey
I – in-line skating
J – jogging
K – kayaking
L – long jump
M – martial arts
N – night hikes
O – orienteering
P – press ups
Q – quick cricket
R – roller skiing
S – swimming
T – tennis
U – unicycling
V – volleyball
W – walking
X – cross country
Y – yoga
Z – zorbing

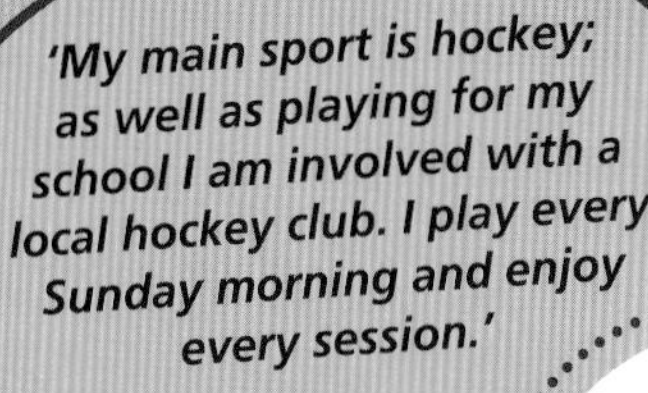

'My main sport is hockey; as well as playing for my school I am involved with a local hockey club. I play every Sunday morning and enjoy every session.'

Ben

'At school we do netball and basketball. At Scouts I took part in a 25 mile bike ride.'

Charlotte

'I play for a bowls club and have been doing so for around 4-5 years. Some think it's not a game for young people, but it is becoming quite a competitive sport with a youth league.'

Darren

SIX WEEK LOG

Week	1						2						3					
	Mon	Tue	Wed	Thu	Fri	w/e	Mon	Tue	Wed	Thu	Fri	w/e	Mon	Tue	Wed	Thu	Fri	w/e
Pulse (bpm)																		
Detail of exercise																		
1 km run	5:20		5:14		5:10		5:12		5:01		4:37							
5km cycle		22:48		22:30				22:35		22:17								
100m swim						4:50						4:20						

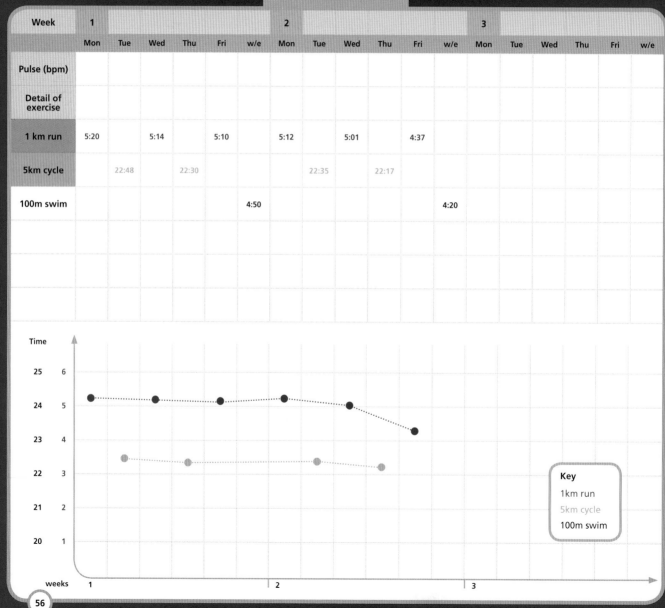

Time

25 6

24 5

23 4

22 3

21 2

20 1

weeks 1 2 3

Key

1km run

5km cycle

100m swim

4						5						6					
Mon	Tue	Wed	Thu	Fri	w/e	Mon	Tue	Wed	Thu	Fri	w/e	Mon	Tue	Wed	Thu	Fri	w/e

4 5 6

SIX WEEK LOG

Week		Detail of exercise	Pulse after exercise (bpm)	Target for improvement
1	Mon			
	Tue			
	Wed			
	Thu			
	Fri			
	w/e			
2	Mon			
	Tue			
	Wed			
	Thu			
	Fri			
	w/e			
3	Mon			
	Tue			
	Wed			
	Thu			
	Fri			
	w/e			
4	Mon			
	Tue			
	Wed			
	Thu			
	Fri			
	w/e			
5	Mon			
	Tue			
	Wed			
	Thu			
	Fri			
	w/e			
6	Mon			
	Tue			
	Wed			
	Thu			
	Fri			
	w/e			

ASSOCIATED ACTIVITY BADGES

Athletics

Orienteer

Cyclist

Physical Recreation

Life Saver

Winter Sports

Martial Arts

Sports Enthusiast

Master at Arms

Swimmer (Staged)

'For my Creative Challenge I enjoyed the 'making things' parts most. I constructed mousetraps and paper aeroplanes, and then got adventurous by designing my own ice cream flavours - triple chocolate was the best!'

Darren

Creative

REQUIREMENTS

!

Complete activities from three of the six following areas:

Area 1 – Performing

> Take part in a performance in front of an audience.

For example: short play, series of sketches, performing magic tricks, singing, playing a musical instrument, a Scout Show, a dance, or a puppet show.

Area 2 – Crafts

> Have a go at some creative crafts.

For example: glass painting, macramé, art-straws, leatherwork, photography, sweet making, decorative knotting, or candle making.

Area 3 – Promotions

> Promote local Scouting.

For example: a newsletter, poster, video, website, audio-based broadcast, or display.

Area 4 – Problem solving

> Take an active part in activities requiring a number of problem-solving skills, effective teamwork and creative thinking.

For example: incident hikes or timed challenges, mental, physical or skill.

Area 5 – Construction

> Construct a model.

For example: model aircraft, 3-D jigsaw, model pioneering project, and model campsite.

Area 6 – Worship

> Take a leading role in preparing and participating in an Act of Worship or Scouts' Own.

For example: selecting or creating readings, prayers or music. This could be at a Troop meeting, residential experience or event.

MAGIC TRICKS

Wow your family and friends with some simple but effective magic tricks...

Magic can be scientifically explained, so it is known as a 'trick'.

Magic has played an important part in history:

> The Egyptians are thought to have been the first to create magic tricks and simple deceptions.

> Ancient Greeks and Romans built devices into temples to create miraculous effects, such as automatically-opening doors. Audiences believed the priests were using special powers from the gods.

> In medieval times, magic was thought to be witchcraft, with those performing it burned at the stake or drowned. It was later proven that anyone could perform such illusions.

> In the 19th century, magic became widely acceptable by society. A watchmaker called Robert Houdin turned his hand to magic, developing tricks with explanations. His influence encouraged many more magicians, including Harry Houdini (real name Erich Weiss), probably the most famous magician, who performed death-defying illusions and escapes.

Magic tricks were also used in theatres to create special effects, such as making ghosts appear on stage. Magic is now a popular form of entertainment. As the audience we are normally baffled with what we see, although we know it's a trick.

A good magic performance will distract the audience from how it actually works. The most common way of doing this is by saying magic words or waving a magic wand.

Try the following tricks, and see if you can fool your audience.

The gravity-defying card

You will need:

> a piece of card or paper (you could use a playing card)

> a volunteer

> a carpeted room.

The trick:

1. Challenge your volunteer to stick the card to the wall, without using anything to attach it. They won't be able to, as it will just fall down
2. Go to the wall yourself, rubbing your feet on the carpet on the way over. Push the card against the wall and as if by magic, it will stick
3. You can get your volunteer to inspect the card, to make sure nothing sticky has been used.

How it works:

> The card sticks because when you rub your feet on the carpet you generate static electricity. This gives the card a small positive charge, which attracts it to the negative charge of the wall.

> You might disguise your shuffling along the carpet by saying some 'magic words.' Make sure that you are wearing rubber soled shoes and that the wall is not made of metal.

Disappearing water

You will need:

> a jug of water

> a plastic cup

> a piece of card (you could use part of a cereal packet)

> a towel – just in case!

The trick:

1. Allow your audience to inspect your cup and piece of card to check that there is nothing unusual about them.
2. Half fill the cup with water.
3. Place the piece of card over the top.
4. Holding onto the card, turn the cup upside down. Then say some 'magic words'.
5. Carefully remove your hand from the card – and as if by magic the water remains in the glass.

How it works:

> The water stays in the glass because of air pressure. The air pressure pushing up against the card is greater than the gravity pulling on the water. Therefore, it doesn't come out of the cup.

> To make the trick more interesting, you might try it over the head of a volunteer. Just make sure that you have practised it first or they may get a nasty surprise!

Magic mind reading

You will need:

> a pack of coloured crayons

> a volunteer.

The trick:

1. Give the pack of crayons to a volunteer in the audience. Ask them to inspect the pack, to make sure that they are all the same (except for the colour).
2. Turn around and place your hands behind your back. Ask them to put a crayon into your hands and then put the rest of the crayons out of sight.
3. Turn back around to face the audience.
4. With your hands still behind your back, scratch the chosen crayon with your nail (getting some of the colour into your nail). Make it look like you are trying to concentrate on the colour of the crayon. Then bring the hand with the marking in front, placing it on your forehead, making it look like you are really concentrating hard. Whilst doing this, take a sneaky look at the colour in your nail – you'll then be able to tell the colour of the crayon they chose.
5. Amaze your audience with the answer.

CIRCUS SKILLS

Juggling

Juggling can be difficult to start with, but practice makes perfect.

> Start with one ball. A tennis ball, beanbag or apple is ideal.

> Imagine two spots in front of your head about 20cm apart. These are the points you will be aiming to throw your juggling balls to.

> Hold your hands at waist level and toss the ball to the other hand, via the imaginary point. Then throw it back again.

> Try not to touch the ball with your fingers. Clutching it will make it harder to control. Just catch and throw it, using the palm of your hand.

> Once you are confident, try adding in a second ball, throwing them between your hands. The second ball shouldn't be thrown at the same time as the first. When the first ball passes through its imaginary spot, then the second ball should be thrown, so there will be a slight delay between throws.

Note: Resist the temptation to pass the second ball between hands while the first ball is in the air. This is cheating! Both balls must be thrown in a similar fashion.

Next you can try three balls.

1. Hold two balls in your right hand and one in your left. Toss one of the balls from your right hand.
2. As it passes the imaginary spot, toss the ball from your left hand and catch the first ball.
3. As the second ball passes its imaginary spot, throw the other ball from your right hand and then catch the second ball.
4. Keep repeating this process and you're juggling. If it doesn't quite work, keep practising and maybe go back to practising with two balls.

Tip: Juggle facing a wall; it will stop you throwing the balls forward (and if you do, they will bounce off the wall).

Poi

Poi is a type of juggling using a traditional Maori dance prop from New Zealand. The word poi means 'ball' in Maori. Women used poi to maintain the flexibility of their hands for weaving, whilst Maori men would use them for developing the strength and co-ordination required for battle.

The poi are swung around rhythmically at speed, creating different patterns in the air.

Make your own:

You can make your own poi using a pair of football socks and two tennis balls.

- Put a tennis ball inside each sock. Hold the sock at the top. It should be around the length of your arm (if not, hold the sock further down or wrap it around your hands).
- You now have your own poi to practise some moves with. You may shorten or lengthen your poi as you get used to them.

Forward swing:

Hold your poi, one in each hand, using a couple of fingers. With your palms facing down, swing the poi either side of you in a forward motion.

Backward swing:

The same as forward swing, but with your palms facing up. Swing the poi in a backwards motion.

Butterfly:

Hold out your arms in front of you. Start to swing your poi in equal timing. Slowly rotate your palms inwards, towards each other. The poi will start to cross over each other in different directions.

There are lots of other poi moves which you can try out. Why not try and create some of your own?

CANDLE MAKING

You will need:

- newspaper
- a flat surface
- two stainless steel saucepans
- heat source (oven hob or gas stove ring)
- candle wax (you can use old candles)
- towels / kitchen roll
- wicks
- pencil
- measuring jug
- moulds (use plastic containers, plant pots, etc.)
- scientific thermometer (a normal household one won't be good enough)
- additives (such as stearin, which helps the candle to burn longer; and vybar, which hardens the candle and helps add to the scent)
- colour dyes.

(Some of these items you will have, others can be bought from candle making shops and specialist craft websites quite cheaply.)

Safety: Before you start working with hot wax read these rules:

- Always wear old clothes, cover work surfaces with newspaper and avoid working on rugs and carpets
- Keep a pile of newspapers nearby in case of spillage
- Always give yourself plenty of room to work in and keep your workspace clean and tidy
- Have all materials and equipment to hand
- Keep equipment clean and unused materials in sealed containers away from dirt and dust.

Using wax.

- When using wax, treat it like cooking oil. Below 100°C is fairly safe, but higher than that it is likely to catch fire as the wax turns to vapour. Remember wax will not boil, it will just get hotter and hotter
- Never leave hot wax unattended
- After use do not pour excess molten wax down the sink as it will set and block your drainpipe. Instead pour it into an old container – it can be remelted later.

Spillage!

- Wax on carpets and items of clothing – scrape off the excess wax and remove the rest by placing a paper towel over the stained area and pressing with a hot iron. This will transfer the wax to the towel
- Wax on metal or plastic objects - place in a freezer for an hour to make the wax brittle. Then crumble the hardened wax, or scrape off.

In the event of a fire:

- do not move the pan
- smother flames with the saucepan lid or a damp towel
- do not attempt to extinguish with water. This will only spread the fire as the wax will float on the surface of the water
- if wax overheats it begins to smoke and give off an acrid smell. If this happens turn down the heat source immediately and allow the wax to cool. Then turn off the heat source completely

There are two basic ways to create a candle:

> using a mould

> dipping a wick into wax to build up layers

The first method is described below.

Using moulds

> You do not need to buy special moulds. Have a look around the house and garden and you will find suitable objects, eg terracotta plant pots, foil containers, ice cream tubs. Make sure whatever you use can withstand the temperature of the wax, has no holes for the wax to leak through, and is at least as wide if not wider at the top as it is at the bottom, otherwise the candle will not come out. An empty juice or milk container makes an ideal mould as it can be torn away as the candle cools.

> To melt wax, use a double boiler (two saucepans, one inside the other). Never leave a double boiler unattended as the water will quickly evaporate unless you keep topping it up. You need to heat the wax to a temperature of 82°C (use a specialist thermometer to measure - normal household ones will not go high enough).

Instructions:

1. Calculate the amount of wax needed by filling the mould with water and measuring it.
2. Put the wax into the top of the double boiler and fill the outer pan a third full with water. Heat on a medium setting on heat source.
3. Melt the wax to 82°C.
4. Prime your wick by placing required length into the melted wax until it starts to release bubbles. This means that the wick has absorbed sufficient wax. Carefully remove it (don't use your fingers – the wax is hot!). Let the wick dry.
5. When the wick is hard (after a couple of minutes) insert it through a small hole at top of mould and pull it through. Secure it around a pencil at the open end and plug the small hole to prevent wax from leaking out.
6. Add your additives. For 500g of wax you will need to add three tablespoons stearin and ½ teaspoonful vybar. These will help the candles burn more effectively. Add your colour dyes a small amount at a time.
7. Pour wax into mould. Before the wax sets tap the side of the mould several times to release trapped air bubbles.
8. When the wax has set to a tacky consistency, poke small holes in the candle around the wick. This will help to prevent air pockets inside the finished candle that can be a fire hazard.
9. Leave to set for a few hours.
10. As the wax sets it will shrink so you will need to remelt left over wax and top up the mould. When it is set, remove from mould.

PHOTOGRAPHY

Taking photographs can be a great way to record an event. For many, it is also a hobby. Knowing how to use the features of your camera will help you to get the most from it.

Know your camera!

There are three main types of camera:

- Single use cameras. Single use cameras are an inexpensive way to take photos and great for camping with, as it doesn't matter as much if they get broken. They are built with a film inside and once this is used up, the whole camera is sent for processing.
- 35mm and APS compacts. Compacts have a built in lens and normally include features such as a flash and auto-focus. Compacts can be used over and over again by either replacing the film or formatting the memory. Compacts are good for taking general photos.
- Single lens reflex (SLRs). SLR cameras give greater artistic control as they can be combined with a vast range of interchangeable lenses and accessories. You can also adjust almost every setting on the camera.

Digital cameras come in both compact and SLR formats. You will most probably have a compact digital camera.

Parts of a camera

Your camera may include some or all of the following features:

- flash
- zoom
- lens
- viewfinder
- mode dial
- macro mode
- flash settings.

Taking a photograph for the Scout Handbook. Can you spot the photo he took?

Memory cards

Digital cameras save images onto memory cards. This allows you to view your image straight away, normally on a liquid-crystal display (LCD) screen. If you don't like the picture you can delete it.

Tiny sensors in the camera convert the image to 'pixels' (short for picture elements) and then save it onto the memory card. The amount of photos a card will store will depend on the size of the card, the resolution of the camera (measured in megapixels) and the amount of compression applied when storing the photos.

The higher the number of megapixels, the better the resolution and printing quality.

Resolution guide

Megapixels	Print size
≤1 megapixel	On screen use
1.3 megapixels	6″x 4″
2 megapixels	8″ x 6″
4 megapixels	10″ x 8″
≥5 megapixels	10″ x 12″

Composing a photograph

When taking your photographs, experiment! Try shots from different angles and using different settings. Try using height or lying on the ground to get a different style of shot. Try using the time delay to take pictures of yourself.

Find an interesting subject, good colours and use of light. The subject doesn't always have to be in the centre.

Most digital cameras will have specific modes for different situations:

> sport. A faster shutter speed, helping it to take faster action shots, such as a volleyball match

> night

> portrait.

Try mixing modes and see what effects you can get.

Macro mode

When taking photographs of detailed objects close up, use the macro mode found on most cameras. This changes the cameras focus distance. You should find that you get a much clearer photograph.

Photo editing

Photographs can be edited and enhanced using computer software. Different images can be joined together, creating a panorama. You may also want to edit out or add in backgrounds, objects, text and people. Tidy up your photos, removing red eye, sharpening colours. Then crop and resize your image, ready to be used.

PROMOTIONS

There are numerous places where Scouting can be promoted in your local community: at local shops, libraries and even bus stops; using local media (newspapers, radio, television); through word-of-mouth; on the internet or even at school.

Our world is full of advertising, and everyone seems to want to sell something, whether it's an idea, an event or the latest 'best thing since sliced bread.' If you are going to promote Scouting successfully, then you will need an idea that stands out from the crowd – something creative, original and eye-catching.

Here are some tips to help you with your Scouting promotion:

1. Firstly, decide exactly what you are trying to say. If you don't know what your message is, how are you going to convey it to your audience?
2. Next, know your audience. Who is the message for? Are you telling other people your age about Scouts? Is your message for younger kids? Are you trying to attract adults to become new leaders? Does your audience know anything about the Scout movement? If you don't know your audience (also called your 'market'), you won't be able to connect with them.
3. Once you've got your message and identified your market, choose your method. This could be a newsletter, poster, video, website, audio-based broadcast, or display. Your method should be the most suitable for the place you will use it. For example, you wouldn't use a website to advertise Scouting on the side of a bus, just like a podcast isn't ideal for a Parents' Evening at a local school. While choosing your method, make sure that you'll be able to advertise where you want to. It often costs money to place an advert, so this might need to be considered.
4. Let your imagination take hold! Get your ideas down on paper. Perhaps having a brainstorming session at a Troop Forum will give you just the inspiration you need. Some things to consider when promoting Scouting are:

> **Get to the point!** Don't use ten words when you can use three

> **Play with words**. Wordplay such as puns (eg Scout of the ordinary) and alliteration (eg Find Friends Fast at 1st Falkirk)

> **A picture is worth a thousand words**. You will get your point across with a well chosen photograph better than a paragraph of text.

5. If your aim is to get people to join Scouting, make sure there is a contact telephone number (You can use 0845 300 1818, which is the Scout Information Centre, set up to help people join anywhere in the UK).

5
THE CREATIVE CHALLENGE

i.CLIMB
i.ROCK
i.SKATE...
i.SCOUT!
scouts.org.uk/shop

i.SCOUT

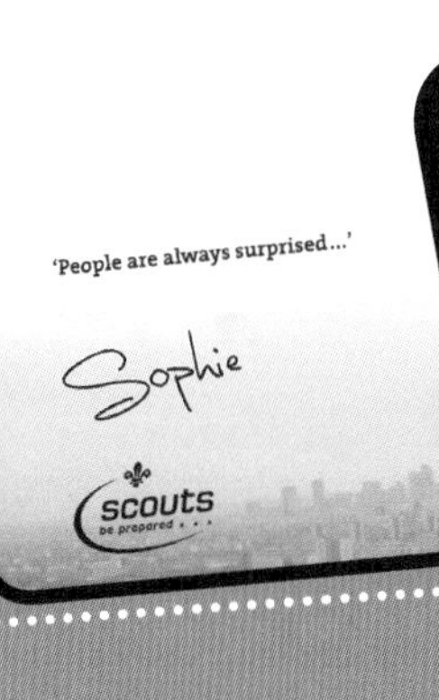
'People are always surprised...'
Sophie
scouts
be prepared

SCOUTS
GOING FOR GOLD
For more information:
scouts.org.uk/join or 0845 300 1818
SCOUTS
BE PREPARED...
TO TAKE THE CHALLENGE
scouts
be prepared
For more information call 0845 300 1818 or visit www.scouts.org.uk
or local contact:

PROBLEM SOLVING

There will be many occasions as a Scout when you will try and solve problems.

This may be when you are a Patrol Leader dealing with your Patrol at camp or at Troop meetings. Like all things it is good to practise solving problems and thinking about how to overcome them.

Here are some examples of problems that you can try and solve:

> real life scenarios that require quick-thinking, such as a first aid situation

> challenges and wide games that revolve around a problem that needs tactical thinking to solve it

> problems that rise out of relationships within the Troop or the Patrol, which may need to be solved so that you can all get along.

For your Creative Challenge, it is likely that you will be set a series of problems to solve in one go, perhaps in the form of an incident hike.

Here are some examples of problems that need to be solved. How would you deal with them?

1. Physical – Radioactive waste

You come across an area that is marked out with cones as out of bounds, and you have to recover a number of radioactive items without entering the area, using only the items that are lying around (rope, bamboo canes, hooks, etc).

2. Logic/Mental – Lateral thinking problems

> Match and fuse

You have a string fuse which will burn from end to end in exactly one minute. The fuse will burn erratically – slowly at first, then quickly, then slowly, and so on. You have matches but no watch. How, using just the fuse and matches, do you measure exactly 30 seconds?

> An enlightening problem

In one room there are three light switches, which turn on three lights in another room of the house. You have to work out which switch turns on which light. You know that all the switches are in the OFF position when you arrive. You can turn as many lights on and off before entering the room. You can only enter the room once to check, and then you must say which switch is for which light. How is it done?

3. Skill – Water problem

Make two equal amounts of water using containers of different volume. See next page.

4. Teamwork – Newspaper task

This task is a race against another team. You are given identical editions of the same newspaper. Behind a screen is a Leader, who will start reading from the newspaper at random. Your task is to find the article he/she is reading before the other team! How will you work together as a team to break down the task and be the most efficient?

Solutions for challenge two are at the end of this chapter (page 81). Once you've mastered them, test your friends!

Water problem

The challenge:

Three different sizes pots are supplied to the team:

> 9 litres
> 5 litres
> 3 litres

There is 8 litres of water in the 9 litre pot.

The team has to produce two equal amounts of 4 litres

The fastest team wins, or the score the team gets is related to their time.

One solution

1 Fill up the 3 litre and empty into 5 litre. Fill up the 3 litre again from the big pot

2 Fill the 5 litre pot with the 3 litre pot (leaving 1 litre in the 3 litre)

3 Empty the full 5 litre pot back into the 9 litre (making 7 litres of water) Empty the 1 litre into the 5 litre pot.

4 Fill up the 3 litre pot from the 7 litres (leaving 4 litres in the 9 litre pot) Add the 3 litres to the 1 litre making 4 litres in each pot.

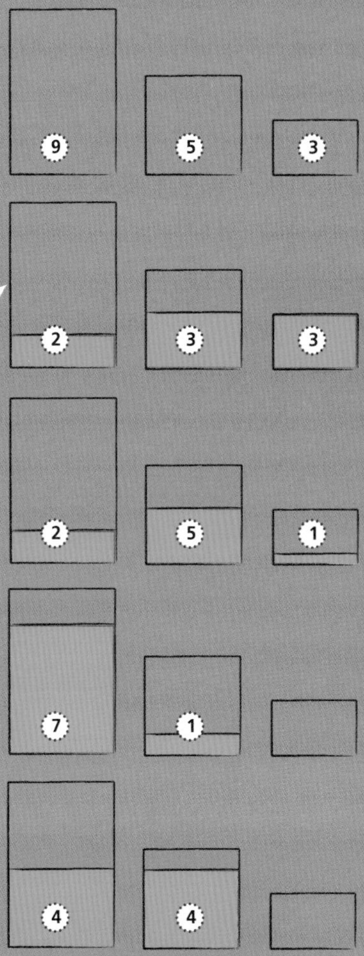

CONSTRUCTION

ELECTRIC LANDFLYER

You will need:

- a piece of balsa wood 200mm x 80mm x 10mm (off-cuts will do as sizes do not need to be exact)
- 4 plastic wheels
- 4 bead-headed pins
- 4 small beads
- A 4.5 volt battery
- 2 matchboxes
- 2 thick elastic bands
- 2 paper clips
- A propeller
- Sticky-backed plastic
- A 3 volt motor

Tools

- Sharp modelling knife
- Hand drill and small twist drill the diameter of the motor shaft.

NB: Only use power tools such as drills under the supervision of an appropriate adult.

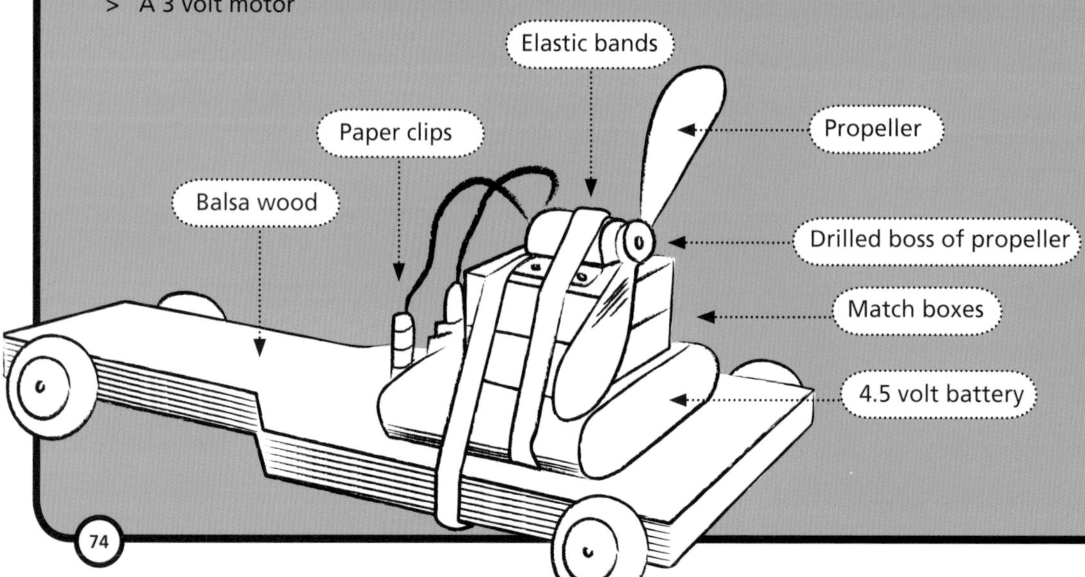

Instructions:

1. Mark out the balsa as shown in fig 1, using the steel rule and pencil. Cut to size with modelling knife.
2. Fix the four plastic wheels onto the balsa using the bead-headed pins for axles and a small bead for the bearing (fig 2). Because of the pins, the landflyer will not be suitable for small children to use.
3. The power unit is built up from a 4.5 volt battery, two empty matchboxes and the 3V motor. For neatness, cover the boxes and battery with sticky backed plastic (the heavy duty kind). Fix all three together with a strong elastic band, then fasten a paper clip to each battery terminal for connecting to the motor.
4. To fit the propeller onto the motor you may need to enlarge the hole in the propeller. To do this, place the propeller onto a firm wooden off-cut and drill through, using a twist drill (see fig 3).
5. Push the pointed end of the propeller boss onto the motor shaft. It is important to put it this way round as the propeller is pushing not pulling the landflyer.
6. Fix the power unit to the chassis with the second strong elastic band. Connect the leads from the motor to the battery with the paper clips. If your landflyer shoots backwards, swap the clips around!

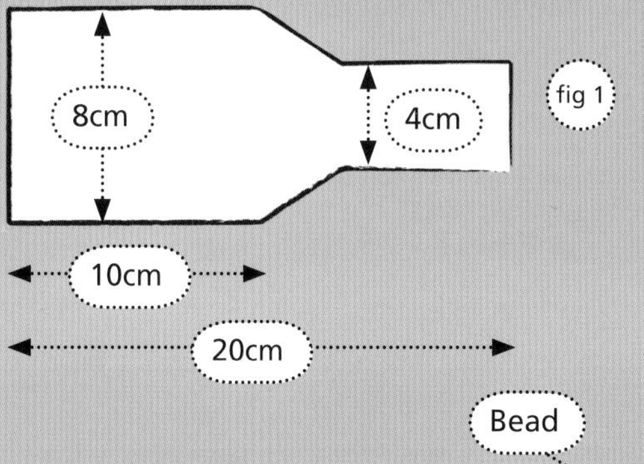

fig 1

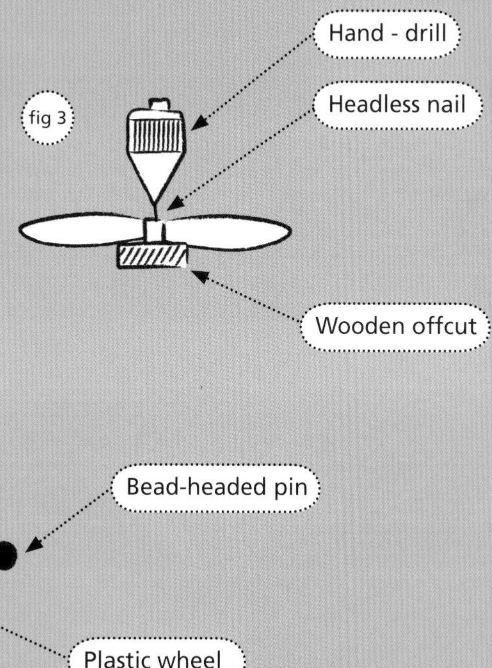

fig 3

fig 2

INTRUDER ALARM

Protect your room from family intruders with a simple alarm.

You will need:

- > tin foil
- > two cereal packets
- > wire
- > 9 volt battery
- > buzzer
- > scissors
- > stapler

The alarm is set off by using a pressure pad. When somebody walks on the pad (which can be hidden by a mat), the buzzer will sound.

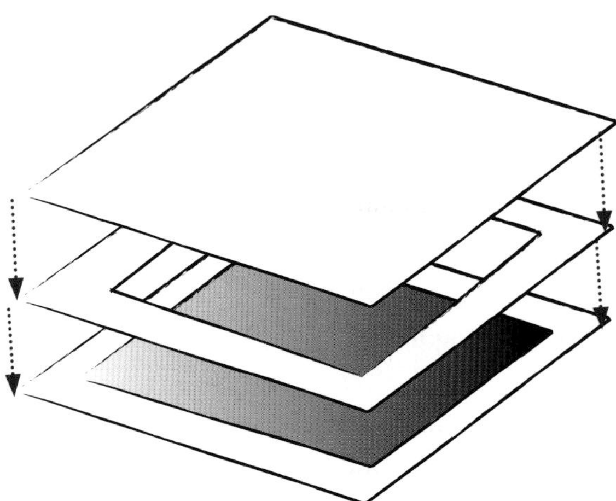

Building the pressure mat

1. Cut up your cereal packs so that you have three rectangular pieces of cardboard about the size of an A4 piece of paper.
2. Cut two squares of tin foil, just smaller than the cardboard. Stick a tin foil square to two of the pieces of cardboard. These will form the bottom and top of the pressure mat.
3. With the third piece of card, carefully cut a square in the middle about 18cm wide. This will form the middle divider between the top and the bottom.
4. Assemble the different layers, so that the two pieces of card with tin foil on face each other. The piece of card with the square cut-out should go between these.
5. To hold the different layers together, use a stapler on one edge. Make sure that you only staple through the cardboard edge and not the tin foil.

Building the circuit

1. Using wires, connect the battery, buzzer and pressure pad together, as shown in the following diagram.
2. When connecting the pressure pad, attach one wire to the top piece of foil and one to the bottom. If you are able to use crocodile clips and battery holders, it will be easier to connect everything!

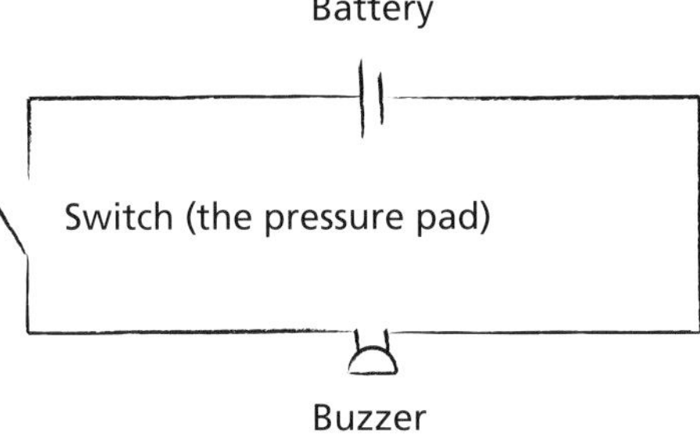

How it works

The pressure pad works as a switch in the circuit. When it is stood upon, the two foil sides touch, completing the circuit, and connecting the battery to the buzzer. The divider helps to prevent the foil touching when someone is not standing on the pad (you may need to use extra pieces of card as a divider, to make it less sensitive).

NB: Tin foil is made out of aluminium, a metal. This makes it a good conductor of electricity.

Now set your alarm and wait for an unsuspecting family member!

WORSHIP

You can be very creative in putting together or leading a Scouts' Own or an Act of Worship. A Scouts' Own is a time when a group of Scouts come together to reflect on what they have done, to think about each other, about nature or their God.

A Scouts' Own or an Act of Worship can include prayers, readings, poems, songs, music or drama. There is a huge range of possibilities to make this time really meaningful to everyone who takes part.

A good way to start is to pick a theme for your Scouts' Own, eg friendship, camping or adventure. Then you can look for readings or prayers that fit it. For example, here are some prayers and teachings from different religions on the theme of peace.

The Prayer of Saint Francis

Lord, make me an instrument of Thy peace;
where there is hatred, let me sow love;
where there is injury, pardon;
where there is doubt, faith;
where there is despair, hope;
where there is darkness, light;
and where there is sadness, joy.
O Divine Master,
grant that I may not so much seek to be consoled as to console;
to be understood, as to understand;
to be loved, as to love;
for it is in giving that we receive,
it is in pardoning that we are pardoned,
and it is in dying that we are born to eternal life.
Amen.

Baha'i

Be generous in prosperity, and thankful in adversity. Be fair in judgment, and guarded in thy speech. Be a lamp unto those who walk in darkness and a home to the stranger. Be eyes to the blind, and a guiding light unto the feet of the erring. Be a breath of life to the body of humankind, a dew to the soil of the human heart, and a fruit upon the tree of humility.

Buddhist

May all beings everywhere plagued with sufferings of body and mind quickly be freed from their illnesses. May those frightened cease to be afraid, and may those bound be free. May the powerless find power and may people think of befriending one another. May those who find themselves in trackless, fearful wilderness – the children, the aged, the unprotected – be guarded by beneficial celestials, and may they swiftly attain Buddhahood.

Jewish

Come, let us go up to the mountain of the Lord, that we may walk the paths of the Most High. And we shall beat our swords into ploughshares and our spears into pruning hooks. Nation shall not lift up sword against nation – neither shall they learn war any more. And none shall be afraid, for the mouth of the Lord of Hosts has spoken.

Hindu

Oh God, lead us from the unreal to the real. Oh God, lead us from darkness to light. Oh God, lead us from death to immortality. Shanti, Shanti, Shanti unto all. Oh Lord God almighty, may there be peace in celestial regions. May there be peace on Earth. May the waters be appeasing. May herbs be wholesome, and may trees and plants bring peace to all. May all beneficent beings bring peace to us. May thy Vedic Law propagate peace all through the world. May all things be a source of peace to us. And may thy peace itself, bestow peace on all and may that peace come to me also.

Muslim

In the name of Allah, the beneficent, the merciful. Praise be to the Lord of the Universe who has created us and made us into tribes and nations that we may know each other, not that we may despise each other. If the enemy inclines towards peace, do thou also incline towards peace, and trust God, for the Lord is the one that hears and knows all things. And of the servants of God, most gracious are those who walk on the Earth in humility, and when we address them, we say 'PEACE'.

Native African

Almighty God, the Great Thumb we cannot evade to tie any knot; the Roaring Thunder that splits mighty trees: the all-seeing Lord up on high who sees even the footprints of an antelope on a rock mass here on Earth. You are the one who does not hesitate to respond to our call. You are the cornerstone of peace.

Native American

Oh Great Spirit of our Ancestors, I raise my pipe to you. To your messengers the four winds, and to Mother Earth who provides for your children. Give us the wisdom to teach our children to love, to respect, and to be kind to each other so that they may grow with peace of mind. Let us learn to share all good things that you provide for us on this Earth.

Shinto

Although the people living across the ocean I believe are our brothers and sisters, why are there constant troubles in this world? Why do winds and waves rise in the oceans surrounding us? I only earnestly wish that the wind will soon puff away all the clouds which are hanging over the tops of mountains.

Sikh

God judges us according to our deeds, not the coat that we wear. Truth is above everything, but higher still is truthful living. Know that we attain God when we love, and only victory endures in consequences of which no one is defeated.

Christian

Blessed are the peacemakers, for they shall be known as the Children of God. But I say to you that hear, love your enemies, do good to those who hate you, bless those who curse you, pray for those who abuse you. To those that strike you on the cheek, offer the other one also, and from those who take away your cloak, do not withhold your coat as well. Give to everyone who begs from you, and of those who take away your goods, do not ask for them again. And as you wish that others would do to you, do so to them.

ASSOCIATED ACTIVITY BADGES

Artist

DIY

Arts Enthusiast

Electronics

Chef

Entertainer

Circus Skills

Hobbies

Craft

IT (Staged)

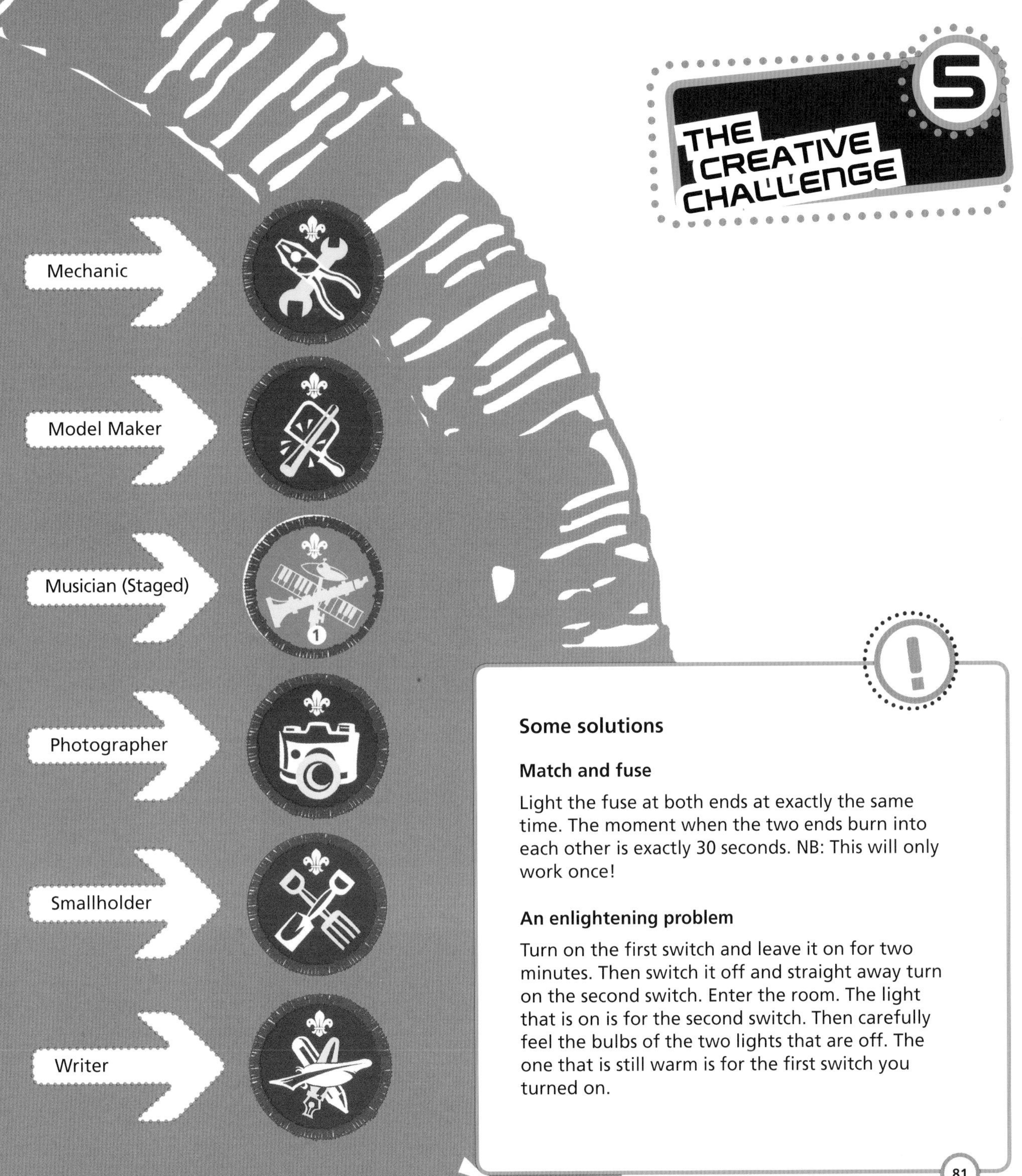

Some solutions

Match and fuse

Light the fuse at both ends at exactly the same time. The moment when the two ends burn into each other is exactly 30 seconds. NB: This will only work once!

An enlightening problem

Turn on the first switch and leave it on for two minutes. Then switch it off and straight away turn on the second switch. Enter the room. The light that is on is for the second switch. Then carefully feel the bulbs of the two lights that are off. The one that is still warm is for the first switch you turned on.

'At the Dutch National Jamboree I met lots of Dutch and German Scouts. We're still in touch via the internet. We talk about football, school, anything really. They don't go camping as often as my Troop, but they do the kind of activities we do at camp at ordinary meetings.'

Michael

MAKE FRIENDS ALL OVER THE WORLD!

REQUIREMENTS

Complete all the activities in one of the following areas:

Area 1: International Contact

> Make contact with Scouts from another country outside the United Kingdom.

Then

> Take part in a Troop or Patrol activity with these Scouts.

OR

> Take part in a Patrol or Troop activity based on things found out during the International contact.

This can be done a number of ways, for example through Nights Away in the UK or overseas, the Internet, pen pals, Jamboree-on-the-Air (JOTA), Jamboree-on-the-Internet (JOTI), or Lands of Adventure.

Area 2: International Issues

Choose and investigate an international issue.

For example:

a. Trade
b. Health
c. Water and sanitation
d. Environment
e. Conflict
f. Refugees
g. Peace
h. Tourism
i. Homelessness
j. Poverty
k. Animal welfare
l. Conservation.

Then complete the following:

a. Show an understanding of the issues involved
b. Take some action as a result of research
c. Compare how the issues affect the UK and countries overseas.

INTERNATIONAL CONTACT

The Scout Movement is the largest mixed sex youth movement in the world – there are over 28 million Scouts worldwide – and Scouts can be found in nearly every country of the world. As a Scout you will have opportunities to experience the 'international' flavour of Scouting in many ways :

- You might take part in activities in your Troop that are international (eg cooking a meal from another country, playing sports and games from around the world, exploring customs, playing a musical instrument from another country).
- International camps are held in many parts of the UK, which are attended by Scouts from other countries – perhaps you will attend one of these.
- You might take part in a camp abroad with Scouts from other countries.
- Your Patrol or Troop might 'twin' with a Patrol or Troop from abroad.
- You could take part in an annual world event like Jamboree-on-the- Air, Jamboree-on-the-Internet or Jamboree-on-the-Trail.
- You could arrange a link-up with a Scout from another country of your choice.
- You could have a go at some badges, like the World Faiths Activity Badge or the International Partnership Award. See your *Scout Badge Book* for more details.
- You could enter the Lands of Adventure challenge.

JOTA

Jamboree-on-the-Air

When Scouts want to meet young people from another country they usually think of attending a World Jamboree or another international gathering. But did you know that that each October about half-a-million Scouts and Guides 'get together' over the airwaves for the annual Jamboree-on-the-Air (JOTA)? Modern communication technology offers Scouts the exciting opportunity to make friends in other countries without even leaving home...

'At the time of the World Scout Jamboree, we were learning about radio transmitters and Morse code, and we were given a challenge to find 50 radio stations and talk to them. I spoke mainly to local people, but I did get in touch with one American called Jamie and spoke to him for ten minutes. It wasn't what I expected to do at Scouts, but it was a good experience to be talking to other Scouts around the world using the radios.'

Darren

JOTA is an annual event where Scouts and Guides all over the world make contact with each other by amateur radio. It is a real Jamboree during which Scouting experiences are exchanged and ideas are shared.

Since 1958 when the first Jamboree-on-the-Air was held, millions of Scouts and Guides have met each other through this event. Not only is it fun to talk to Scouts from other parts of the world but it provides also a chance to find out about other countries and about Scouting elsewhere. Many contacts made during the JOTA have resulted in pen-pals and links between Scout Troops that have lasted for many years.

There are no restrictions on age or the number that can participate. JOTA also happens at little or no expense. The radio stations are operated by licensed amateur radio operators. Many Scouts and Leaders hold licences and have their own stations, but the majority participates in the JOTA through stations operated by local radio clubs and individual radio amateurs. Some operators also use television or computer linked communications.

Date and duration of the event

The worldwide JOTA takes place on the third full weekend of October each year. The event starts at 0000 hours local time on the Saturday and concludes 48 hours later at 2400 hours local time on the Sunday. Each station can choose its own operating hours within this period.

JOTI

Jamboree-on-the-Internet

Jamboree-on-the-Internet (JOTI) happens at the same time as JOTA and is a very similar event except that at JOTI, Scouts and Guides communicate via the internet.

During JOTI, thousands of Scouts from all over the world meet and communicate with each other over the internet, using any technologies locally available, from web browsers to email, chat programs, microphones, scanners and digital cameras. Most of the communication takes place over email and in a chat network called Internet Relay Chat (IRC). JOTI allows you to build friendships with Scouts in other countries and to find out more about their lives and their Scouting. Often, these contacts last for years and lasting friendships are made.

It's fairly easy to participate in JOTI. All you need is a computer, a modem and a phone line. As software you will need at least:

> **a web browser**

such as Netscape or Internet Explorer

> **an email program**

Or you can use the built-in email feature of the web browser

> **a chat program (IRC client)** to meet and chat with other people in real-time.

There are many other items that you could use to enhance your JOTI experience. Check with your friends what you have at hand. Here are some ideas:

> Use a fax to send handwritten greetings to other groups

> Use a scanner to scan pictures and logos of your scout group, home town and scout meeting place

> Connect a microphone to your computer's sound card and talk with other people using a voice-capable chat program such as virc or by joining the egroups chat area

> Ask a local amateur-radio club for help and talk or morse with other scout groups from all over the world via radio and tv waves

> Use a digital camera to take snapshots of the participants

> Use a webcam to post regular images of your location on the web during joti.

Find out more about Jamboree-on-the-Internet by going to the official website - **www.joti.org**

Make sure you know how to keep safe online. For more information on using the internet safely go to www.thinkuknow.co.uk

JOTT

Jamboree-on-the-Trail

Jamboree-on-the-Trail (JOTT) is an annual day for Scouts all over the world to hike together. All Scouts, whatever their age and wherever they may be in the world, are invited to take part in whatever way they can.

You might check out a hiking trail while working on an activity badge, challenge or the Hikes Away Staged activity badges.

JOTT is held on the second Saturday of May each year and more information can be found on the JOTT website - **www.jott.org**

LANDS OF ADVENTURE

Lands of Adventure - You Are Europe

Lands of Adventure is a European programme for Scouts and Explorer Scouts aged 11 to 16. It adds a European dimension to the Scout Programme.

Lands of Adventure works well with the programme, helping you with the Global Challenge, the Creative Challenge, and the International Friendship Partnership Award. It could also be a good linking activity with Explorer Scouts.

Lands of Adventure is a challenge open to patrols of Scouts from all over the European Scout Region (see image below).

There are three challenges within the Lands of Adventure:

> Express EURself
> EUR Hopping
> Europe@EUR.door

Express EURself - Your creative step into Europe

Express EURself is a project planned and undertaken by patrols in their own programme, based on the theme of 'Discovery'. Patrols produce their project in any media format of their choice - such as video, music, sculpture, art, dance, and mural. All the results will be included on a CD-Rom, which will be sent to all patrols that take part. It will also be streamed on the Lands of Adventure website and so it can be seen by anybody anywhere in the world.

EUR Hopping - make new friends in Europe.

The aim of EUR Hopping is to encourage Scouts from different countries to make contact and design a common project which involves:

> establishing contact
> regular communication
> joint decision on a common project
> agreeing a project implemented in co-operation between the Scout patrols/groups which involves planning the project together, putting it into action and assessing how well it went afterwards.

The patrols/groups might meet 'really' or 'virtually'.

Europe@EUR.door - Europe is closer than you think

Europe@EUR door aims to encourage Scouts to learn more about Scouting and explore the culture of other European countries. Scouts from all over Europe are invited to plan and carry out a project that is specific to the chosen host country (or if they wish, any other country of their choice).

To find out more and to register your patrol for Lands of Adventure, go to **www.landsofadventure.eu**

6 Dear Susan, how are you?

SCOUT PENPALS

One way of making contact with Scouts across the world is to get a Scout penpal. Even with the internet, social networking sites and communication tools that allow you to chat with people in other countries through your computer, there can be a special thrill from receiving a letter through the post. Luckily, there is already an International Links Scheme set up to help you find a penpal.

What do I need to do?

> Decide on the country you would like to find out about.

> Contact the International Links Postbox Secretary – you can do this via international@scout.org.uk and use the subject 'Scout Penpal' in your email. Alternatively complete an application form. Visit www.scouts.org.uk and search 'international links'.

> Be patient! The country you want to contact may not have any suitable links, and you may have to wait some time before a penpal comes forward. It is worth applying for the scheme well in advance of when you want to make contact.

> Be flexible! If you're not too fussed which country you make links with, you can view a list of the countries waiting to find UK contacts on the website, which is updated every month.

> If you want to write in English, make sure you put on your form that you want your link Scout to reply in English. Having a penpal can also be a good way of practising your foreign language skills, if you fancy the challenge!

Remember there are many ways of making international contact through the Scout Programme:

> If family members or family friends travel abroad as part of their work, ask them to look out for contacts.

> Ask people who have moved into your community from another country or have family connections abroad.

> Check out existing links through twin towns, school links and faith communities.

> Visit a UK International Camp on their open day and link with a visiting foreign Scout.

> Use contacts made by attending an international camp in another country.

> Establish a contact through Explorer Scouts or Scout Network members in your District who have attended a World Jamboree.

Hannah and Charlotte writing a letter to a Scout penpal

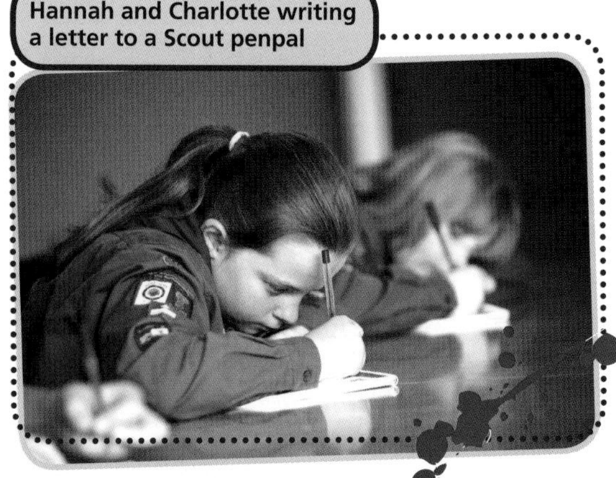

INTERNATIONAL ISSUES

To complete this part of the challenge, you need to select an international issue that interests you. The list on page 83 is only a starting point for your ideas. Firstly, you should undertake some research, possibly on the internet, to discover as much as you can about your chosen issue.

Once you have done your research, you must take some action about your issue. This could be through fundraising, volunteering time to a charity concerned with the issue or through raising awareness about the issue in your community.

You should then compare this issue in another country to the situation in your own – perhaps even within your own local community or how people that you know are affected by it.

On the following pages are some examples of issues you might find thought provoking.

TRADE

Fair trade

International trade may seem not to affect your life, but when prices of goods fall dramatically it has a disastrous impact on the lives of millions of small scale farmers, forcing many into crippling debt and others to lose their land and their homes.

For many farmers when they come to sell their crops they may have to accept a price which could be less than it cost to grow.

Development charities recognise the important role we as consumers can play to improve the situation for food producers. They pay workers a fair price, helping to strengthen their organisations and marketing their produce through their own One World shops and catalogues. By doing this, the charities offer consumers the opportunity to buy products which are bought on the basis of a fair trade.

Bananas

Bananas are the most popular fruit in the UK. Almost half a million Fairtrade bananas are eaten everyday in the UK. They are a healthy fruit full of potassium and fibre.

In the know

Most bananas are produced by small farmers in the Caribbean and on plantations in Latin America and parts of Africa. Many small farmers and banana workers endure unacceptable working and living conditions and their surrounding environment is ruined by toxic chemicals and intensive farming.

Meet Conrad

Conrad is a banana farmer

He is married and he has three grown-up sons

'Fairtrade has made great changes for me and my country'

Banana farming

Conrad's passion is banana farming, though it is tough work. His farm is about 5.6 acres and he works hard on his farm to grow quality bananas which are exported to the UK. He harvests his bananas every week – about 100 boxes – and takes them from his farm to the reception centre, where they are weighed and loaded into crates to go on the ship to Southampton.

Fairtrade and Conrad

Fairtrade means that Conrad is able to get a good price for his bananas and that the price doesn't change when things get tough. It also means that Conrad has to look after the environment and not use dangerous chemicals on his farm. When the hurricanes hit St Lucia recently and many of the farms were very badly damaged, Fairtrade helped the farmers get back on their feet quickly.

'Continue buying my bananas. They are good and sweet. By doing that you'll be helping a lot of people.'

The Fairtrade premium

As well as getting a fair and stable price for the bananas that covers the cost of production, Fairtrade farmers also get a little bit extra – the Fairtrade premium – which they use for community projects. Banana farmers in St Lucia are organized into groups. Each group decides democratically how they will use the Fairtrade premium in their community. In Conrad's community, they have used this to build a new fence around the local school – to keep the children in and others out! They also bought some fans for the local medical centre, which previously had nothing to keep the patients cool in the tropical heat.

How this might affect you

The FAIRTRADE Mark

The FAIRTRADE Mark is an independent consumer label that appears on products as a guarantee that producers and workers have received a fair price for their work. The Mark is licensed by the Fairtrade Foundation in the UK, a registered charity set up by CAFOD, Christian Aid, Oxfam, Traidcraft Exchange and the World Development Movement.

The purpose of Fairtrade is to improve the terms of trade for poor producers and workers in developing countries and make a real improvement in people's lives. Fairtrade is based on an internationally agreed set of Fairtrade standards which are independently assessed and monitored. Producers and traders in the system are certified and audited. The FAIRTRADE Mark is the only independent guarantee of Fairtrade.

How to get involved

The FAIRTRADE Mark appears on over 3000 different products. They are available in most major supermarkets, wholefood and fair trade shops, and by mail order. If your store doesn't have the product you want, ask the manager to stock it!

> Find out more about Fairtrade

> Try different types of Fairtrade chocolate

> Encourage others to buy Fairtrade goods.

More info

Fairtrade – **www.fairtrade.org.uk**

Dubble Fairtrade Chocolate – **www.dubble.co.uk**

Oxfam's Cool Planet - **www.oxfam.org.uk/coolplanet/kidsweb**

Look for this Mark on products when you shop

HEALTH

Health is not just about avoiding diseases; it is about having a good mental and physical state and general wellbeing. Different parts of the world face a variety of health related issues. The plain fact is that in some parts of the world people are dying of starvation, while in others people are dying of obesity. Measles, tetanus and HIV/AIDS are among other global health problems.

Blindness

> Globally, 314 million people are visually impaired. Of those, 37 million are blind and 124 million people have low vision.

> Worldwide for each blind person, an average of 3.4 people have low vision, with country and regional variation ranging from 2.4 to 5.5.

Distribution of poor sight

By age: Visual impairment is not equally distributed across age groups. More than 82 per cent of all people who are blind are 50 years of age and older, although they represent only 19 per cent of the world's population. However, childhood blindness remains a serious problem, because an estimated 1.4 million blind children below the age of 15 will have to live with their blindness for many years.

By gender: In every region of the world, and at all ages, females have a significantly higher risk of being visually impaired than males.

Geographically: Poor sight is not distributed uniformly throughout the world. More than 90 per cent of the world's visually impaired live in developing countries.

How this might affect you

More than two million people in the UK are at risk of needlessly losing their sight. More than half of all sight loss is avoidable. Unknowingly, 1.9 million people with diabetes who aren't having regular eye tests and 250,000 people with early-stage glaucoma are at high risk of losing their sight.

Few people understand that eye tests are important because they identify potentially blinding conditions. Most people give the reason for not having an eye test as 'they didn't have a problem with their eyes'.

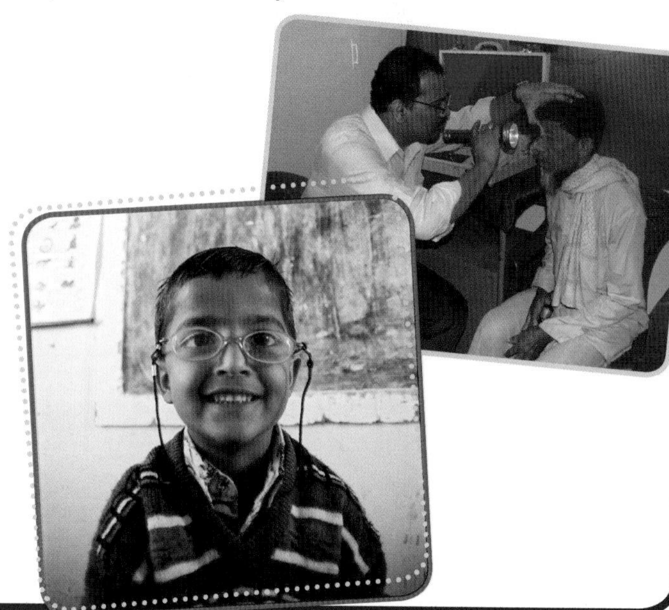

A further half a million people in the UK are needlessly living with sight loss by not seeking treatment for cataracts (a routine operation that is successful in 90 per cent of cases) or by simply wearing the wrong prescription glasses.

One of the most common causes of sight loss amongst young people is as a result of an accident. Smoking has been shown to be a major contributing factor to visual impairment.

How to get involved

> Have an eye test every two years.

> Encourage others to have an eye test.

> Help with a local voluntary society for the blind.

> Collect old spectacles to send overseas.

> 'Befriend' and help a partially sighted person.

> Help to make your community more accessible to people with visual problems.

More info

> World Health Organisation **www.who.int/topics/blindness/**

> UNICEF Youth Voice **www.unicef.org.uk/youthvoice/**

> RNIB - **www.rnib.org.uk/youngpeople**

> Fight for Sight - **www.fightforsight.org.uk**

> Sight Savers International - **www.sightsavers.org**

WATER AND SANITATION

Clean water is essential for life, but one in eight people in the world do not have it. 2.5 billion people do not have access to adequate sanitation.

The lack of clean water close to people's homes also affects people's time, livelihoods and quality of life.

Many women and children in developing countries spend hours each day walking miles to collect water. This water can be dirty and unsafe but they have no alternative.

Carrying heavy water containers is an exhausting task, which takes up valuable time and energy. It prevents women from doing other things at home or earning money and stops children from going to school.

Sanitation

Diarrhoea claims the lives of around 5,000 children a day. These children are dying because they do not have access to adequate sanitation or safe water. Their deaths, from common diseases such as typhoid, are preventable.

Where there is nowhere safe and clean to go to the toilet, people are exposed to disease, lack of privacy, and indignity.

Bad health caused by poor sanitation has a knock-on effect on the family economy and nutrition.

In many cultures women who have no access to a latrine must wait until it is dark to go to the toilet or have to walk long distances to find an isolated spot. Where there are no toilets, girls are prevented from going to school.

Credit: WaterAid/Abir Abdullah

Ruby stands by an open rubbish ditch in Balar Math Slum, Bangladesh. Hanging latrines feed in to the ditch too.

The international charity WaterAid interviewed people in Bangladesh about life without sanitation. Ruby (pictured above) talks about the toilets in the slum where she lives near Dhaka:

'This slum has existed for 10 years and is in a shocking state.'

'Hanging latrines feed straight into a rubbish-filled ditch in the middle of the slum. Five thousand households here have no clean water and no sanitation.'

'Many people get very ill here and I think it all stems from the open latrines. Smell the stench, it's disgusting. We get fevers, coughs and terrible diarrhoea and there are no healthcare facilities that we can use.'

How this might affect you

Dehydration - A Major Health Concern

Water is the most important nutrient in our bodies, making up roughly 70 per cent of our muscle and brain tissue. Only oxygen is needed by the body more than water.

Most people do not drink enough water every day to meet their body's basic requirements, leaving them dehydrated. Dehydration itself is responsible for a wide range of common ailments experienced by just about everyone in today's busy, fast-paced world, including headaches and fatigue.

When we breathe, we lose moisture to the air every time we exhale: as much as two cups a day! Our bodies lose water through evaporation from the surface of our skin even without rigorous exercise, and, of course, we also pass water in our urine. During the course of an average day, a healthy adult can lose eight to 10 cups of water. Add in exercise, and this number rises considerably.

If we fail to replenish the water we lose through these natural processes, we set off a physiological reaction that can have serious health effects. The following is the natural progression of dehydration and its effects on the body (symptoms):

Mild

- because your kidneys will begin to conserve water, your urine will become concentrated and will be amber-coloured as opposed to a normal light-tinted yellow colour
- constipation and/or bloating may be noticed
- dry skin, mucous membranes, and lips
- thirst, often extreme
- flushed face

Moderate

> fatigue
> sunken eyes or sunken fontanels (soft spot on head) in infants
> lack of tears in crying infant
> 'doughy' skin that doesn't bounce back when pinched
> dizziness / vertigo / lightheadedness
> up to 30 per cent decline in physical labour capacity, muscle cramping
> headache
> cold hands and feet
> problems concentrating
> drowsiness
> fainting
> impatience and extreme irritability
> major reduction in urine production

Severe

> weak irregular heart beat (often racing) and low blood pressure
> rapid breathing
> failure of body's heat regulation systems (sweating, for example)
> confusion
> vomiting and/or diarrhoea
> shock, collapse or unconsciousness
> seizures
> coma and death

To prevent dehydration, experts recommend that everyone drink at least six to eight glasses of water a day.

Information and image from **www.wateraid.org**

How to get involved

By drinking more water, you will be healthier and become aware of the daily struggle faced by 884 million people who do not have access to clean water in the developing world. You could find out how much water your family or Scout Troop uses and investigate how you could conserve water.

Get involved with a charity that helps people dig wells. Buy ethical bottled water, which raises funds and awareness for projects in Africa and Asia.

More info

WaterAid - **www.wateraid.org**

Oxfam's Cool Planet
www.oxfam.org.uk/coolplanet/kidsweb

Pump Aid - **www.pumpaid.org**

Thirsty Planet - **www.thirsty-planet.com**

WaterAid's mission is to overcome poverty by enabling the world's poorest people to gain access to safe water, sanitation and hygiene education.

Environment

The earth's climate is changing. In the past these changes were slow, happening over thousands of years. Today, however, our actions have sped up climate change and this is creating problems.

Every time someone turns on a light switch or uses the car, carbon dioxide is emitted into the earth's atmosphere, and the sheer global scale of humankind's energy use is causing the temperature of the world to rise. This is known as global warming, and there are many factors that contribute to the phenomenon. Experts have a term for the amount of energy we use - a carbon footprint. In recent years, these words have become commonplace as we have been encouraged by environmentalists to be more careful about the energy we use.

The consequences of climate change are alarming. If the Earth's temperature continues to rise, the polar ice caps (in the Arctic and Antarctic) that help keep the planet cool, will melt at catastrophic rates. Not only could this mean extinction for native wildlife, such as the polar bear, but the likelihood of natural disasters such as floods and tsunamis will increase.

Environmental campaigners have challenged multinational corporations and industrial nations to reduce their energy use. Innovators are looking for ways to make products more energy efficient. However, there is still a huge reliance on fossil fuels (coal, oil and gas) and the move to renewable sources is potentially too slow to help reduce climate change. Action needs to be taken on an individual and global scale if we are to protect our planet for future generations to enjoy.

How this might affect you

Some of the problems we may face in the UK as a result of climate change are:

> **rising sea levels** – coastal regions will suffer flooding

> **severe weather** – here in the UK we would experience more extreme weather: droughts in some areas and flooding in others. Summers are likely to become hotter, uncomfortably so, and winter much colder, causing problems for the elderly

> **loss of biodiversity** – many species of plants and animals will not be able to adapt to their changed ecosystems.

How to get involved

One way to be more considerate about the environment is to start the Green Footprint Award. You could do this with your Troop, Scout Group or with a group of friends.

Though the challenge is great, every person can take action in their homes and with their lifestyle that can make a difference. If millions of people take tiny steps, think of the total distance that can be travelled. The same is true of looking after our environment. A good Scout cares about planet and people, and looks for ways to help protect their environment. Schools, Scout Groups and families are all helping to make better choices about the energy they use, and it is not too late to do something to help.

Green Footprint Award

The award is in three stages and helps you to:

> learn about climate change

> look at the energy you use, with the green-o-meter

> take a climate change pledge to reduce your carbon footprint

> tell others in your community about the importance of combating climate change.

On top of this, you could:

- Write an environmental policy for your Scout Troop
- Adopt an animal from an endangered with an animal conservation charity or zoo
- Take charge of the recycling in your home or classroom
- Adopt an environmental issue and join a related campaign.

More info

Scouts Climate Change website
www.scouts.org.uk/climatechange

Green Footprint Award
www.greenfootprintaward.org.uk

Climate Change special at **www.bbc.co.uk/cbbc**

REFUGEES

A refugee is someone who has been displaced (forced to leave their home) by war. As you read this, literally millions of people, often women and children, are fleeing their country because it is too dangerous to stay where they are. There are many reasons people become refugees: political troubles, famine, economic crisis or natural disasters are just some. People attempting to settle in another country as refugees are called asylum seekers.

Under international law the word refugee has a very precise meaning: someone who is forced to flee their home and country; who escapes to another country and is given refugee status by the government of that country. Only the government of a country can decide whether a person should be granted refugee status and they use the 1951 United Nations Convention on refugees.

Refugee statistics

- There are approximately 50 million uprooted people around the world: refugees who have sought safety in another country, and people displaced within their own country. Around half of this displaced population are children.
- An estimated 1.2 billion people worldwide survive on less than $1 per day. Half of them are children.
- An estimated 45,000 households in Rwanda today are headed by children, 90 per cent of them girls.

The United Nations High Commission for Refugees, along with other charities and agencies, campaign for rights for refugees, and work to give refugee children and families access to medical aid, shelter, and the tools to become free citizens.

How this might affect you

In the UK, schools help refugee pupils develop, succeed and contribute to the community. Some schools ensure refugee pupils achieve their potential in a variety of ways.

- In building on the knowledge and skills refugee pupils bring, schools enable them to experience success and establish a sense of belonging to their school community. This assists their integration.
- By supporting language and learning, schools ensure refugee pupils learn to communicate effectively in English, and acquire the skills and qualifications they need to gain employment or to access further and higher education.
- Going to school, making friends and developing a sense of belonging all support refugee pupils' positive coping and resilience after their difficult experiences. Schools are promoting emotional well-being through curriculum activities, projects and pastoral care.
- By encouraging refugee parents to play an active part in the education of their children, schools and pupils will benefit from their talents and skills. Parental involvement and family learning initiatives in school can also provide real opportunities for refugee parents to acquire important skills that will assist their integration as well as that of their children.

How to get involved

- Support refugees and asylum seekers – you could sell your unwanted toys and games and give the proceeds to a refugee charity to help children who don't have any toys.
- Campaign on the issues facing refugees and asylum seekers.
- Get involved in volunteering and practical action.

More info

United Nations High Commission for Refugees **www.unhcr.org**

Refugee Council - **www.refugeecouncil.org.uk**

Star Network - **www.star-network.org.uk**

Amnesty International - **www.amnesty.org.uk**

TOURISM

International Tourism now takes visitors to previously inaccessible places in the world as well as traditional holiday destinations. International tourism is forecast to nearly treble over the next 20 years. Members of the World Tourism Organization believe that the Global Code of Ethics for Tourism is needed to help minimize the negative impacts of tourism on the environment and on cultural heritage while maximizing the benefits for residents of tourist destinations.

Case study

- In East Africa, native Maasai tribes have been evicted from their traditional lands to make way for safari lodges and tours.
- In Natal, South Africa, the park service works to ensure that villagers have free access to parks for local needs and have the opportunity to sell their handicrafts at local lodges. Proceeds from the sales of handicrafts make it possible for parents to buy better clothing and school supplies for their children. They have designed rainforest tours where visitors walk high in the canopy on suspended walkways to look at rare birds and other natural wonders without harming the fragile forest floor or the trees.
- The growth of tourism centred on water sports such as snorkelling and scuba diving is endangering coral reefs, which are home to a quarter of all marine species. Coupled with this, the effects of climate change are causing the temperature of the oceans to rise, which causes the reef to 'bleach' and kills corals. Some countries have laws in place to protect the habitat, but where these don't exist, tourism is having a negative impact. It has been predicted by marine biologists that nearly a third of corals (the organisms that build reefs) face extinction.

How this might affect you

Ecotourism

More than just 'green travel', ecotravel is mindful travel: personally fulfilling, challenging and enlightening. It is travel with purpose - a personal purpose and a global one. Ecotourism is responsible travel to natural areas, which conserves the environment and improves the wellbeing of local people because it:

> minimises impact

> builds environmental and cultural awareness and respect

> Provides positive experiences for visitors and hosts

> Funds conservation

> Provides financial benefits and empowers local people

> Raises sensitivity to host countries' political, environmental, and social climate

> Supports human rights and labour agreements

How to get involved

Everyone has a role to play in creating responsible travel and tourism. Governments, businesses and communities must do all they can, but as a traveller you can make a difference:

> Open your mind to other cultures and traditions: it will transform your experience, and you will earn respect and be more readily welcomed by local people. Be tolerant and respect diversity – observe social and cultural traditions and practices.

> Respect human rights. Exploitation in any form conflicts with the fundamental aims of tourism.

> Help preserve natural environments. Protect wildlife and habitats and do not purchase products made from endangered plants or animals.

> Respect cultural resources. Activities should be conducted with respect for the artistic, archaeological and cultural heritage.

> Your trip can contribute to local economic development. Purchase local handicrafts and products using the principles of fair trade. Bargaining for goods should reflect an understanding of a fair wage.

> Learn about the destination's current health situation and access to emergency and diplomatic services to ensure your health and safety. Make sure that your specific requirements (diet, accessibility, medical care) can be fulfilled before you decide to travel this destination.

> Familiarise yourself with the laws so that you do not commit any act considered criminal by the country visited.

> Calculate your carbon footprint and think of what steps you can take to offset or reduce it.

More info

World Tourism Organisation - **www.unwto.org**

International Ecotourism Society
www.ecotourism.org

Carbon Calculators
www.carbonfootprint.com
www.energysaving.org.uk
www.co2balance.com

ANIMAL WELFARE

Being kind to animals has always been an aspect of good Scouting, and was in the original Scout Law written by Baden-Powell in *Scouting for Boys*:

'A Scout is a friend to animals. - He should save them as far as possible from pain, and should not kill any animal unnecessarily, even if it is only a fly - for it is one of God's creatures'.

However, there are people who deliberately harm or hunt animals that are protected or endangered, and animal cruelty exists in every continent of the world. Perhaps you could use your Global Challenge to find out about animal welfare and take action to protect wildlife.

Polar bears under threat

Human activities pose many threats to polar bears and their environment, namely hunting, pollution and habitat destruction, and human-induced climate change.

Global warming

Global warming is considered to be a great threat to polar bears. Global warming means ice is melting earlier in the summer and freezing later in the winter. As a result, bears have less time to hunt for seals, have a longer summer fast and must wait longer before they can resume hunting, causing stress and loss of condition.

Hunting

Polar bears are hunted throughout most of their range. Hunting is regulated in Canada and is banned in Russia, but the remoteness of much of the polar bear's range can make illegal hunting difficult to control.

Habitat destruction

The Arctic is being exploited for its mineral wealth and is threatened by pollution and mining for petrochemicals. It is not known how these activities affect polar bears. Other possible problems include contamination of ice, water, food species and bears themselves by toxic chemicals, pollutants and nuclear waste.

Conservation status

The world population is estimated to be between about 22-27,000 bears, of which 15,000 or more are in Canada. The polar bear is 'conservation dependant', which means conservation efforts are needed to ensure its future.

How this might affect you

Circuses with wild animals in the UK

The keeping and use of domestic and wild animals in circuses is currently permitted throughout the UK.

There are circuses that display wild animals to the public. They have wild animals that include lions and tigers, zebra, camels, a bear and an elephant. There is nothing to stop other animal circuses from the continent touring the UK.

At the moment circuses with animals are licensed under the Performing Animals Act 1925 but this sets no standards for the care and welfare of animals travelling with menageries or circuses, or in their winter quarters. This law refers to the trainers but not the animals.

The Animal Welfare Act introduced in 2006 raises the standards of care and welfare for animals in all circumstances where they are kept, owned or managed by humans. This means that a circus has to demonstrate that each individual animal is provided a suitable environment in which it can behave normally and receive protection from pain and distress. Local authorities and animal welfare agencies frequently make inspections of animals' living conditions. The Born Free Foundation, which opposes the keeping of animals in circuses, believes that a travelling circus can never provide wild or domestic animals with their daily needs. However, the Act does not ban the use of non-domestic animals in circuses.

How to get involved

> Adopt an animal through an animal adoption charity.

> Persuade friends not to go to circuses that have animals.

> Save energy and reduce waste to reduce global warming and preserve animal habitats.

> Eat less meat! – or choose free range and ethically reared products.

More info

RSPCA – **www.rspca.org.uk**

Compassion in World Farming – **www.ciwf.org.uk**

Born Free Foundation – **www.bornfree.org.uk**

HOMELESSNESS

Definition: Someone who is homeless is without a fixed home.

Homeless people may live on the streets, or may move from shelter to shelter, or may be required to live in temporary accommodation

Examples include:

> People who have either been forced to leave home because of fear or danger, or who have chosen to leave home and cannot support themselves

> Street children

> Refugees and internally displaced people.

> People who may have a job, but no fixed abode, and so sleep at friends' houses, shelters, squats, or on the streets at night.

Why the situation occurs?

Young people may leave home because they are threatened, mistreated, mentally and/or physically abused. Some young people leave home following a disagreement, which they feel can not be resolved. Others may be forced to leave home by their families if they have done something that their parents and family cannot accept and cope with, for example, underage pregnancy, drug addiction, and abusive behaviour.

They may have little or no means to support themselves and will have to rely on their own survival skills as well as assistance from government and charitable organisations. They may not know what assistance is available and may end up living rough on the streets and facing other dangers every day.

Children in some parts of the world may be rejected by their parents who can not afford to support them. They may be left to wander the streets and survive by themselves, or the whole family may be homeless and live on the streets.

Refugees and internally displaced people flee their homes due to danger or fear, and automatically become homeless. See page 97 for more information.

Some people may fall on hard times and not be able to make rent payments or pay bills. They may still have a job, but may not be able to continue living in their homes. They then have to rely on social support, charities, the assistance of their friends or families, or even live on the streets.

The Extension Scout Programme in Kenya

In Nairobi and the other big cities in Kenya, over 60,000 children are living on the streets because their families have broken up, often when one or both parents dies from AIDS. These children have to survive by scavenging waste food, begging, stealing and committing other petty crimes. They have little or no access to clean water so they do not wash.

The Kenya Scout Association has found a way to help these children get back into society. They have set up 24 special units which use Scout methods to teach these children life skills, which will allow them to find a job, as well as have fun like other young people of their age. The leaders are trained to deal with the special needs of the street children - helping them to stop sniffing glue for example. When they can, they reunite the children with their families. The children learn skills such as how to use computers and bake bread in a bakery which has been set up on a campsite. One of the Scouts passed his driving test and now has a job as a driver. A clinic has also been set up on the campsite.

The project is mainly supported by generous people outside the country. One of them runs a tourist company which offers young people from the UK a tour and a 10 day Jamboree with street children.

The project is making such a great difference that the Uganda Scouts are starting a similar scheme.

In Kenya, Scouts help unload Shelterboxes sent from the UK to areas where people have been made homeless by violence, following the country's disputed elections.

How this might affect you

You may think that homelessness does not and will never affect you, but no-one decides to be homeless, particularly young people. This true story is about a girl called Tara who became one of the UK's 'hidden homeless' after her parents separated.

Case study – Tara

Tara came from a happy family but when her parents separated and she remained with her mum problems in their relationship started. Tara felt her mum was to blame for her father not being around anymore and she was annoyed when her mum started interfering in her relationship with her then boyfriend. Things got really bad and after one particularly heated argument Tara left home and went to live with her maternal aunt.

Tara's aunt helped her to access help through Connexions and they suggested she talked to Reconnect, Depaul Trust's family mediation project. The Reconnect worker listened to Tara's concerns about her relationship with her mum and with her consent set up a meeting with her mum to hear her side of the problem. It was apparent that they shared each other's concerns, but from very different perspectives. It was recommended, and both agreed to joint mediation sessions, which were held at a neutral location with the Reconnect worker acting as impartial sounding board.

Tara and her mum have been attending mediation sessions regularly and it has been an emotional journey for them both. Although they have been unable to agree on a number of issues, they have been willing to make the effort to see things from each other's perspective.

Tara has not yet returned home but they are continuing, with the help of the Reconnect project, to work through difficult and challenging discussions.

Recently Tara and her Mum have started to meet for a coffee and to talk outside of these mediation sessions. They have even spoken about Tara spending Christmas at home with her Mum - the first time in three years.

How to get involved

> Tackle the issue - learn about the issue and how to identify with the situation. Why do people become homeless and what difficulties do they face? What support can they receive? What attitudes need to be changed and how can you help this?

> Your Troop could get involved in volunteering with a homelessness project, at a soup kitchen, shelter or Christmas shelter

> Hold a sponsored sleep out to raise money for a homelessness charity.

More info

Shelter – **www.shelter.org.uk**

Crisis – **www.crisis.org.uk**

Habitat for Humanity – **www.habitat.org**

Depaul Trust – **www.depaultrust.org**

Childine – **www.childline.org.uk**

ASSOCIATED ACTIVITY BADGES

Air Researcher

World Faiths

Astronomer

Interpreter

Global Conservation

Communicator

'I got very involved with sports day; I was the sports captain for my team. I had to try and encourage my friends and myself to do their best at whatever event they were doing.'

Hannah

MAKE YOUR

PROMISE!

REQUIREMENTS

Complete five activities in total, taken from at least two areas. Examples are provided below but other similar activities can also be undertaken:

Area 1 - Commitment to the Promise and Scout Law

a. Explain how you have recently 'done your best' on at least three occasions and how this made a difference.

b. Explain to a new Scout in your Troop the meaning of the Scout Promise and Law.

c. Assist with the planning and take part in an Investiture ceremony or similar.

d. Demonstrate that you can be trusted by taking on a special responsibility on behalf of the Troop. This might involve the management of money, or the Troop's reputation.

Area 2 - Relationship with your God

a. Take part in a number of acts of worship with others in the Troop, such as Scout parades at your place of worship, and/or Scouts' Owns.

b. Complete a course that furthers your understanding of your own faith community.

c. Choose and read prayers and /or reflections for you Troop's opening and closing ceremony.

d. Hold the My Faith Activity Badge.

Area 3 - The life of the Troop

a. Take an active part in at least two Troop Forums and express your views on at least one item being discussed.

b. Contribute to the writing or reviewing of your Troop's 'Code of Conduct'.

c. Play a full part in at least two Troop Leadership Forums and help to implement a decision of the forum.

d. Run successfully a learning experience for other Scouts.

e. Successfully lead a group of Scouts at a two-day camp or other similar event.

Area 4 - Developing Beliefs and Attitudes

a. Honestly review an event or activity and decide how it might be done better in the future.

b. Visit an act of worship of another faith community and compare the traditions and customs with your own.

c. Investigate a political or world issue, such as climate change, smoking, fairtrade and explain your views to others on the subject.

d. Take part in a debate on a topic of local or national interest.

e. As a Scout, give freely of your time to help someone less fortunate than yourself.

COMMITMENT TO PROMISE AND LAW

What is a promise?

If you promise to do something, you say you will definitely do it. If you promise something to someone, you guarantee they will get it. This is called making a promise. Everyone makes the Scout Promise when they become a full Member. If you think carefully you can probably think of other times that you have made a promise or heard other people making a promise.

People make promises every day in different situations:

Family – parents and children often make promises to each other: 'I promise to be back home by 5pm'. 'If you keep your bedroom tidy all week I promise we can go and watch the match on Saturday'.

Faith – In churches that baptise infants, there usually follows a service of dedication or confirmation when the child becomes an adolescent. In baptism, parents make promises about the Christian faith on behalf of the baby. The time comes when the young person is old enough to make their own commitment to the Christian faith. This happens at a service called Confirmation (they confirm the promises made on their behalf by their parents and godparents).

During the Sikh Amrit ceremony a special liquid called amrit is used. It is a sweet mixture of sugar and water prepared in a steel bowl. The mixture is stirred by five Sikhs with small swords. Some of the mixture is drunk and some is sprinkled on the eyes and hair. It promises the person being initiated that if they obey the teachings of Sikhism they will live for ever, even after their bodies have died.

Community – When couples get married in the Church of England they make a promise or wedding vows to each other 'I Stuart, take you, Elizabeth to be my wife, to have and to hold from this day forward, for better, for worse, for richer, for poorer, in sickness and in health, to love and to cherish 'til death us do part, according to God's holy law. In the presence of God I make this vow.'

After making vows and exchanging rings, the promise is sealed by signing the register.

Political – After election to the House of Commons a Member of Parliament (MP) must swear an oath of allegiance before taking their seat. While holding a copy of the New Testament (or, in the case of a Jew or Muslim, the Torah or Koran) a Member swears: 'I.....swear by Almighty God that I will be faithful and bear true allegiance to Her Majesty Queen Elizabeth, her heirs and successors, according to law. So help me God.' Members who object to oath swearing may make a solemn affirmation instead.

Houses of Parliament

Courts – Seeing a person give evidence helps the judge to decide whether or not that person is telling the truth. Witnesses will normally be asked to swear (take an oath) that what is said or used as evidence to prove your case is true. An oath is taken on the appropriate holy book. If a witness objects to being sworn, they can give a promise to tell the truth (called 'affirming').

Commercial – Every time we buy something with a Bank of England note we are handing over a piece of paper on which the Bank has written 'I promise to pay the bearer on demand the sum of...'

Personal – Think about who you have made a promise to this week. Did you keep the promise you made? How does it feel when someone makes a promise to you and they don't keep it?

Our whole society works most of the time because we can rely on the promises people make to us, and other people rely on the promises we make to them. Promises require the person making them to tell the truth and do what they said they were going to do.

Sometimes we find it hard to keep promises because circumstances change which make our good intentions harder to put into practice, but as Scouts we need to help each other to keep our promises. Sometimes we need other people to motivate us to keep our promises.

Someone who keeps their promises can be relied on by other people and helps make society a place where we can trust each other. Some people find it helpful to make promises with themselves or to their God.

What promises could you make to yourself that you would want to keep for the rest of your life?

Can you think of any other promises that you would want to make to yourself?

Remember … If you don't intend to keep your promise you shouldn't make it in the first place.

I promise to myself that ....

I will never take illegal drugs

I will always try to put other people's needs before my own

When I get a job I will maintain a healthy work-life balance

I will always study hard for my examinations

I will always try to forgive those who have treated me badly

RELATIONSHIP WITH YOUR GOD

In the Jewish faith, it is customary to write G-d as a mark of respect, so that the name of G-d may not be defaced or erased. In Judaism, G-d makes many promises and in the book of Genesis, Chapter 17, verse 10 G-d says: 'This is My covenant, which you shall keep, between Me and you and your posterity after you: Every male among you shall be circumcised.' This is why all Jewish boys are circumcised. For Jewish men this is an outward sign of the promise they make with G-d.

Some promises are made without any outward sign – can you think of any?

The six main religions in the United Kingdom all require believers to make a commitment.

Why not try and meet someone of a faith which you do not know very much about? On the next page are some basic facts to get you started:

Muslims preparing to pray at a Scout camp

Buddhism

Founder	Siddhartha Gautama (The Buddha)
Place of origin	North East India
Sacred text	Tripitaka
Sacred building	Stupa
Major festivals	Wesak
Main denominations	Theravada, Mahayana, Tibetan, Chinese and Japanese groups including Soto and Zen

Christianity

Founder	Jesus Christ
Place of origin	Israel
Sacred text	The Bible
Sacred building	Church, Chapel, Cathedral
Holy places	Jerusalem, Bethlehem, Nazareth, Rome, Canterbury, Lourdes (a popular place of pilgrimage)
Major festivals	Easter, Christmas, Pentecost (also known as Whitsun)
Main denominations	Anglican, Free Churches, Orthodox, Reformed, Roman Catholic

Hinduism

Founder	Developed out of Brahminism
Place of origin	India
Sacred text	Vedas, Upanishads
Place of worship	Mandir
Holy place	River Ganges
Major festivals	Divali

Islam

Founder	Mohammed
Place of origin	Saudi Arabia
Sacred text	The Qur'an
Sacred building	Mosque
Holy places	Mecca, Medina, Jerusalem
Major festivals	Eid-al-Fitr, Eid-al-Adha
Main denominations	Sunni, Shia

Judaism

Founding forefathers	Abraham; Moses
Place of origin	Israel
Sacred text	The TeNaKh (Torah, Nevi'im, Ketuvim)
Place of worship	Synagogue
Holy place	Jerusalem
Major festivals	Rosh Hashanah and Yom Kippur, Pesach (Passover), Shavuot (Pentecost), Sukkot (Tabernacles)
Main denominations	Orthodox, Reform

Sikhism

Founder	Guru Nanak
Place of origin	The Punjab, North Western India
Sacred text	The Guru Granth Sahib
Sacred building	Gurdwara
Holy place	The Golden Temple, Amritsar
Major festivals	Divali, Gurpurbs

Meditation and worship

In Buddhism, meditation is a conscious effort to change how the mind works. The Pali word for meditation is 'bhavana' which means 'to make grow' or 'to develop'.

Look at the pictures of people worshipping. Think about how people might feel in different kinds of worship situations? How do you think these different emotions can make people feel closer to God?

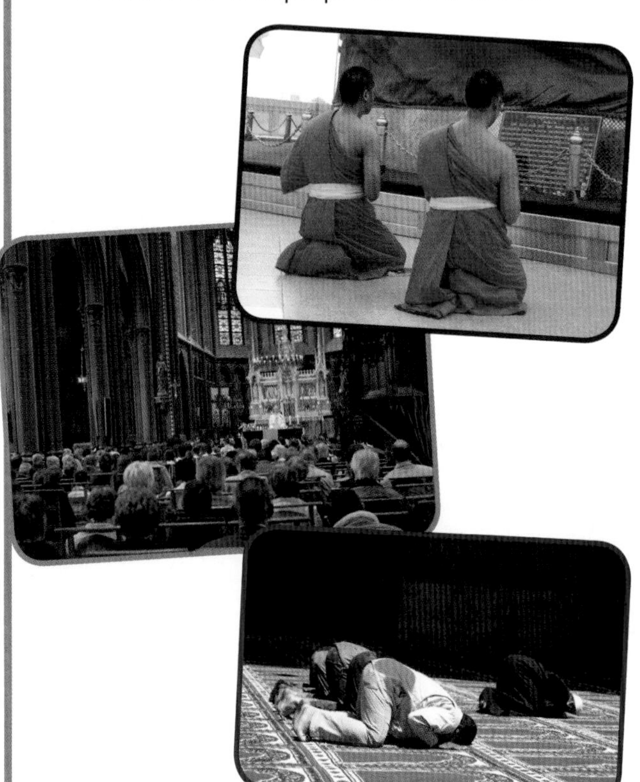

Have you ever sat quietly in a cathedral, temple or other place of worship, or a place that is special to you? Think how you felt while you were there. Write a poem, or paint a picture to express how you felt.

Some religions (Christian, Muslim, Jewish) meet together to worship, but Hindu worship is primarily an individual act rather than a communal one, as it involves making personal offerings to the deity. Worshippers repeat the names of their favourite gods and goddesses, and repeat mantras. Water, fruit, flowers and incense are offered to God.

Whether you have decided on your beliefs, or are still discovering faith, it is important that you feel able to live life in accordance with your faith and learn how to put your faith into practice in your daily life. Many people find ways of taking time out each day or week to spend in prayer, meditation, worship, learning scriptures, listening to teaching or discussing their faith with others. Why not get into the good routine of taking five minutes every day to sit and just be. Go on try it now!

Every religion has its own calendar of religious festivals and holidays or holy days - but what is a religious festival?

Religious festivals

A religious festival is a time of special importance marked by followers of that religion. Religious festivals are commonly celebrated on recurring cycles in a calendar year or lunar calendar. This means that, because ancient calendars were not hugely accurate, the exact date of the festival changes each year.

On the next page is a table of religious festivals and holidays.

Table of religious festivals and holidays

Religion	Festival	Significance
Buddhist	Asala	Turning of the Wheel of Teaching by the Buddha
	Wesak	Celebration of the Buddha's birth, enlightenment and final passing
	Kathina	Monks receive new robes at the end of three months' retreat
Christian	Christmas	Celebration of the birth of Jesus Christ
	Easter	Celebration of Christ's resurrection
	Pentecost	Coming of the Holy Spirit on the apostles of Jesus
Hindu	Diwali	Festival of Lights: start of the Hindu new year
	Navratri	Nine nights of devotion to the Mother Goddess
	Janmashtami	Celebration of the birth of Krishna
Jewish	Rosh Hashanah	Jewish new year
	Yom Kippur	Day of atonement – solemn day of prayer and fasting
	Pesach	Passover festival remembering the exodus of Israel from slavery in Egypt
Muslim	Ramadhan	Forty days of fasting in daylight hours – celebrates the revelation of the Qu'ran to Mohammed
	Eid-al-Fitr	Festival marking the end of Ramadhan
	Eid-al-Adha	The festival of sacrifice, remembering Abraham's offer of Ishmael as a sacrifice to Allah
Sikh	Baisakhi	Sikh new year
	Diwali	When Sikhs remember the release of Guru Hagobind from prison
	Gurpurbs	Number of festivals celebrating the birth or passing of the 10 Gurus

THE LIFE OF THE TROOP

Forums

Forums are occasions when the Troop, or representatives of the Troop, gather to discuss various aspects of Troop life. These can take many forms, be it interest groups or whole Troop or Patrol discussions. The Forum could be used to plan meetings or activities or look at how the troop is run.

Troop Leadership Forum

The Troop Leadership Forum is a meeting of the Patrol Leaders and older Scouts, with one or more Adult Leaders. Any Young Leaders working with the Troop can also be invited, and it may be useful from time to time to invite one or more of the Assistant Patrol Leaders (as it will prepare them for their time when they become Patrol Leaders).

The Troop Leadership Forum should be involved as much as possible in the day-to-day running of the Troop. It will meet as frequently as is necessary, but usually about once a term would be appropriate. The Troop Leadership Forum could have any of the following responsibilities:

- Planning the Troop programme
- Considering the ideas and suggestions raised by the Troop Forum
- Reviewing the structure of Patrols
- Appointing Patrol Leaders
- Approving a Patrol Leader's choice of Assistant Patrol Leaders
- Agreeing a Troop Code of Conduct

Having an effective Troop Leadership Forum will help to share the leadership amongst a number of people.

'We have a PL/APL meeting before the Scout meeting most weeks. During this we discuss activities coming up and changes that need to be made. We meet up 45 minutes before the rest of the Scouts arrive and just get on with it.'
Cameron and Darren

Code of Conduct

Many Troops have a code of conduct which is contributed to by everyone in the troop. They are important as they outline the accepted behaviour of the Troop. To ensure they are kept relevant to all members they would normally be reviewed annually.

Here are two prime examples on which you might like to base your own Troop's Code of Conduct:

Example 1:

To get the most out of Scouting we suggest that you take an active part in Troop life.

The following is what we would consider as a minimum commitment from Scouts:

1. Attend all Scout meetings unless ill or away.
2. Take part in at least one of the three Group Church parades.
3. Take part in the District St George's Day parade in April. This parade is on a Sunday afternoon and the date is normally published in the Troop diary sheet in December.
4. Attend at least two Scouting events outside of the normal Troop meeting during the year.
5. Help with at least one fundraising activity.
6. Look after your own and Group equipment.
7. Wear your uniform smartly and with pride.
8. Enjoy your Scouting.
9. Let the Patrol Leader know if you have any ideas for activities for the Troop.
10. Let a Leader know if you are unhappy with anything within the Troop.

Example 2:

At all times we should:

> Listen and follow the instructions given by our Leaders, Patrol Leaders and Assistant Patrol Leaders.
> Turn up on time, so we can start and finish on time, and be prepared to join in.
> Be intolerant of bullying, swearing and not do it ourselves!
> Wear sensible clothes and footwear for the activities we're doing.
> Be honest and say what we think, feel, want or need, provided it is at an appropriate time and not hurtful towards others.
> Set a good example to younger Scouts or Cubs.
> Remember to say please and thank you, and most importantly, smile and have fun!

During meetings we should:

> Turn our mobile phones off or keep them silent.
> Put sweets or chewing gum away, so we're not tempted to eat them.
> Turn up in smart uniform, unless we're told otherwise by a Leader.

Above all we should:

> Show loyalty to our Troop and the worldwide Movement.
> Be able to be trusted and trust others.
> Be a considerate friend to others.
> Be brave, even when the going is tough.
> Be careful with other people's stuff as well as our own.
> Treat each other with respect.

Rushil
Patrol Leader

Running a learning experience for other Scouts

As a Scout you will have learned lots of new skills and teaching these to others can be fun. You might like to teach younger Scouts a specific skill or help them to achieve a Challenge or an Activity Badge. You may even think about trying to achieve an Instructor Activity Badge.

Lead successfully a group of Scouts at a two-day camp or other similar event

As a Scout you will have the opportunity to lead younger Scouts. You could do this to achieve your Outdoor Plus Challenge.

'We went to a disabled school to help others where they were short of leaders. The students were really happy to have new people there and enjoyed the company. It was satisfying to see the looks on their faces.'

Cameron

DEVELOPING BELIEFS AND ATTITUDES

Reviewing activities

Sometimes, however hard we try, things we plan go a bit wrong. When that happens, it is important to be honest with yourself and ask what you could have done better, rather than blaming other people. If you get into the habit of reviewing each activity, and writing down the results, you will be to make sure that they are even better next time.

Some people call this W6 – what went well, what went wrong.

Help someone less fortunate than yourself

As a Scout, you promise to help other people. There are lots of ways in which you can do a special 'good turn'. Your local authority may be able to tell you about groups who are already working with disadvantaged people and you can contact them to see how you can be most useful.

Here are a few ideas:

> Visit an old person who lives alone. They might need help with shopping and odd jobs, or just someone to talk to

> Help to renovate flats for families with low incomes

> Organise a sponsored activity to raise money for a charity. This could be a walk, car-wash, silence or fast (going without food). Whatever you do, involve your Leaders in the planning so that everything takes place safely.

Visit an Act of Worship of another faith community

You will need to plan this in advance, and find out about any special customs and behaviour (taking off your shoes, covering your head) so you don't upset people. As well as looking for differences with your own culture, look for things that are similar of equivalent. Maybe you will find some ideas that you could use to make your Troop prayers, Scout's Own or Church Parade a bit more interesting!

Your town may have ecumenical celebrations, in which people from different faiths and denominations worship together. Your Patrol or Troop might help out with this.

'I visited a synagogue because we were doing a topic on Judaism. We had to get caps for our heads and their book of worship was called the Torah, but it wasn't a book it was like a scribe which you had to read backwards. It was pretty interesting to observe a different way of worshipping.'

Darren

ASSOCIATED ACTIVITY BADGES

My Faith

'Camping is one of the best activities you can do at Scouts. You learn the skills to survive outdoors. If you can live outdoors, you can live anywhere. In my Outdoor Challenge I learnt knots and lashings, how to cook on an open fire and some lifesaving first aid. Doing all this while camping made it much more enjoyable.'
Rushil
Outdoor

8 THE OUTDOOR CHALLENGE

REQUIREMENTS

Take an active part in one or more Nights Away, totalling at least two nights, preferably camping, to include many of the following activities:

a. Help to pitch and strike your tent.
b. Light a fire and cook at least one meal using an open fire.
c. Set up a suitable stove, and prepare a meal using a stove.
d. Demonstrate personal hygiene.
e. Keep your belongings organised and tidy within your accommodation.
f. Maintain a tidy and orderly site.
g. Take part in a wide game.
h. Take part in a campfire or other entertainment.
i. Build a simple pioneering project.
j. Build a useful camp gadget.
k. Explore the environment of your camp.
l. With others, successfully complete a two hour activity or project.
m. Provide a service commitment to the site for about an hour.

This list gives an idea of the type and style of the activities that the Nights Away should include. Depending on the activity there may be extra ideas that could be included, which can be agreed in the Troop Forum.

In addition to the above, demonstrate the following basic emergency aid skills during the Nights Away experience:

a. Understand the initial actions to take in the event of an accident.
b. Understand the importance of getting adult help and when to call the emergency services.
c. Know how to treat minor cuts, burns and scalds, stings and insect bites.

PITCH AND STRIKE A TENT

Pitch, strike and store a tent

Every tent is different and has its own best way of being **pitched** (put up) and **struck** (taken down), but here are some general points which will help if you ever have to pitch a Patrol tent which is new to you.

> As you unpack the tent note how it is folded and what bits go in which bag – this will help with packing it up.

> Find a suitable piece of ground – flat, with no sharp objects, and no ant nests. Check that the door of the tent does not face into the wind and that you like the view! Avoid pitching the tent under a tree or you will be dripped on long after any rain has stopped. In some woodland sites it can't be avoided but do avoid old oak trees as they lose branches with no warning in a strong wind.

> Lay out the groundsheet which will define the area of the tent and help you locate the position of its pegs.

> Fit the poles together and attach them to the tent. For large tents with wooden poles they probably go inside; for small tents with metal, fibre-glass or carbon fibre poles they probably go outside the tent but under the flysheet. If your tent has a ridge pole, make sure it goes through the loops provided. Watch out for any metal spikes which might tear the material. Always make sure the doors are closed up before you put it up or you may find the doors won't close when it is pitched.

> Use two or three other Scouts to hold the tent while you put the largest pegs in place for the main guy ropes. Once these are tight your helpers should be able to let go and help you put the rest of the pegs in.

- Set the corner guy-ropes at right angles to each other (pegs following the lines of the guys)

- Set other guy-ropes in line with the seams in the canvas (pegs in line with each other too!).
- Brailing pegs (corners first, pulling the walls tight so that the walls are vertical). Brailing pegs should go in at 90°.
- Pegs should go into the ground at an angle of 45 degrees and the guy-ropes should pull on them at right angles.
- Adjust all the guy ropes until the material of the tent is pulled just tight enough to look smooth and not sag.
- Fit the groundsheet.

Once your Patrol has mastered the way to pitch your tent, try these activities:

- Try pitching a tent you have never pitched before.
- Pitch a tent with everyone blindfolded except the Patrol Leader.
- Record the time it takes to pitch your tent and then see if you can beat this time without being careless.
- Make up a scrapbook of tents: use pictures from catalogues, describe each tent you have use of.

Tent care

Your tent is your home and at camp it needs looking after if you are going to enjoy living in it. Here are a few simple rules about tents. If you stick to them everyone will be happy and the tents will last much longer.

A good Scout is someone who knows how to be comfortable at camp.

Comfort includes keeping dry and warm and your tent will only keep out the wind and rain if it stays waterproof and does not get torn.

> Keep everything (and everyone) from touching the inside of your tent because it will leak when it rains.

> Never walk on the tent while you are pitching it or striking it as this will take the waterproofing off and may damage the canvas.

> Always remove your shoes at the door and avoid walking on the groundsheet – especially when conditions are wet and muddy, but even in dry conditions this will bring dust and pollen into your sleeping area.

> Pitch it correctly. This way the canvas will not be under strain. If the tent looks well pitched (everything neatly in line and nothing sagging) then it probably is!

> Always pack the tent away bone dry. If not, it will rot very quickly and be ruined. If you have to strike camp in the rain, always spread the tent out to dry as soon as you get home, ideally by hanging it up if possible.

> Always clean the pegs. Even when they are put into a separate bag, mud dries and then gets everywhere. Clean the pegs by scraping one peg with another and leave them spread out to dry.

> Always count the number of pegs before and after camp so that none are left behind.

'I clean the pegs and then stack them in a square so that they dry.
Hannah

Parts of a tent

The traditional Patrol tent consists of two or three upright poles, a ridge pole, green canvas plus a flysheet in many cases, all secured by four main storm guys and a number of side guys. Lightweight tents consist of aluminium or glass fibre flexible poles; nylon, polyester or poly-cotton and nearly all have a flysheet. It is important to familiarise yourself with the parts of a tent. Tents share many common features with the same function.

Guy lines — These may also be known as 'guys' or 'guy ropes'. A guy line is a single line or rope which creates the familiar tent shape when the tent is pegged into the ground and the guy lines are pulled tight. Badly tensioned lines cause a tent to sag and when raining, pockets of water form which may then drip into the tent. Rope guy lines made from natural fibres should be slackened at night to prevent them from snapping due to becoming wet and then shrinking. These lines also help to keep the tent down in high winds. Synthetic materials, however, can slacken when they are wet so guy lines may need tightening.

Runner — This is a wooden, metal or plastic bracket attached to the guy line which aids the shortening of the line (and, therefore, the tightening of the line). The guy line goes from the tent, around the peg and back up to the runner where it is tied off. The runner has a second hole which the line can freely run through: it is this part which holds the line in position.

Becket — There are several forms of becket, and they are the means by which you close or tie up the door. Some beckets take the shape of a wooden toggle and loop, others consist of a loop passing through an eyelet on the other side of the door.

Pegging point — On a ridge tent, these points are the brailing loops at the bottom of the tent's wall or at the end of a guy line. On a lightweight hiking tent, the pegging points are rubber bands that are fixed to the tent through a canvas loop that is stitched to the tent. A pegging point is usually located at a strong point on a tent, such as on a seam line.

Ridge — This is the top of a tent from where the two sides slope away. On a Patrol tent this is identified by the top cross pole (also known as the ridge pole). It is important not to put anything between the canvas and this pole, as this causes leaking when it rains.

Flysheet — This is an outer covering layer to the tent made from a heavier material than the inner. For frame and lightweight tents the inner tent is a very light, breathable cotton layer, and so needs this waterproof outer to protect it from wind and rain. On a ridge tent, you place the flysheet over the poles before raising the canvas.

Sod cloth — This is a border of hessian or plastic material attached to the bottom of a patrol tent. It is tucked under the groundsheet to prevent rainwater or dew soaking equipment and personal kit inside the tent.

Groundsheet — This is made of a heavy waterproof material placed on the ground inside the tent and, in effect, becomes the floor. A single groundsheet to fit the floor space of the tent is more effective than a patchwork of individual groundsheets. It stops damp and water from getting into the tent from the ground and also provides protection from insects. Some tents have these sewn into the inner tent. On many lightweight tents the sewn-in groundsheet may not be of a heavy quality, and may benefit from having a protection sheet laid underneath it to prevent punctures occurring. Remember to always check the camping area for sharp stones before pitching your tent, to avoid damage.

Tentbag or valise — This is the bag that the tent is stored in. These vary in size, but it is worth practising folding up the tent before going away to check that your tent does actually fit inside! Once you have pitched your tent, make sure you put the tent bag and any other bags for the poles or pegs in a safe place – ready for when you strike the tent.

Dolly — This is a wooden cap that goes on top of each upright pole; attached to it are long guy lines which are used to hold the main body of the tent up. These lines are also known as storm guys, as they provide stability in high winds.

Brailings — The brailings are small loops at the bottom edge of a patrol tent. They are used to peg down the vertical walls so the rain and the wind and rain are kept out. They are also used to air the tent, by lifting or rolling the side walls up, which is known as brailing the tent. It is important to air the tent when you can to help ventilate it and to prevent the grass underneath from drying out during longer camps.

To pitch a lightweight 'dome' tent

1. Find a suitable piece of ground: flat and with no sharp objects sticking out.
2. Empty the bag or valise of the tent and all its parts and lay them out so that you can see what the tent consists of.
3. Assemble the poles which are often held together by elastic shock cord. Make sure the doors are closed then attach the poles to the tent by sliding them through the sleeves provided.
4. Peg out the groundsheet. Metal pegs can often be pushed into the ground by hand. Set the pegs at 45 degrees to the ground and 90 degrees to the loops.
5. Peg out all the remaining loops around the base of the tent and guy lines. Remember that the loops should be stretched in line with the seams of the tent. The tent should then be upright and free of creases.
6. Place the flysheet over the poles of the tent to form an outer 'shell'. Take care not to damage the flysheet and make sure that it does not touch the inner tent.

In some tents, the poles go through sleeves in the flysheet which is then pitched first. The inner is then attached and is hung inside the flysheet.

1 2

3

3

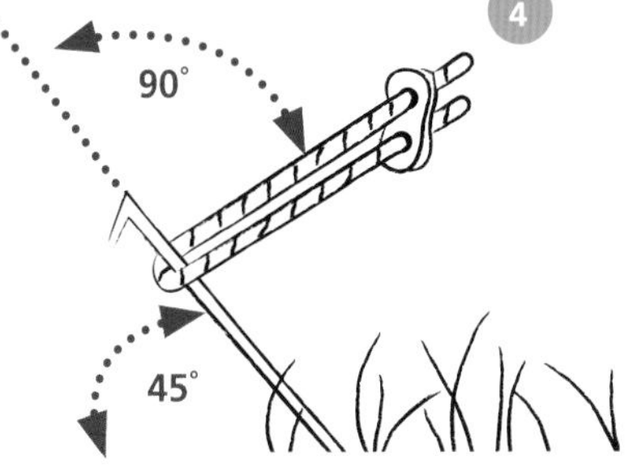

LIGHT A FIRE

Decide where to set the fire – well away from tents, trees and hedges which might also catch fire. Frequently used campsites often have designated areas of rough ground where you should lay your fire.

If there is no fire place and you have the land owner's permission, lift enough turf (about eight centimetres thick so the roots are not destroyed) to give a patch of bare ground for the fire with a good gap around it. Keep the turf in a cool damp place so that you can put it back when you have finished.

If the turf must be kept for more than a day or two, store it upside down with the roots on the top and keep it well watered.

Altar fires are very common. Usually this is a metal frame with a metal tray on top of it. You build the fire on the tray in the same way as a ground fire.

The fire needs to be built carefully – don't just pile on lots of wood and hope for the best! Collect all the wood you need first, before you light the fire. You will need small pieces of kindling and large pieces for when the fire is burning well.

For the wood and kindling to burn they need oxygen (which is in the air) but too much wind can blow out a small flame. Watch the fire carefully and shield it from strong winds. Blow gently to help the flames to spread.

Once the fire is alight, put a few larger pieces of wood at the end of it where the wind blows the flames on to them. When they are well alight, add more wood to the other end. The fire will be hottest and best for cooking when the wood has burnt for a while and has red and glowing embers rather than flames. When you add more wood aim to keep at least one part of the fire just right for cooking on. An ideal cooking fire is both flameless and smokeless.

Equipment for building a fire

You will need:

> punk or tinder – dry leaves, paper, bark, birch, wood chippings

> kindling – dry, dead twigs and sticks

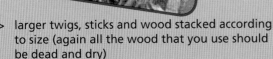

> larger twigs, sticks and wood stacked according to size (again all the wood that you use should be dead and dry)
> logs or stones
> matches (kept in a plastic bag or waxed in case of wet weather). If you build a fire carefully, you should be able to light it with one match
> knife or spade if turf needs lifting (always check the local rules for fire lighting before starting to cut turf)
> a safety bucket of water, sand or fine soil
> a 'wafter' such as an old enamel plate to fan air onto the fire during lighting.

Safety checklist

> Paraffin, petrol and methylated spirits are very volatile and highly inflammable. **Never** use them to light or revive a fire. If the vapour from them catches fire, you could become engulfed in flames.
> Never leave a fire unattended.
> Never underestimate a fire or the strength of the wind.
> Never put sealed pressurised containers such as deodorant cans on a fire.
> Ensure you are not wearing anything that is dangling which could catch fire.

Keeping the wood pile well stocked

It is important to prepare a supply of wood ready before lighting your fire. Site a wood pile near but not next to the fire, graded in piles of kindling, twigs, branches and logs. Use plastic sheeting to cover the wood pile and to keep it off the ground. Ensure that you always have a supply of burnable, dry wood no matter what the weather.

Building and lighting a fire

1. Stand the first twig upright in the ground and surround it with tinder or 'punk'.
2. Build a wigwam shape by surrounding your tinder with dry kindling.
3. Use progressively thicker twigs, expanding the shape but leaving a gap at the windward side for lighting so that the wind will blow onto the fire.
4. Light a match, shielding the flame in your hand and getting as near as possible to the base of the fire.
5. Light the tinder or punk and any small pieces of kindling.
6. Add more twigs as necessary, maintaining the wigwam shape until it spreads to thicker wood.
7. If you need to blow the fire, get in close and blow gently.
8. Once alight, add larger and larger twigs and sticks continuing to maintain the wigwam shape. Then add a few pieces of wood at one end so that they catch light. When these are well alight, add more wood to the other end.
9. When it is firmly established, and the wigwam shape has been abandoned, lay bricks of thick logs parallel with the wind direction on either side of the fire. These logs will support a metal grid for cooking on.

Feed a fire – don't smother it. Fires are fickle and will go out if they are not looked after in the early stages. Replenish fuel frequently. Leave the fireplace as you found it, so that there is no trace that you have been there.

If the earth at the base of your fire is wet, build your fire on top of a sheet of aluminium foil or layers of dry sticks placed on the ground.

BURNING PROPERTIES OF WOOD

Collecting wood for your fire

Not all wood burns well. The list below will help you to identify the best wood for lighting and burning.

Wood burning properties

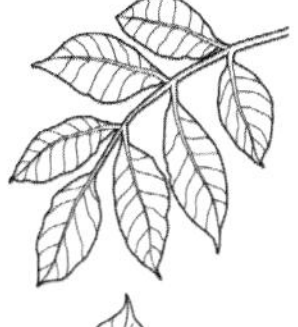

Ash
Kindling – average
Cooking – good

Beech
Kindling – average
Cooking – average

Birch
Kindling – good
Cooking – good

Horse Chestnut
Kindling – poor
Cooking – poor

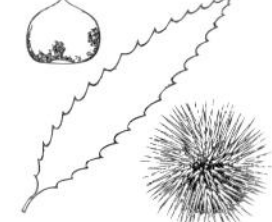

Sweet Chestnut
Kindling – poor
Cooking – average

Elm
Kindling – poor
Cooking – poor

Hawthorn
Kindling – good
Cooking – good

Hazel
Kindling – average
Cooking – average

Holly
Kindling – good
Cooking – good

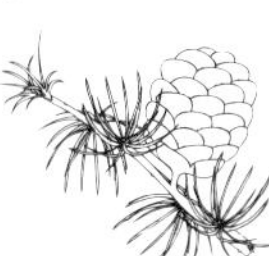

Larch
Kindling – good
Cooking – good

Lime
Kindling – average
Cooking – average

Oak
Kindling – poor
Cooking – average

Pine

Kindling – good

Cooking – good

Poplar

Kindling – poor

Cooking – poor

Spruce

Kindling – good

Cooking – good

Sycamore

Kindling – poor

Cooking – average

Use this rhyme to remember which woods are best for fire lighting and which to avoid.

These hardwoods burn well and slowly,

Ash, Beech, Hawthorn, Oak and Holly;

Softwoods flare up quickly and fine,

Birch, Fir, Hazel, Larch and Pine;

Elm and Willow you'll regret,

Chestnut green and sycamore wet.

Only use dead wood for fires

Learn to recognise live and dead wood. As a rule of thumb green is live and will not burn well. Remember to only use fallen dead wood – never damage living trees. If you have access to a wooded area, you may be surprised how much suitable wood can be collected from the forest floor.

Different grades of wood

Before you start, collect plenty of wood of different sizes. This is probably the most important thing to remember as you will be surprised how much wood you need to keep the fire going.

You will need dry kindling to get the fire started – dead, dry leaves, paper, birch bark and so on. These will not burn for long and you must use the heat from them to make the wood catch fire – thin twigs first, which will in turn help to light the bigger stuff.

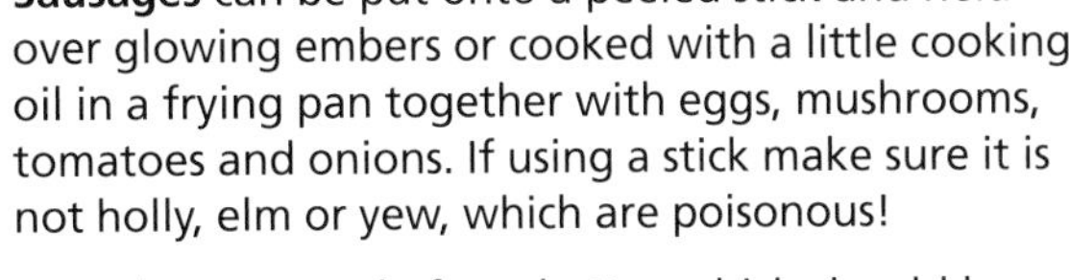

COOK A MEAL ON AN OPEN FIRE

Cooking

Remember that metal pots and frying pans will get hot when cooking on an open fire. Take care when handling them.

When you are using pots and pans it is helpful to put washing up liquid on the outside. Soot will come off much easier when you wash up.

Here are some ideas for simple meals:

Twists are made using a stiff dough of flour and water. But first you need to find a thick green stick. Peel the bark off and then heat the stick over the fire before you wind the dough around it. When it is cooked, the twist should slide cleanly off the stick. Add jam and it's delicious.

Potatoes can be baked in foil in the glowing embers which are left after the flames have died down. Bananas and apples as a dessert can also be cooked this way, nice with raisins or chocolate buttons.

Sausages can be put onto a peeled stick and held over glowing embers or cooked with a little cooking oil in a frying pan together with eggs, mushrooms, tomatoes and onions. If using a stick make sure it is not holly, elm or yew, which are poisonous!

Pancakes are made from batter which should be made about one hour before you need it. To make about eight pancakes you will need an egg, a mugful of flour, a pinch of salt, a mugful of milk and a little fat.

Put the flour and salt in a bowl and make a well in the centre. Drop the egg and half the milk into the well and stir gradually until all the flour is mixed in. Try to make sure the mixture is smooth with no lumps, then slowly add the rest of the milk, beating all the time.

Put a tiny amount of cooking oil into a frying pan and wait until it is really hot. Tilt the pan so that it is evenly coated with oil. Pour just enough batter into the pan to cover the bottom with a thin layer. As the pancake cooks through, it should come unstuck from the pan and you can then turn it over to cook on the other side.

Serve with lemon and sugar.

After your meal you might like to try twists for fun.

Do not forget, you have not finished until the fire is put out, the turf put back level, and all the washing up done.

SET UP A STOVE

Gas Stoves

1. Disposable gas containers should be changed outside the tent, away from naked lights. Shake first to make sure they are empty and turn the tap hard off.
2. Unscrew the burners completely before removing the cartridge.
3. Unscrew the base or other retaining device.
4. Place the empty containers in a sack, well away from the tent. Never dispose of them on a fire!
5. Insert the new cartridge and close the base firmly before screwing back burner.
6. Make sure that the stove is firm and level. Hold lighted match to burner while you turn on the gas.

PREPARE A MEAL USING A STOVE

In truth, there is little difference between cooking on gas and using an open fire. The timings may be different between the two, and you will not be able to cook certain things on a stove that you can on a fire (and vice versa). Stove cooking generally comes with less hassle, so many Scouts will rely on their stove to cook a quick breakfast.

Try using fires and stoves for camp cooking and you'll soon find out which method works best for what meal.

FOOD HYGIENE

When your kitchen and dining room is outdoors, you soon learn the importance of food hygiene, as what may not be a big issue at home soon becomes a tourist attraction for pests and vermin. If you're going to enjoy food at camp, you need to keep cooking and food preparation areas clean at all times. You will also pick up tips on how to improve hygiene levels around food.

'Colour coded chopping boards are a really effective way to prevent contamination when preparing meals. Hygiene on camp is really important, and having different colours for different food groups helps to stop you using a dirty board. Plus, when you've got more chopping boards, more members of the patrol can help cooking, and dinner is prepared even quicker!'

Hannah

Colours to use

Red: raw meat
Blue: raw fish
Yellow: cooked meat
Green: salad and fruit
Brown: vegetables
White: bread and dairy

DEMONSTRATE PERSONAL HYGIENE

All your kitchen hygiene becomes even more important when you go to camp and you'll also need to know how to keep yourself healthy and comfortable.

> Have a good wash all over every morning – you will feel much better! Do not expect to have a hot wash every day in camp, although some Patrols get themselves organised and use just a little hot water to take the chill off the water.

> Make sure you have enough changes of clothes with you. Camping can be hot and sticky work and underclothes and socks must be changed daily.

> Don't go to bed in the clothes you have been wearing all day – you'll feel awful in the morning! Bring a pair of pyjamas or clothes just for night time.

> To clean your teeth you can rinse your toothbrush in some water in your mug. You should clean your teeth every morning and again last thing at night and if possible after every meal.

> Make sure you wash your hands with soap (or an anti-bacterial gel) after using the toilet and before handling any food.

If you are a Patrol Leader make sure your younger scouts who may never have been camping before, know where the washing and toilet facilities are. Always remember to leave those facilities as you would wish to find them.

Inspection

Air your sleeping bag and night clothes as soon as you get up. It should be well-aired before being put away.

Whatever way your leaders ask you to do your inspection the main reason this is done is to make sure you stay healthy and take home the equipment that belongs to you.

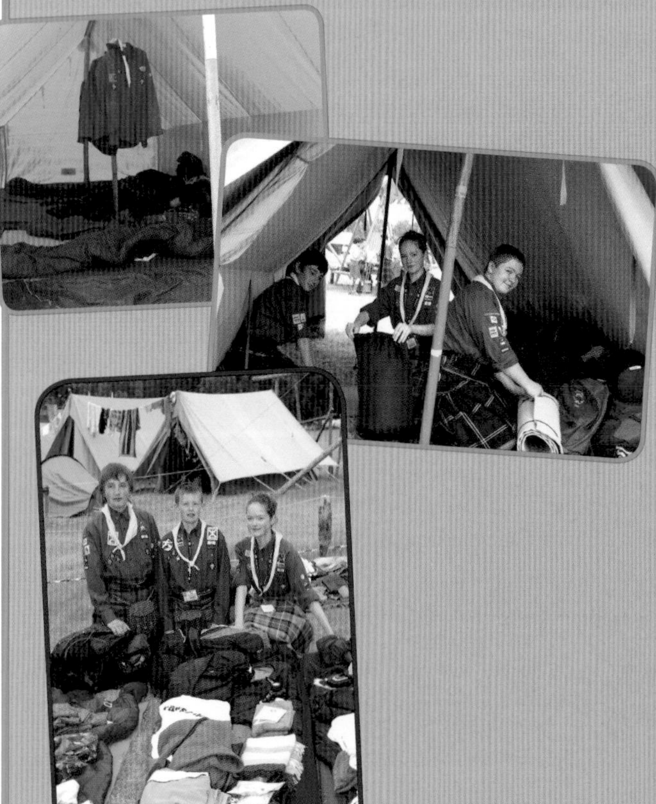

KIT AND EQUIPMENT

Make sure that your name is on all your personal equipment.

Uniform

Uniform includes navy activity trousers, Scout Belt, Scout shirt and your group scarf.

Kit bag or rucksack

For most camps a 50-70 litre rucksack should be big enough. Where there are no scheduled hikes a kit bag or holdall will suffice but remember you are responsible for carrying your kit bag!

Rucksack liners

No rucksack or kitbag is 100% waterproof and few attempt to be, therefore a strong liner to your bag is vital. Bringing used carrier bags is always useful on any camp or expedition.

Waterproofs

A good waterproof jacket and a pair of waterproof trousers should see you through all but the worst weather conditions, breathable are best as it will keep you drier. Ensure that these really are waterproof. You will be outside for a long time and many garments are only 'showerproof'.

Tents

Bring enough tents for all those in your patrol. If you are not using a patrol tent, a sensible combination of 2-5 people hike tents that are easily portable is best. Each patrol should also have a dining shelter or similar.

Sleeping bag

A good sleeping bag is essential for a good night's sleep – choose one with a season rating suitable for the conditions you will be using it in.

Sleeping bags are typically categorised into Season Ratings, but these ratings should only be considered as a guide and not a guarantee of the bag's suitability for your needs.

This table shows what is generally meant for each season rating.

Season	1	2	3	4	5
Rating	Summer	Spring/ summer	Spring to autumn	Winter	Expedition
Rating (C)	+5	0	-5	-10	-15

Although sleeping bags are grouped into season ratings, you should bear in mind that other factors need to be considered such as the additional use of a roll or sleeping mat, whether you are in a tent or completely outside, and of course the thermal efficiency of the night clothing you are wearing.

Sleeping mat

A sleeping mat will help keep out the cold, aiding your sleep and conserving heat. A blanket underneath also helps with insulation and blocks out cold from the ground.

Boots

A good pair of boots is essential for both hiking and other activities at camp. Ensure they are comfortable and fit well. They should be 'worn in' before prolonged use. More than one pair of footwear is essential in case they get wet.

Trousers / Shorts

Choose trousers made from quick drying fabric, not denim. Make sure they will keep you warm and are comfortable.

Tops

The key to upper clothing is to wear layers so you can regulate heat: go for lots of thin layers rather than one thick one. More T-shirts will be required in summer and more jumpers in winter, although even in summer evenings can be chilly, so make sure you have plenty of warm clothes.

Hats

You lose a lot of heat through your head. In winter and at night choose a thermal hat that will retain this heat. In summer go for a hat that will protect you from the sun eg baseball cap.

Gloves

Your hands can get very cold especially when wet, so a pair of gloves will help you retain that extra bit of warmth. Fingerless gloves will help to keep you warm and allow you to handle fiddly objects eg a compass.

Socks

At camp some people go for two pairs of socks, some for just one. It's up to you to go for what you find comfortable. Bring enough for the duration of the camp and a spare pair. When you are wearing thermal or hiking socks, sometimes it is a good idea to wear a thin pair underneath to prevent rubbing.

Underwear

Bring enough for the duration of the camp and a spare set.

First aid kit

A personal first aid kit is always a good idea. Include plasters and anything else that you will need. Ensure that you tell your leader if you are taking any medication.

Cutlery

Knife, fork, spoon and teaspoon for eating and preparing your food.

Plate, bowl and mug

A mug is essential, for hot drinks and it can be used to hold your food if space is at a premium – on camps a plate and bowl are important too – go for plastic or metal.

Stove and cooking pots

Bring a small portable stove (three per Patrol should suffice) and fuel. Trangias with gas adaptors are best as they come with cooking pots as an integral part. Get resealable gas canisters for use on future camps. More substantial double gas stoves are also an option (one or two per patrol). If you are hiking, make sure that your fuel is carried in a suitable sealed container.

Cooking utensils

Wooden spoon, ladle, draining spoon, spatula, sharp knife, colander, jug and bowl will suffice but if you are desperate to try out your new 100 piece camp cook set then feel free to bring it along too!

Towels

A tea towel is essential for camps and expeditions. Depending on the nature of the camp and its duration, a bath towel will be useful for swimming and showering. A hand towel may also be useful if space is not at a premium.

Wash kit

Brush, comb, toothbrush, toothpaste, flannel, soap, deodorant plus anything else you need to make you feel human again (including contact lens solution if appropriate).

Torch

A torch is essential if you are caught in failing light, have to pitch your tent in the dark or are taking part in any night activities. Remember to take spare batteries.

Camera

A disposable camera is the safest and cheapest way to capture those moments that need recording for posterity!

Chairs

There will be some 'down time' so why not bring a fold-up camp chair to make you more comfortable?

These are often items which are brought by your Troop or Patrol and you should check with your leaders which, if any, of these that you need to bring.

'Keep tidying the kitchen as you go along. That way it's easier to keep on top of things. It's also important to keep the surfaces clean, just like you would at home.'

Ben

MAINTAIN A TIDY AND ORDERLY SITE

Your campsite should be well laid out and will have lots of different areas to it which each have particular and important functions to make sure that everything can take place safely.

When laying out your site, consider the wind direction and pitch your tent upwind of anything which will produce smoke or smells.

Good, enjoyable camps are well organised and tidy. There will be nothing left lying around that might cause a hazard and the site will certainly be litter free.

As well as the sleeping tents, there will be an eating area and a cooking area. This could include a wood pile, chopping area, fire or a stove as well as storage areas. You should help to make sure that your site is organised and tidy. Try to find out how these different areas are arranged. For example, you could find out about how stores are organised.

TAKE PART IN A WIDE GAME

Wide games

A wide game is an outdoor activity, usually between two or more teams which have to achieve specific objectives in order to win the game. This might be simply preventing the other team(s) from finishing or collecting certain items. Wide games are organised in a large area and can be played either on a Troop night or at camp and at night (or at least in the dusk) as well as daytime.

Wide games usually have a theme or storyline which helps set the scene and can provide the highpoint to a camp. Apart from having fun, wide games provide an opportunity for the participants to develop teamwork, planning skills, endurance, resourcefulness, initiative and physical fitness!

There are no hard and fast rules to wide games which is what makes them flexible and allows you to be as creative as you like.

'Night is the best time to play wide games, really, because it's harder to find people in the dark and it's a bit of an adventure. One time we played a game where we started out at a base by the campfire. The Leaders gave us 30 seconds to hide. I hid on the field, wearing my friend's jacket so they wouldn't know it was me. After that they came out with torches, and when they shone it on you they had to say the name of the person. The object of the game was to get back to base without being caught and identified. In a wide game there are no prizes, but it doesn't matter because it's so much fun.'

Charlotte

Lord of the Rings

Buy some cheap glow sticks (the 22 inch ones are the best to use) and make them into rings. Throw the rings into a large field. One team must defend the field whilst the other team has to try to sneak in to get the rings.

General rules:

> You can only carry one ring at a time.

> Rings cannot be hidden.

> Rings must not be thrown.

> When tagged you have to go quietly.

> You need to create a 'prison' for those who are caught and they must remain there for two minutes.

> A base is needed for the attackers to use to store the rings.

An ace wide game

Equipment needed: One pack of playing cards

Aim of the game:

To capture the other team's ace player

How to play:

> The Troop splits into two equal teams.

> Give every player in Team A one red playing card (suits don't matter), making sure one player has the ace.

> Give every player in Team B a black playing card (suits don't matter), making sure one player has the ace.

> Define the area for the game and make sure everyone understands it.

> Each team tries to capture the other team's ace.

> Scouts individually challenge opposing team members; the Scout with the highest value card wins. The Scout with the lowest card loses their 'life' and returns to central base for a new life (and exchanges their card for a new one). If both have equal value cards, disregard and carry on. The ace is the highest value card in the team and can only be captured by two Scouts together from the opposing team who have picture cards.

> The ace is therefore the most powerful card because it beats any card it challenges, but of course it is the most vulnerable as the opposing team is trying to find out who has the card and capture it.

There is plenty of opportunity here for teams to plan tactics and strategy.

TAKE PART IN A CAMPFIRE

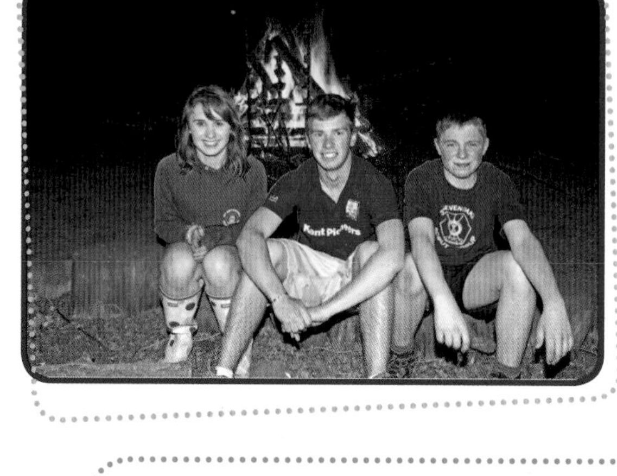

Campfires have always been a part of camp life. Different Scout Troops have their own favourite songs, stories and sketches and taking part in a campfire with other Scouts can be particularly good. After you have been to a few, you will be confident to lead a song or a sketch yourself!

The tradition of collecting the ashes

Collect the cool ashes of the previous night's campfire and add them to the base of your next campfire. You will be taking with you the fun and friendship of each fire and the people you met and sang with.

Campfire blankets

Blankets are really to keep off the evening chill. It is always colder away from a campfire than sitting at the fire. However, they can also be a record of camps and activities you have been on. You could make a poncho or cape from a blanket and then add whatever badges, patches or decoration you wish.

SIMPLE KNOTS

People have been tying knots for thousands of years. Today, despite technology, knots are still as necessary as ever. In sports such as sailing, climbing, caving and angling, and in work such as fire fighting, fishing, truck driving and even surgery, the ability to tie the right knot is essential. All knots have a purpose and it is just as important to understand what that purpose is, and when the knot is used, as having the ability to tie it. The wrong knot at the wrong time can be dangerous.

Here are details of nine knots commonly used in Scouting. It explains what the knots are used for and how to tie them. In order to help us with knotting, it is also useful to understand a little bit about ropes.

Types of rope

Laid ropes - These are ropes normally consisting of three strands which run over each other from left to right. Traditionally, they are made from natural fibres, but nowadays they tend to be made from synthetic materials.

Braided ropes - These are ropes which consist of a strong core of synthetic fibres, covered by a plaited or braided sheath.

Natural ropes - These are made from such natural materials as hemp, sisal, manila and cotton, which are easy and pleasant to knot.

Synthetic ropes - These are relatively expensive but last a long time. They are superior in that they are generally lighter, stronger, less prone to rot, water resistant and better able to withstand difficult and extreme environments. Wire ropes are available but are rarely used in Scouting.

How ropes are measured

Ropes are normally measured by their circumference. For example, a 75mm rope is approximately 25mm in diameter.

Parts of the rope

You won't need to be told that a piece of rope will have two ends! However, in order to work with ropes, it is useful to be able to refer to different parts.

The main parts of a rope are called:

Working end - The end of the rope you are using to tie a knot

Standing end - The end of the rope opposite to that being used to tie the knot

Standing part - Any part between the two ends. It can be a part of the rope already used in the knot

Loop - A loop made by turning the rope back on itself and crossing the standing part

Bight - A loop made by turning the rope back on itself without crossing the standing part.

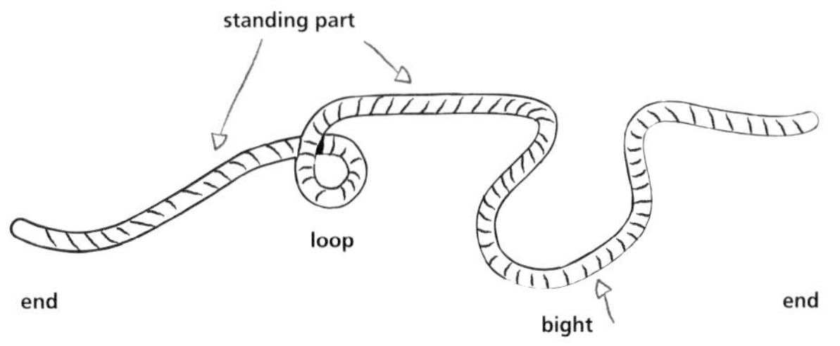

Some other useful definitions

A bend - This is a knot which is used for tying one rope to another.

A hitch - This is used for fastening a rope to another object such as a post, spar, pole, log and so on.

Although there are many different kinds of knots, knowledge of the ones detailed here will enable you to undertake most pioneering projects and activities required in Scouting.

Equipment

You will need a couple of lengths of rope about a metre long and ideally of differing colours. This will help you see the knot as it forms. You will also need a free-standing pole or a wooden chair back, or even a table leg for tying some knots to!

Knot	Purpose
Reef knot	To join two ropes of the same diameter (also used in first aid to join two ends of a bandage together)
Sheet bend	To join two ropes together
Figure of eight	A stopper knot
Round turn and two half hitches	To attach a rope to a pole
Clove hitch	To attach a rope to a pole and to start and finish a square lashing
Timber hitch	To drag a log and to start a diagonal lashing
Highwayman's hitch	A slip hitch
Sheepshank	To shorten a rope or to bridge a damaged section of rope
Bowline	To make a non-slip loop

Common Knots

Reef knot

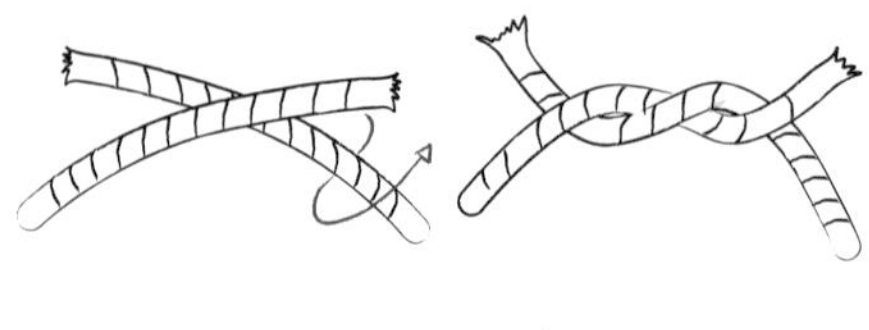

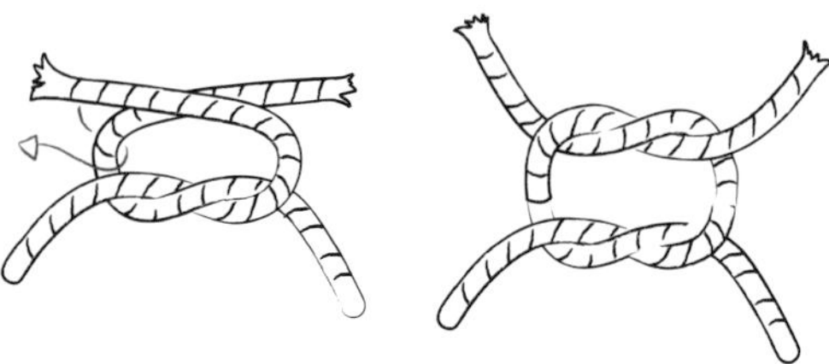

This most common knot is used to tie together two working ends of the same material and size. Take an end of rope in each hand and lay the left hand end over the right. Then, using your right hand, take the end from the left down behind the other rope and up to the front again. Point the ends inwards again, this time the right hand one over the other one, then take it down behind it and up to the front through the loop which has now been formed. Pull the knot tight. This knot is often remembered by, 'left over right and under and right over left and under'.

Sheet bend

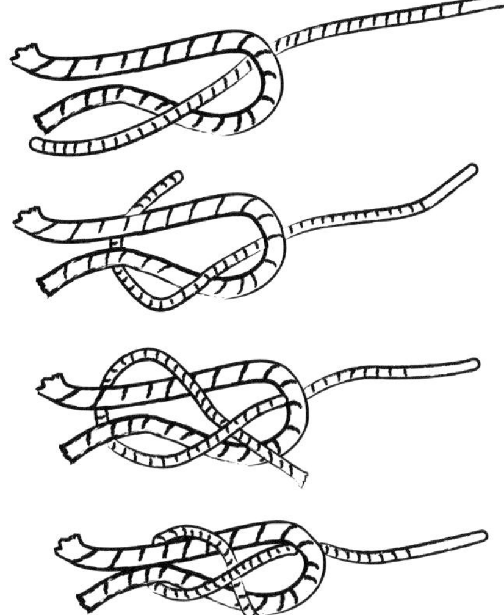

The 'sheet' is the sailor's name for a rope. Form a bight in the working end of the thicker rope. Take the working end of the thinner rope and pass it up through the bight. Take the thinner rope round the back of the bight and trap it under itself. Remember not to take the working end back down the bight in the first rope. Pull tight by holding the bight in one hand and pulling the standing part of the second rope with the other. Make sure the two ends are on the same side of the knot. If the ropes are of very different thickness, take the working end round the bight and under itself twice to form a double sheet bend to make the bend more secure.

Figure of eight

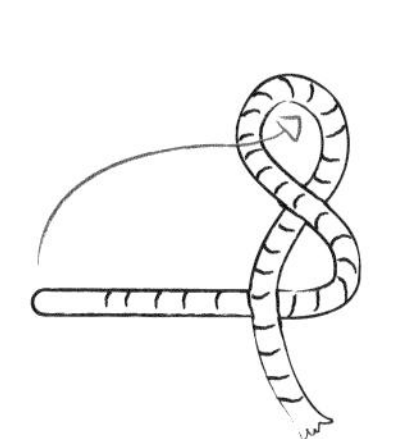

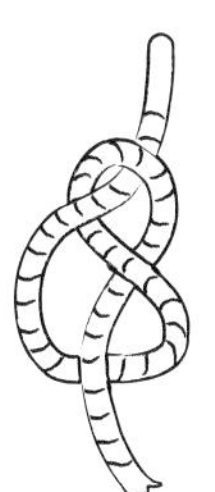

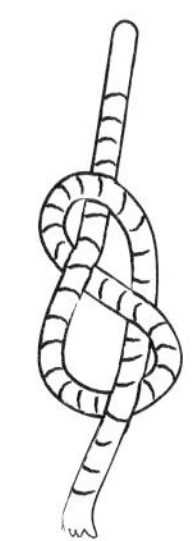

This is a 'stopper knot' that is unlikely to jam or pull loose. It is also used, when doubled, to tie a loop in a rope. Form a loop in the end of a rope. Take the working end behind the standing part and back over itself into the open loop. Finish by pulling both sides of the knot tight. If the knot is correct, it will look like a 'figure of eight'.

Round turn and two half-hitches

This is a long name for a simple hitch used to attach a rope to a post, spar, tree, and so on. It is a composite knot formed from two simple knots. Form a round turn by turning the working end twice around the post. Then form a half-hitch by taking the working end around the standing part forming a crossed loop. Repeat to form a second half-hitch. These should be tied in the same direction and tightened up against the post to ensure that the round turn doesn't slip.

Clove hitch

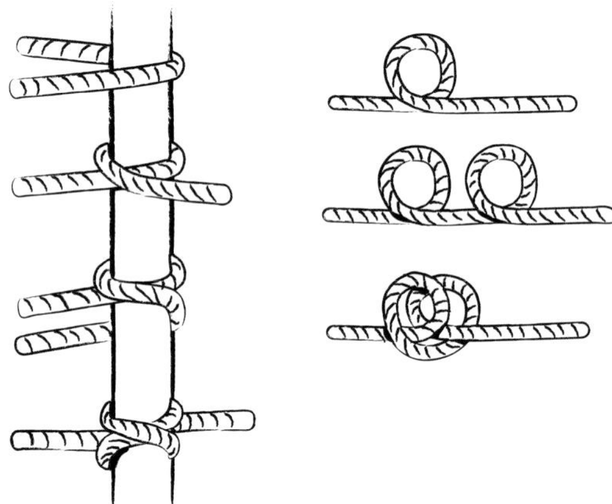

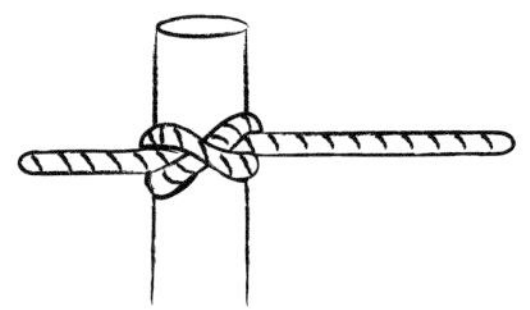

The clove hitch is another method of 'hitching' a rope to a post. Not as secure as the round turn and two half hitches, it is often used to begin other hitches and lashings. There are many ways to tie a clove hitch. However, the one that everyone should know is: pass the working end over and under a rail. Run it across the standing part at the front. Continue round the rail again and bring the working end back to trap it under the diagonal. Thus the two ends of the rope should be laid next to each other under the diagonal but running in opposite directions. The clove hitch looks like a 'N'.

Timber hitch

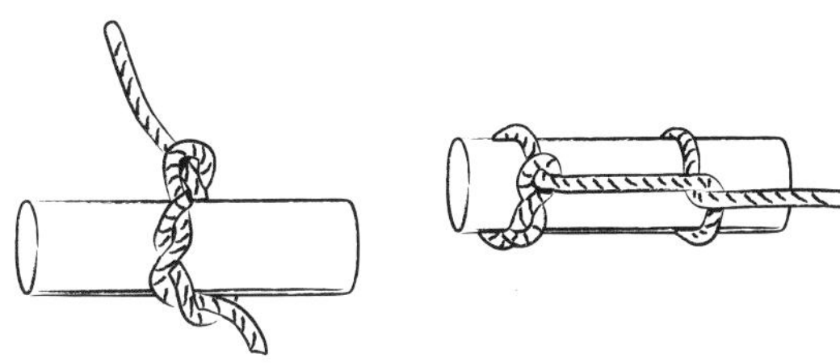

The timber hitch is a temporary knot used to drag, tow or lift a log or pole. Turn the working end round the standing part and then wrap it around itself at least four or five times. A half-hitch can be tied in the standing part further up the log or pole to add some security. The log is dragged by pulling the standing end. Also used to start a diagonal lashing.

'I can tie a clove hitch, reef knot, round turn and two half hitches, square lashing and a friendship knot.'
Rushil

Highwayman's hitch

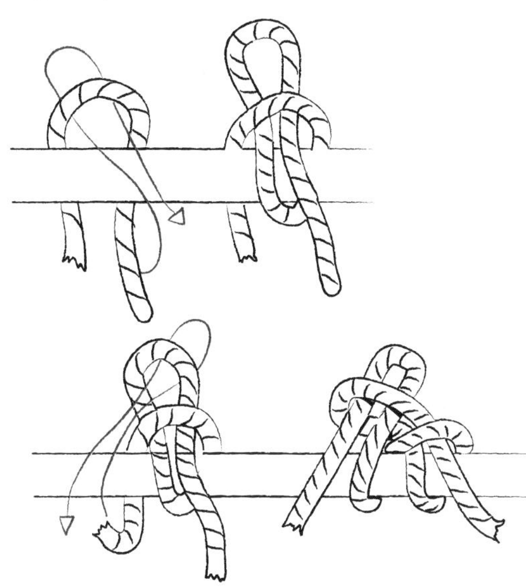

This hitch is a 'slip hitch'. Pulled on the standing end it holds fast. Pulled on the working end it comes free. Thus it is used to tie a boat to a mooring ring or an animal to a rail or post. Start by passing a bight behind the rail. Take another bight in the standing part and pass it in front of the rail and through the first bight. Pull tight on the working end. Then take a third bight in the working end and pass it in front of the rail- and through the second bight. Pull tight on the standing part. Because it is a slip knot, it is not used in climbing or pioneering.

Sheepshank

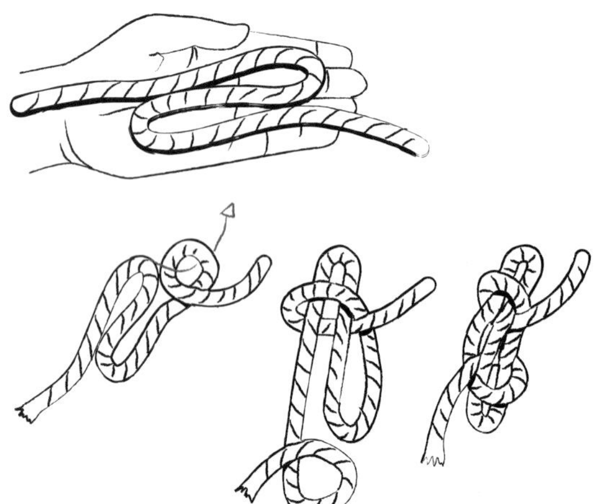

This knot is used to shorten a rope, or to bridge a damaged length, without cutting the rope. It can be tied in the middle of the rope without needing the ends. Form the rope into an 'S', that is two opposing bights. In each free end form a half hitch. Pass the adjacent bight through the half hitch. Pull the two free ends tight at the same time. If being used to bridge a damaged portion of rope, make sure the damaged part goes through both half hitches. That is, the damaged portion should be the centre of the 'S'. The sheepshank should be kept in tension. If loosened it may well come undone so it must not be used in climbing or pioneering.

Bowline

The bowline is used to form a non-slip loop in the end of a rope. It was traditionally the climbers' waist knot before harnesses were used. Form a loop by passing the working end over the standing part. Pass the working end back up through the loop from behind and around the back of the standing part. Pass the working end back down the loop and pull tight. If using synthetic rope, the working end should be locked off against the adjacent standing part with a half hitch. The bowline is invaluable in rescue situations but might have to be tied blind. Once you are comfortable with tying the knot, practise it with your eyes closed. It can sometimes be remembered by 'the rabbit comes out of its hole, round the tree, and down the hole again'!

BUILD A SIMPLE PIONEERING PROJECT

An example of a simple pioneering project is a flagpole. Here are some examples of flagpoles you could build.

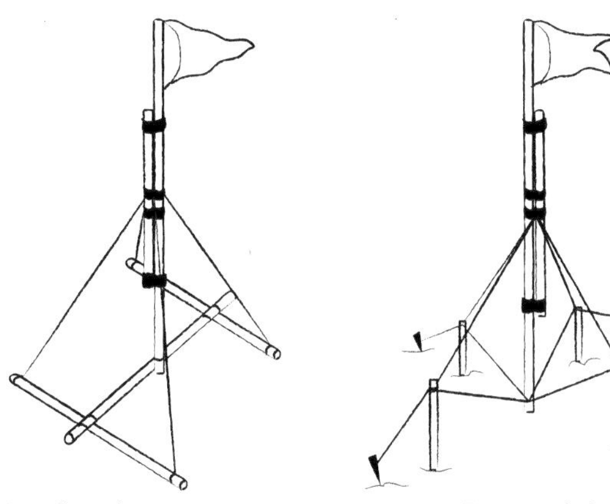

Wigan flagpole

Four stay skylon

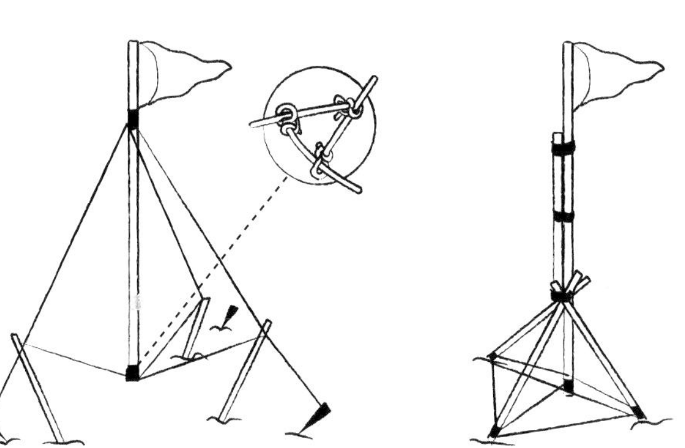

Simple skylon

Tripod portable flagpole

You will need to practise your knots and learn some lashings to construct these.

Clove hitch

Used to fasten a rope to a spar while under strain. Also to start square lashings and all lashings.

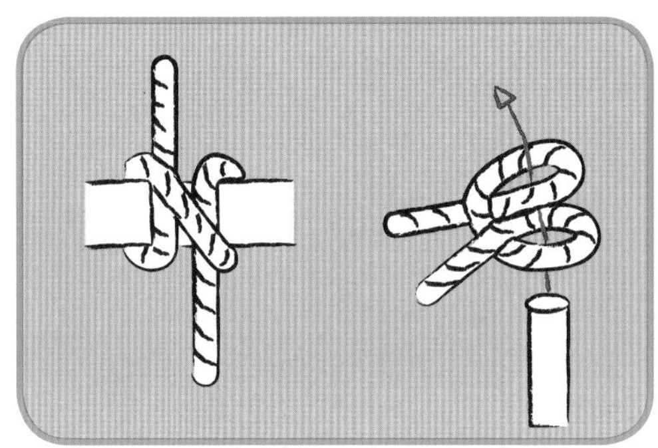

Round turn and two half hitches

Used to fasten a rope to a spar.

LASHINGS

Sheer Lashing

A sheer lashing is used either to join two poles together or to extend their length.

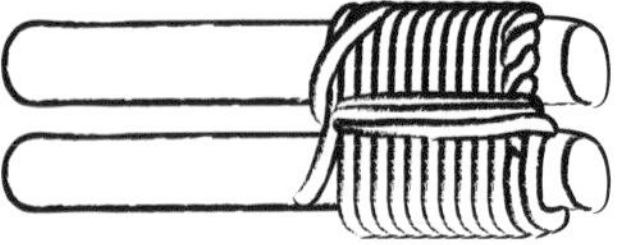

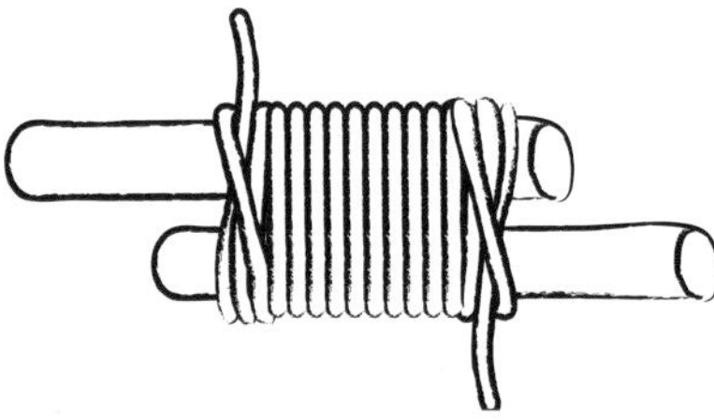

There are two ways of tying a sheer lashing:

1. Start with a clove hitch (and in other instances) around a spar. Follow up with about 10 turns take a few frapping turns. Don't pull tight as this lashing is used for sheer legs. End with a clove hitch.
2. Start with a clove hitch around both spars. Follow with turns, pulling tight after each. There is no frapping turn. Wedges can be used to tighten the lashing. Finish with a clove hitch.

Figure of Eight

Lay spars with two running one way and the third in the other. Start with a clove hitch on one outer spar then take turns over and under. Make frappings between spars-end with a clove hitch on opposite spar to start. Used to make tripods.

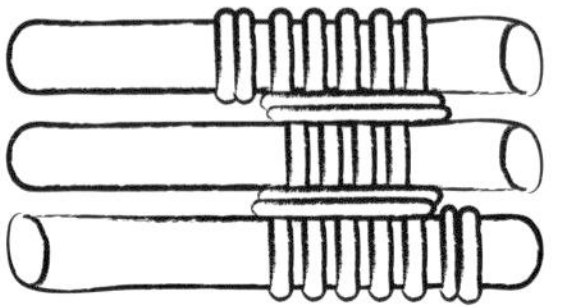

Sheer lashing

SQUARE LASHING

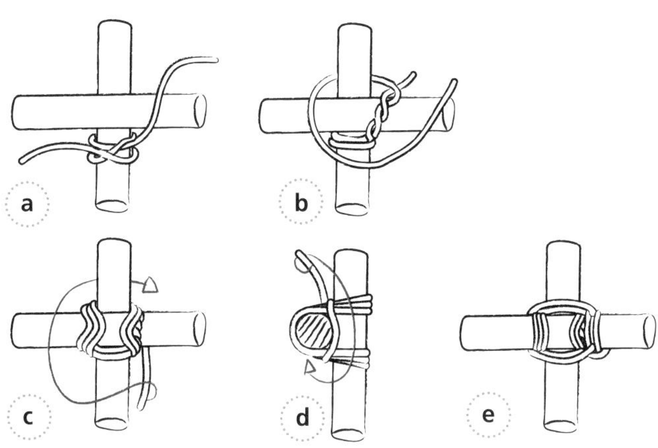

A square lashing is used to hold two poles that cross each other. This is usually (although not necessarily) at 90 degrees to each other.

1. Start this lashing with a clove hitch. Twist the rope end to neaten. (a + b)
2. Wrap the rope first over one spar, then under the other, pulling tight all the time. (b)
3. On the second time round, go inside the previous turn of rope on top, but outside underneath the spars. (c)
4. After three turns, apply two frapping turns, which pull on the rope turns already made, making them even tighter. (d) Finish off with a clove hitch. (e)

Tying a square lashing

BUILD A USEFUL CAMP GADGET

A camp gadget is simply something that is made to make life at camp easier. It can be as simple as a branch used as a mug tree or as advanced as a camp dresser (see page 193). Why not plan and design a gadget, and use some of the knots and lashings you have learned.

Equipment

For most gadgets, poles about the thickness of a broom handle and thick string is all that is needed.

Other camp gadgets:

> hanging larder
> wellie boot stand
> towel rail
> washing-up bowl stand.

TWO HOUR PROJECT

When you go to camp, you will find there are many activities going on. This will of course depend on the site or location that you are going to and many Troops have their own particular favourites.

Here are some examples of things you may do:

> astronomy
> axemanship
> badge work
> build a bivouac
> camp gadgets
> cooking competitions
> day on a farm
> explorations such as visiting a place of worship or a famous bridge
> local geology and archaeology
> mystery outing
> nature conservation
> nature study
> painting or sketching
> photography
> pioneering
> play reading
> sports and games
> swimming
> visit a pottery or country fair
> visit other Scouts.

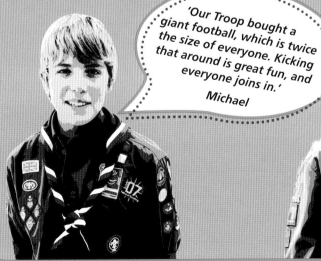

'Our Troop bought a giant football, which is twice the size of everyone. Kicking that around is great fun, and everyone joins in.'
Michael

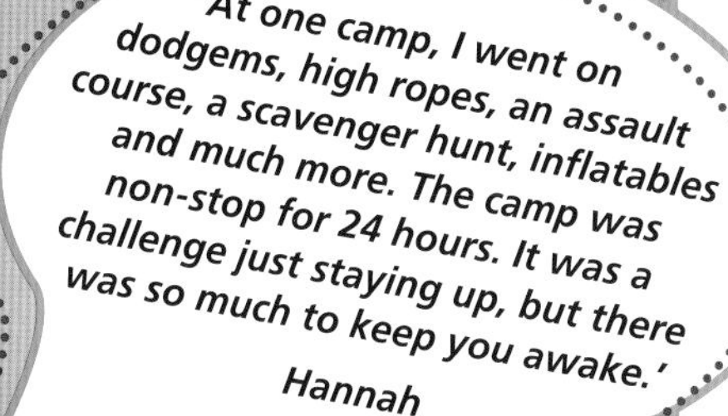
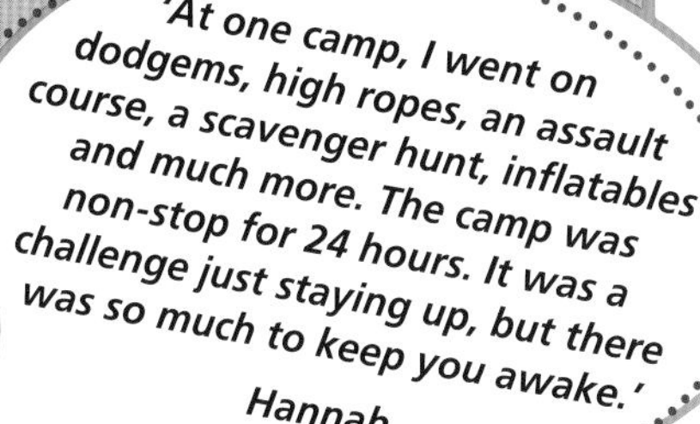

'At one camp, I went on dodgems, high ropes, an assault course, a scavenger hunt, inflatables and much more. The camp was non-stop for 24 hours. It was a challenge just staying up, but there was so much to keep you awake.'
Hannah

ASTRONOMY

Have you ever stood on a clear crisp night gazing up into the heavens at all those thousands of stars?

If you're into astronomy you may have your own telescope, but there are other opportunities to get a better look at outer space, through visiting an observatory, planetarium or even by using a telescope online through the National Schools Observatory (see below). Looking out at the stars can make us feel small, as we are not just part of planet Earth, but the solar system (which includes Mars and the other planets) our own galaxy (the Milky Way) and the entire universe, which is everything that physically exists.

Stars are burning gaseous balls, emitting light. How bright a star appears depends on many factors including the age of the star, distance from the earth, temperature, movement and size. The sun is a star close enough to the earth to provide us with light and warmth.

Stars in the night sky can be grouped into constellations, a way to recognise collections of stars. Some of these constellations can be seen in the diagrams below.

The North Star (Polaris) is always above the North Pole. This makes it useful for navigation at night, as it can be used for finding which way is north. It can be found by locating the constellation called 'the Plough'. The last two stars in the bucket of the Plough make an imaginary line pointing to the North Star.

The Plough

The North Star

Find out more:

National Schools Observatory
www.schoolsobservatory.org.uk

NASA Kids' Club – **www.nasa.gov/kidsclub**

British National Space Centre Learning Zone
www.bnsc.gov.uk

BBC – Space
www.bbc.co.uk/science/space

GEOCACHING

Geocaching is an outdoor activity with a technological twist, which you can try at your camp. It combines Scouting Skills like navigation with a hide-and-seek game, and allows you to find hidden treasures (called caches) that people have placed, leaving their co-ordinates on the internet.

To go geocaching you will need a GPS receiver. GPS stands for the Global Positioning System, which is a set of satellites owned by the US government, which communicate with a handheld receiver to tell you exactly where you are on the planet. Using the GPS, you can plot co-ordinates of caches you find online, and travel to them.

When you get to the correct spot, the game is far from over. You will need to hunt for the cache, and upon finding it you get to look inside at the messages other cachers have left and you can also exchange trinkets (called Geocoins or Geobugs) before hiding it back where you found it.

If you get to go geocaching, try the following activities:

> find your position using the GPS

> enter the coordinates (or waypoint) of a cache into the GPS

> find a cache

> place a cache and enter the details into a geocaching website

Like many other outdoor activities, there are guidelines and etiquette for geocaching responsibly. The Geocaching Association of Great Britain (GAGB) produce a list of guidelines for safe caching, which should be followed.

Find out more:

www.geocaching.com

www.gagb.org.uk

SERVICE COMMITMENT

When you are at camp, it can be greatly appreciated by the site manager or landowner if you offer to do a small job of service. This could range from filling in potholes to emptying bins – and during the summer when the site is very busy, they will probably be very grateful for your help. The network of campsites owned by Scouting across the UK are an excellent resource and a good Scout should offer to spend a small amount of time helping to keep them in good shape.

DEALING WITH AN ACCIDENT

The Outdoor Challenge gives you the opportunity to gain some basic knowledge of emergency aid and know the actions to take if someone gets hurt or injured. Even if you have already passed some of your Emergency Aid Staged Badges, it is good to remind yourself again just what you need to do when you are confronted by an injury

a) Understand the initial action to take in the event of an accident

b) Understand the importance of getting adult help and when to call the emergency services.

Have you ever seen a headline which reads something like 'Boy saves father's life'. You may have seen something similar in the local press which is followed by a description of how a young person's quick thinking and proper training have saved a life.

First aid is the very first help or treatment given to someone who is injured or is suddenly taken ill. The injury may be quite minor, such as a burn, a cut or bruise or maybe an insect sting or bite. The treatment will be quite simple and within a few minutes the plaster has been applied, or the burn has been cooled and dressed and the casualty is feeling better. However, some injuries may be more serious, requiring experienced medical aid if the casualty is to survive. If you are first on the scene, your priority is to act quickly and calmly. **If at all possible, get adult help.** If you are at camp, your leaders will have had some first aid training and will be better able to manage the situation. They may however need your help, so stay nearby unless told otherwise.

The first aid priorities are:

> Assess the situation

In a first aid scenario, the most important thing is never to put yourself at risk. Ask yourself how many people have been hurt and who might be available to help. Observe what has happened and be aware of any further dangers – both to the casualties and yourself. It is important that you don't add to the problem by becoming a casualty yourself. So for example, check for traffic, or whether something might fall and injure you or whether the electric power has been switched off.

> Make the area safe

Do what you can to protect any casualties from further injury and to prevent causing injury to others. This may involve leaving the casualty where they are.

> Give emergency aid

Assess the condition of the casualties. If there is more than one person hurt, decide who you need to help first. It is often the case that the 'quiet' casualty may be more seriously hurt than one shouting and complaining. Deal with life threatening conditions. It is vital to open airways and maintain breathing, to restart blood circulation by cardiac massage if the heart has stopped pumping and to stop the flow of blood from any serious wounds.

> Get help from others.

It is essential to get the medical services involved as quickly a possible, either by getting the casualty to hospital or by calling the Ambulance Service.

MAKING AN EMERGENCY CALL

With many people now carrying mobile phones, contact with the emergency services is usually very easy. However there are some parts of the country where the phone reception is poor and you may need to use a landline. All calls to the emergency services are free. Dialling 999 in the UK (or 112 anywhere in the European Union) will connect you to an operator who will ask you which service you require. If people have been hurt and need to get to hospital ask for the ambulance service.

Talking to the emergency services

Before you dial, take a deep breath and compose yourself. Try and think and speak clearly, so you can provide all the information needed as quickly as possible.

The operator may need to know who you are and the number you are calling from.

They will need to know the exact location of the incident. If you know the area, be as precise as you can, giving the full address and any local landmarks. If you are a stranger to the location, ask a local person or use an in-car navigation system with a 'where am I?' facility which pinpoints its position very accurately by satellite. Remember also that all phone boxes show their address inside and emergency phone boxes on the motorways are numbered for identification purposes.

The operator will need to know the type and seriousness of the incident, so that they know what help to send.

They will need to know of any other hazards which might affect the rescue, such as leaking gas, toxic waste spillage, and broken power lines or details of any extreme weather conditions.

Don't end the call until the operator has all the information they need. You may need to arrange to meet the ambulance and guide the crew to the scene of the incident.

Never assume that someone else has phoned. The emergency service would rather receive calls from half a dozen people than fail to turn up because everyone assumed someone else had phoned.

MINOR INJURIES

Most injuries at camp will be quite minor and providing the correct treatment will ease any discomfort quickly and aid the healing process.

Cuts

Small cuts will generally lose very little blood and direct firm pressure to the wound, while elevating the injury, will generally be sufficient to stop any bleeding. After washing, an adhesive dressing will be all that is required to keep the wound clean while it heals during the following few days. Care needs to be taken to avoid infection.

> Wash your hands thoroughly with soap and water or use an antibacterial gel, and if you have them put on disposable gloves.

> If there is any dirt in the wound, try flushing it out under running water, or use an alcohol-free wipe. Dry it gently by tapping it with a gauze swab.

> Cover the wound with a sterile dressing, avoiding touching the wound.

> Clean away any dirt from the surrounding area with soap and water or a clean wipe. Dry as before then check for allergies to plasters before applying the adhesive dressing).

wipe away from wound, using a clean gauze swab for each stroke.

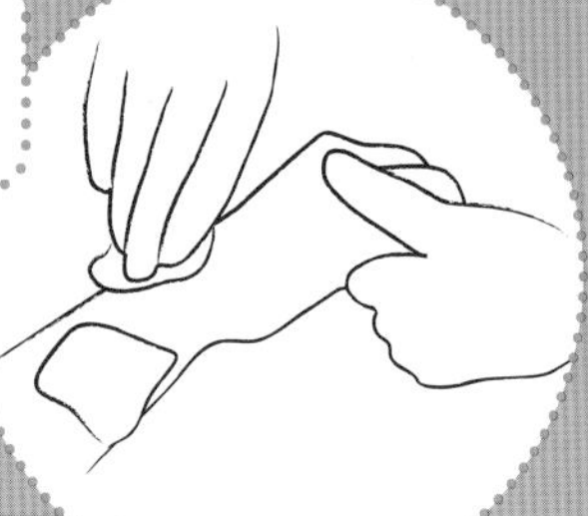

Burns and scalds

Burns are normally caused by coming into contact with something dry and very hot, such as a metal grid on the cooking fire. Scalds are caused by wet heat, such as steam from the mouth of a kettle or by spilling boiling water from a cooking pan onto skin.

Most minor burns and scalds will heal quickly although the skin may redden and blister. Care should be taken not to prick the blisters, as this will increase the chances of infection.

> Cool the injured area with cold running water for at least 10 minutes.

> Put on disposable gloves to limit the chance of infection.

> Remove any clothing or jewellery from the area before any swelling begins.

> Cover the area with a clean, non fluffy sterile dressing, or cling film or a plastic bag.

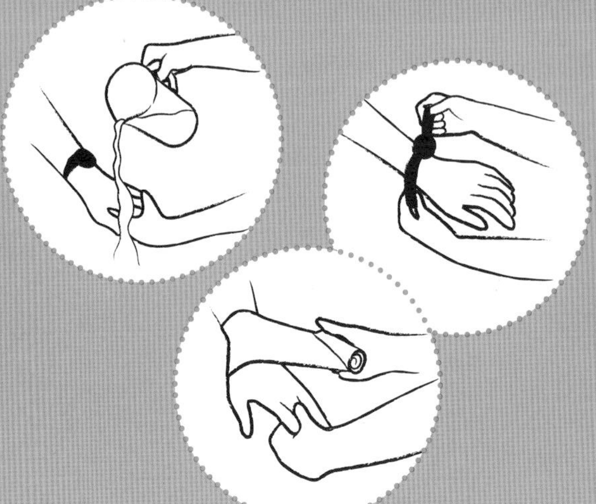

Stings and insect bites

In a camping situation one of the most likely stings is from contact with stinging nettles. This can cause irritations to the skin which become red with a series of small raised bumps. Very often the cure is close by – in the form of a large oval leaf, know as the 'doc leaf'. These should be screwed up and the 'juice' from the leaf rubbed onto the stinging area. There is an alkaline in the leaf which helps to neutralise the formic acid in the nettles.

Bee and wasp stings can also affect campers during the summer months. They are generally painful rather than dangerous. Both insects normally only sting if they are threatened. The bee can often leave its sting in the form of a tiny stem. If it is visible, it can be scrapped away. Avoid using tweezers as they can result in more poison entering at the site of the sting.

> Raise the affected part and apply an ice pack or a cold compress for 10 minutes. Many first aid kits carry a spray to relieve stings and this may be applied if the casualty does not have a condition which prevents its use.

> Some people can go into anaphylactic shock following a bite. They become very anxious, their skin may become red and blotchy and their breathing becomes noisy and the casualty may gasp for air. The pulse becomes very rapid and their skin can feel cold and clammy, and they may break into a sweat.

> You will need to make the casualty comfortable, in a position that makes it easy to breath and phone immediately for an ambulance.

> Stings to the mouth and throat can also be very dangerous, as the resulting swelling can make it difficult to breathe. Give the casualty cold water to drink and get them to hospital.

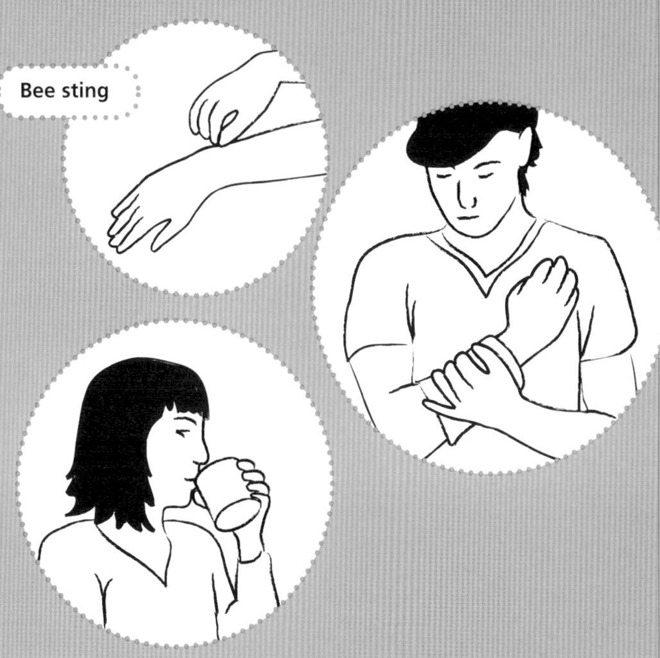

'When we were building a gateway for our campsite once, the Scout Leader was at the top of the structure. He's not the smallest, and his weight caused the gateway to give in. It was like slow motion as he fell directly on top of me. My first reaction would have been to fall about laughing, but I honestly couldn't move! After some first aid treatment for both of us, we were soon alright. We even finished the gateway...'

Darren

'A girl in my Troop only ate a muffin for breakfast before a day of hiking, but didn't tell anyone. After a few hours of walking, she wandered into a bush and fainted! It wasn't funny at the time, and I put h in the recovery position. When she came round, she didn't know where she was, and freaked out a bit. Thankfully, she was okay, and we can all laugh about it now. She learnt the importance of eating properly before exercise, and I learnt the importance of knowing emergency aid.'

Hannah

ASSOCIATED ACTIVITY BADGES

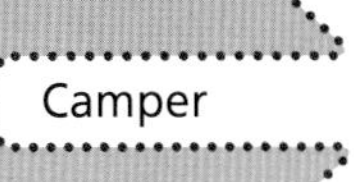

'I can still remember my first camp at Corfe Castle, completing a scavenger hike and making lots of new friends. I've now completed over 40 nights away and am a Patrol Leader. In completing my Outdoor Plus Challenge I have built Bivvis (natural shelters), learnt new cooking techniques and practiced first aid which I have since used in real life. Being a Patrol Leader gives you responsibility and the chance to put into practice the things you have learnt, teaching others.'
Hannah
Outdoor Plus
NIGHTS AWAY
AND MUCH MORE...

9 THE OUTDOOR PLUS CHALLENGE

REQUIREMENTS

Complete the following activities:

Hold the Outdoor Challenge.

Spend at least eight nights away as a Scout, four of which must be camping.

Take an active part in further camp(s), which should include many of the following:

a. Lead or help to lead a group of Scouts in setting up a well-organised site that includes sleeping tents, food and equipment stores, fire/stove, kitchen and eating area.

b. Plan a balanced menu for a short camp.

c. Show how to use safely an axe and/or a saw.

d. Lead the cooking of a meal for the group.

e. Show knowledge of the safety precautions for the use of lamps and stoves.

f. Cook a backwoods meal with the group.

g. Build a working camp gadget, such as an altar fire, camp oven or a gateway to a campsite.

h. Take a leading role in the construction of a pioneering project.

i. Build a bivouac and sleep in it.

This list gives an idea of the type and style of the activities that the Nights Away should include. Depending on the activity there may be extra ideas that could be included, which can be agreed in the Troop Forum.

In addition to the above, demonstrate knowledge in emergency aid for the outdoors and be able to:

a. Demonstrate how to open an airway and give CPR.

b. Know how and when to put a patient in the recovery position.

c. Know how to recognise and treat fractures and severe bleeding.

d. Know how to use direct pressure to stop bleeding.

e. Demonstrate an awareness of the dangers of temperature extremes such as sunstroke, dehydration, heat exhaustion and hypothermia and know how to prevent and treat them.

SET UP A WELL ORGANISED SITE

The campsite layout

Consider these locations when planning the layout of your campsite.

- Sleeping areas
- Kitchen areas
- Chopping area
- Dining area
- Cooking area/fire
- Washing-up area
- Central camp area
- Equipment store
- Food store
- First aid tent
- Flagpole
- Waste disposal area
- Rubbish bins
- Wet pit
- Toilet and ablution area

This way to toilets

Central camp area

- Sleeping tents should be at least two metres apart.
- Pitch any sleeping tents on the flattest ground you can find. Avoid natural dips for sleeping areas – these tend to become waterlogged during heavy rain.
- Try to visit your site in winter to check how well it drains.
- Leave a reasonable amount of space for recreation.
- Site toilets so that the prevailing wind blows towards them.
- Include a separate area for personal washing.
- Site the chopping area away from overhanging trees.
- Site your kitchen tent close to a water supply.

SLEEPING TENTS

At camp, many Scout Troops may have an inspection and the level of formality of this inspection varies greatly between Troops. The main purpose of the inspection is to make sure that everyone is enjoying the camp by looking after themselves, each other and their equipment.

Here is a list of guidelines that will help you to ensure that you are camping to a good standard.

Ridge tents

> The tent should be pitched properly with all guys taut and pegs in line. This will ensure that the tent is doing its job properly – keeping you sheltered from wind and rain – and that it will last as long as possible.

> In the morning, if the weather is fair the tent should be allowed to air. If the canvas is dry, the walls should be rolled up to allow more air in. If the canvas is damp, it should be brailled, without the sod cloth touching the ground, to allow it to dry.

brailing

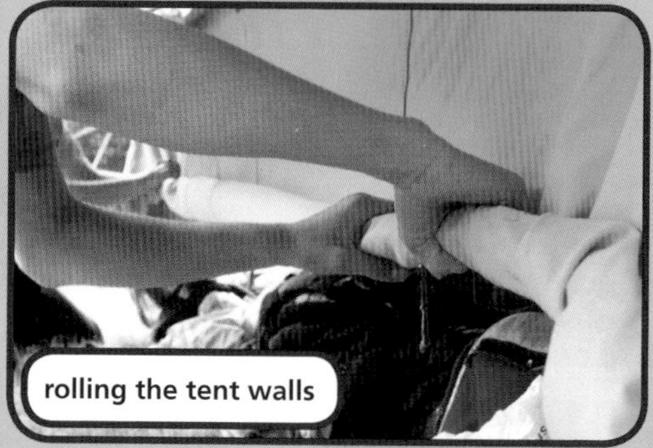
rolling the tent walls

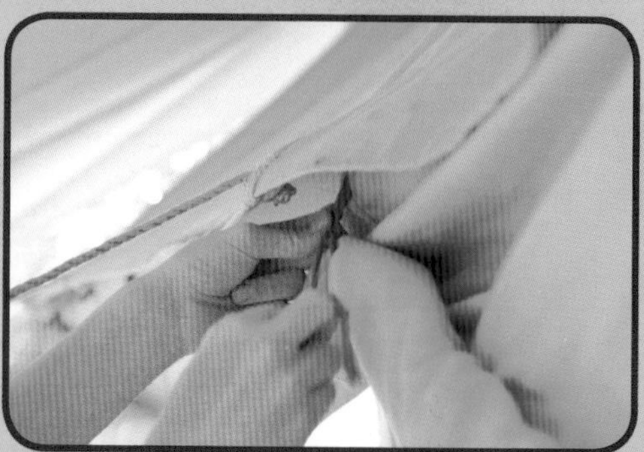

> Sleeping bags should be stored in bad weather and allowed to air in fine weather. A good airing will ensure a better night's sleep and the sleeping bag will last longer.

> Wash kits should be displayed in order to ensure that they have been used properly. You will enjoy a camp a lot more if you ensure that you wash properly and regularly. Make sure that wet towels are hung to dry wherever possible on a dedicated drying line (but **not** on the tent or its guy lines).

> In fair weather, wet clothes should be hung out to dry. If this is not possible, they should be stored in a separate plastic bag, away from clean, dry clothes.

> One end of the groundsheet should be folded over. This will allow a passageway where you should walk when you have to go into the tent in order to keep mud and grass off the groundsheet.

> The groundsheet should be swept and clean from mud, grass, etc. This is of course where you will be sleeping and it will be much more comfortable if it is clean.

> Spare shoes should be kept along the passageway at the bottom of the groundsheet. At camp, you will find that different activities need different kinds of footwear. It is a lot easier to keep them in a convenient place where you do not need to have shoes all over your groundsheet.

> Each person's belongings should be stored tidily and separately from everyone else's. This will ensure that nothing goes missing during the camp and that your clothes and equipment are a lot easier to find.

> Nothing should be touching the walls of the tent. This will ensure that nothing gets wet: not just the items which touch the walls but things near it, and it will also enhance and lengthen the life of the tent and its effectiveness.

> The whole tent area, including under the groundsheet should be litter free. You should do everything you can to keep your site tidy during (and not just at the end of) the camp in order to deter vermin and small animals as much as possible.

Lightweight tents

> The same principles apply to camping in a lightweight tent. However, you will (obviously) not be able to roll or brail the tent but, depending on the design of the tent, you should do what you can to air it regularly.

> Because you will have less space, it is hugely important that your belongings are kept tidily.

> Because the inner tent groundsheet is not removable, it is even more important you do what you can in order to keep litter, mud and grass out of the tent. Shoes and boots must be kept out of the tent and in a porch area wherever possible.

FOOD STORES

Patrol food stores

> Patrol tables should be wiped regularly. Use an anti-bacterial spray for this.

> All food should be covered or sealed with a tight fitting lid, stored upright and kept above ground level. This will ensure that insects, small animals and moisture from the ground will not get at it. Plastic boxes are very useful, whereas paper and card are easily chewed through.

> Perishable food such as meat, dairy products and vegetables should be stored properly in separate cool boxes. Food will go off very quickly if you have no refrigeration, particularly in warm weather. Use ice blocks, and replace these regularly. Shade and cold water are helpful in prolonging the life of food.

> Items which are not food should not be stored near food. It is important that your stores are kept in an organised manner and that items which may taint food are not kept near them.

> Plates, cutlery, utensils, pots, pans etc should be stored in an organised way and should be cleaned and dried immediately after use. Again, it is important that your stores are organised so that you know where to find anything quickly and hygiene is particularly important. At camp, where you do not have ready access to modern facilities, disease can easily be spread quickly, and it is important that you maintain very high levels of food hygiene. Basins in particular should be clean and dry when they are stored.

> Dishcloths and scouring pads etc which are beyond use should be disposed of. It is sometimes possible to boil wash dishcloths – but it is better to take lots of 'disposables' to camp as they will get dirty and unusable very quickly.

> The groundsheet should be clean, free of mud, grass, food scraps, litter etc. It is important that food and crockery is stored in a clean environment.

> Nothing should be touching the walls of the store tent. This will help to keep the inside of the tent dry and will also protect the tent from damage.

EQUIPMENT STORES

Patrol equipment stores

- The equipment store should be tidy and organised. You will often need to find things quickly and keeping your store organised is the only way to do it. Also, there may be sharp items such as axes and saws or things which may leak, such as fuel. You must know where they are kept and you may miss these potential hazards if your stores are a mess.
- Axes and saws must be covered and stored properly when they are not in use. Apart from being an obvious safety hazard, they will last longer and be more efficient if moisture is kept from them and they are not allowed to rust.
- Nothing should be touching the walls of the store tent. This will help to keep the inside of the tent dry and will also protect the tent from damage.
- Mark your equipment boxes on the outside with a list of the equipment they contain. This will help you identify contents quickly, without rooting around, and also help when packing equipment away.

'In my Troop there's one Scout who is a bit obsessed with cleanliness, and keeps the equipment store tidy by labelling everything and giving everything its own place. It's funny, but it makes it really easy to find equipment, so I can see the advantage of being organised.'

Ben

FIRE

Wood pile and chopping area

- Mark these areas out as soon as you arrive in camp. Then you won't have to have wood chips all over the site. There are obvious safety reasons why they should be marked out clearly. Only one person at a time should be in the chopping area, and it should be three axe lengths (about 2m) plus an arms length as a minimum radius. Naturally, both areas should be close together to save you carrying wood all over your site.
- Keep your wood pile dry. Make your wood pile on one end of an old tarpaulin or groundsheet and fold it over the wood to protect it from moisture above and below. You should be particularly careful that matches and firelighters are kept dry. Ensure that your wood pile always has a good supply of chopped wood and that it is 'graded' ie that you have your wood in order of size from kindling to medium sized sticks to logs.
- Peg your chopping block in position so that it is firm.
- Cover the sharp edges of axes and saws and ensure that they are properly stored when they are not in use.
- Your fireplace should be well away from any tents or canvas. You should have a fire bucket – probably filled with earth - close to your fire, but make sure it is not a trip hazard. Your ashes should be disposed of properly and regularly.

KITCHEN AND EATING AREA

- Be mindful of hygiene. The kitchen and dining area is an especially important area to keep clean and tidy at camp. As you will not have access to the same level of modern conveniences as at home (such as free running hot water) and because you are likely to be more active in an outdoor environment, you will be more exposed to any diseases or infections which are around. However, this does not mean you will eat in a less comfortable way than you would at home.
- Make sure that all your tables and surfaces are clean and organised at all times. It goes without saying that all your cooking utensils, pots, basins, plates, dishtowels, etc. must be kept spotlessly clean (and stored in a box with a lid), and that your preparation surfaces are cleaned with an antibacterial spray. Wash your hands before starting to prepare your food. It is a good idea to have a plentiful supply of hot water whilst you are preparing a meal so that you can wash your hands, utensils and surfaces quickly and easily. Your enjoyment of a camp will be greatly reduced if you have to spend most of it in bed with an upset stomach!

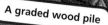

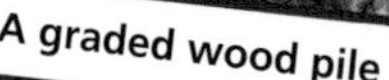
A graded wood pile

- Keep your kitchen free from insects and vermin. You should take care to ensure that there are no scraps of food or other litter left around after meal times as this will encourage vermin which carry diseases.
- Tidy and store after every meal. It is a common mistake to leave lots of things insecurely or improperly stored in the dining area. Make sure that all your plates and cooking utensils as well as fuel, and so on are stored properly in your storage area between mealtimes and especially at night.

'Camp food ... I'd say it's not the nicest thing in the world...'

Michael

'... I love camp food. I've made sweet and sour chicken, chicken chausseur and camp pizzas – the burnt taste is actually quite nice!'

Hannah

'Food at camp is magic!'

Cameron

MINIMAL IMPACT CAMPING

In Scouting For Boys, Baden-Powell wrote:

'Never forget that the state of an old camp ground after the camp has finished, tells exactly whether the Patrol or Troop which has used it was a smart one or not. No Scouts who are any good ever leave a camp ground dirty.

'Remember the only two things you leave behind you on breaking up camp:

1. Nothing
2. Your thanks to the owner of the ground'

Wise words … and even more pertinent now than when they were written.

'Leave No Trace' started as a popular mantra for outdoor recreation fans, but has become a global initiative for preventing permanent damage to the environment from outdoor activities.

Scouts have a reputation, earned over many years, for knowing something about outdoor living. Using the seven principles, here are some tips to show you a better way of doing things, which will hopefully encourage you to change your camping habits, to help the environment rather than obey authority, and to focus on the environmental impact, not rules and regulations. These guidelines apply equally to a weekend camp at your local campsite as they do on remote moorland in the Highlands.

The seven principles of minimal impact camping:

1. Plan Ahead and Prepare

2. Travel and camp on durable surfaces

3. Dispose of waste properly

4. Leave what you find

5. Minimise campfire impacts

6. Respect wildlife

7. Be considerate of other visitors

Be prepared and plan ahead

> Find out about the area you are to visit - get up to date information on maps, paths, water conditions, camping, weather conditions, restrictions, permits regulations and other helpful information.

> Plan your meals so that you use a minimal amount of non-recyclable materials, and have a minimal amount of leftovers. Remove food from bulky packaging or breakable jars and place it in plastic bags and containers to reduce rubbish that you'll have to take away.

> Plan your meals and activities around using a minimal amount of fuel and materials.

> Transportation - reduce the number of vehicles going to and from the site. Make use of public transport if practical.

> Choose earth-tone colours to reduce the visual impact of clothing and equipment (but not at the expense of compromising safety).

> Test equipment before you go to ensure it will be effective in the conditions.

Travel and camp on durable surfaces

> Wherever possible use existing recognised tracks and paths.

> It is generally better to pitch tents on established camping areas.

> Consider the impact pitching a tent in a wild area may have, eg disruption to wildlife and damage to plants.

> Avoid actions which cause unnecessary damage (eg taking short cuts on footpaths) and do not leave unnecessary signs that you have been there.

Dispose of waste properly

> 'If you can carry it in, you can carry it out' should be the general rule when it comes to waste.

> Bag all rubbish and take recyclables home.

> Washing and human waste disposal must be done carefully to avoid pollution and injury to humans, animals, and aquatic life. To deal with human waste, dig a cathole (15-20cm deep) at least 70 metres from camp, paths or any water sources. Deposit human waste here, then replace the soil in the hole.

> Water is easily polluted by soap and shampoo (even if these are biodegradable), by food waste and human waste.

> Flatten cans to save space and take them home.

> Mark any soiled ground or pits with a foul ground sign - a small cairn, a cross made from twigs and laid horizontally, or stuck in the ground to make a vertical cross.

> Be prepared to carry out additional rubbish found on the site.

> If you have any, take food scraps with you. Don't burn or bury them; burying will attract foraging animals like rats and foxes.

> Use natural materials, eg grass, wet sand, seaweed as scourers to reduce the need for detergents. If you avoid cooking greasy foods the pots are even easier to clean.

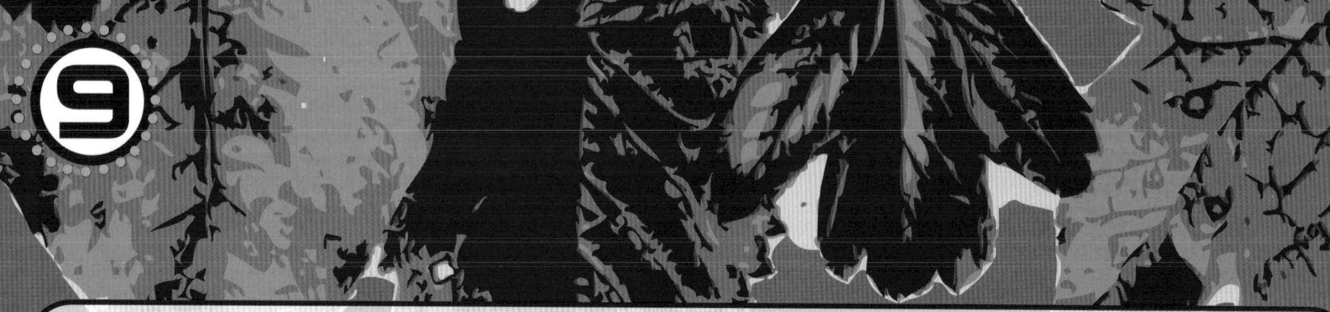

> On a larger camp, have a wet-pit - a hole on which has been laid either a network of sticks that supports a filter made of grass or bracken, or a pegged out piece of sacking. Used washing up water should be drained through the filter, which can then be burnt, or packed away.

> Leave the site in a better condition than when you found it.

Leave what you find

> Do not pick the flowers.

> Avoid damage to plants.

> Leave wild flowers, bones, feathers, and unusual rock formations for others to enjoy.

> Respect cultural aspects of an environment such as historical relics, geological sites or sites of other scientific interest.

> Do not disturb or remove artefacts from historical or archaeological sites.

> Return any collected items to where they were found.

> If you gather edible berries and plants, pick only those that are abundant and make sure to leave plenty for wildlife.

Minimize campfire impacts

> If possible, use established fire sites rather than creating new ones. Pit fires should be avoided, as they usually scorch the ground to the point where it won't support plant life.

> Heed any fire regulation signs.

> Be sensitive to the fact that collecting and burning wood can destroy homes for small plants and animals.

> Use as little wood as you need.

> It is much easier to leave no trace cooking on a stove rather than with a campfire.

Respect wildlife

> Observe wildlife from a distance so they are not forced to change their behaviour due to a human presence.

> Do not disturb nesting birds or other wildlife.

> Do not feed animals without permission.

> Do not tease animals.

> Do not disturb livestock.

> Do not feed wildlife - it spoils their survival instincts and disrupts the order of nature.

> Brush spiders and other creepy-crawlies out of the tent instead of killing them.

Be considerate of other visitors

> Do not enter campsites without permission.

> Do not litter or leave behind items that 'may be of use to the next group' if you don't want them.

> Do not be loud after dark or early in the morning.

> Be courteous to local people, and use local facilities, if you can, to help the local economy.

> Keep pets under control.

> Evaluate your trip and work out how to do it better next time.

Minimal impact camping:

> depends more on attitude and awareness than rules and regulations

> is used to reduce the effects that people have on the environment

> will allow you to enjoy the natural surroundings without causing too much environmental damage.As you build your experience of camps, you will improve your judgment on these matters. Try to minimise your impact on the land and on other visitors, but be sure to enjoy your nights away.

You can find out more about Leave No Trace at their website – **www.LNT.org**

PREPARE A BALANCED MENU FOR A SHORT CAMP

There are six stages to catering for a short camp:

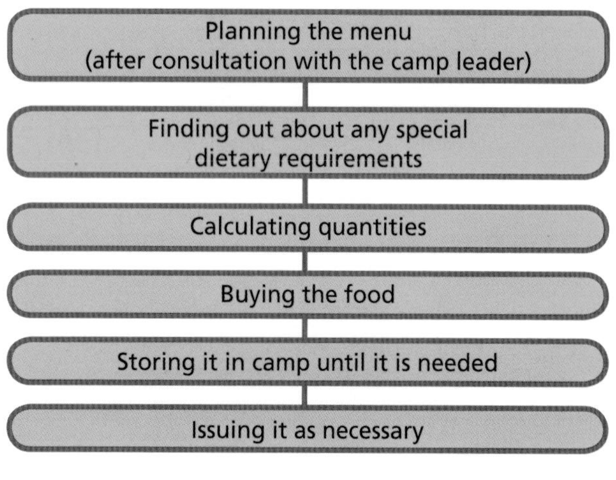
Planning the menu
(after consultation with the camp leader)
Finding out about any special dietary requirements
Calculating quantities
Buying the food
Storing it in camp until it is needed
Issuing it as necessary

Unless you are used to catering for large numbers, this can be quite a big job the first time you do it. The best way to learn is to act as an assistant for one or two camps, after which you might be ready to do the job yourself at a Patrol or Troop camp. Some things to remember:

> Some Scouts, for medical or religious reasons, cannot eat some foods.

> Do consider the programme when you are planning the menu – no hearty meals just before swimming, for example.

> Remember to buy things like salt, jam, sugar, and so on which will not actually appear on the menu. Also, get non-food items such as washing-up materials, bin bags and matches.

> Better to have too much food than too little.

> Large size packets and tins are often better value if you will use that much.

> Keep all this year's price lists, menus, orders and so on – they will help when you plan your next camp menu.

> Ensure that your menu allows for a balanced and healthy diet.

Menus

Work out a menu which fits in with your programme.

It is a good idea to find out what your Patrol likes to eat before planning the menu so that there is more chance that everyone will enjoy the food. Try listing a dozen main meals and asking your Patrol to tick the ones which they like. Then you can choose the most popular.

Camp menus should be balanced. When in camp, the body is called on to do a lot more than usual so enough food should be eaten to keep it 'fuelled up'. Try to include the following:

Proteins – meat, fish, dairy products, vegetables, nut and pulses (including baked beans) contain protein.

Carbohydrates – bread, potatoes, pasta, rice and sugar are sources of carbohydrates.

Fat – milk, cream, butter, bacon or meat fat are examples of fatty foods. You only need fats in moderation.

The best plan for most campers is to start with a good breakfast, a light lunch, a substantial evening meal followed by a hot drink before going to bed.

Be aware that some members of your Patrol might not be able to eat certain foods so check whilst you are planning your menu because:

> Some people have allergic reactions to food or other medical conditions (such as diabetes)

> Some religions have rules about different types of food

> Some people have opted not to eat meat or animal products.

You must accept these restrictions or beliefs and build a menu around them with the Scouts concerned offering advice.

It is also important to remember to drink plenty of fluids, particularly if the weather is hot. Water or squash is far better for you than fizzy drinks.

Example weekend menu

Friday

Supper — Soup, bread, biscuits

Saturday

Breakfast — Cereal
Bread soaked in beaten eggs and fried
Bread and jam
Tea/coffee/juice

Lunch — Sandwiches
Crisps
Apple
Chocolate biscuit
Cold drink

Dinner — Spaghetti Bolognese
Tinned sponge and custard
Tea/coffee/juice

Supper — Hot chocolate, biscuits

Sunday

Breakfast — Cereal
Sausage and beans
Bread and jam
Tea/coffee/juice

Lunch — Fish fingers, peas and carrots
Potatoes
Rice pudding
Cold drink

The following list of foods and their quantities can be used as a helpful guideline to help you calculate how much food you will need.

Bread – allow one loaf per day for 6 persons

Bacon – two rashers per head per meal

Baked beans – 60g (2oz) per head

Butter/margarine - 60g (2oz) per head per day

Cereal – 15-18 servings from 750g box

Coffee (instant) – 60g (2oz) per gallon (18 cups)

Cheese – 8-10 salad servings per 500g (16 oz)

Gravy – eight servings from one pint

Milk – 500ml per head per day

Minced beef – 150-180g (5-6oz) raw, per portion

Porridge oats – 45g (1½oz), dry, per portion

Potatoes – 250g (8oz), unpeeled, per portion

Rice (savoury) – 45-60g (1½ -2oz), uncooked, per portion

Sausages (large) 3-4 per head (as a dinner)

Sausages (small) 4 per head (as part of breakfast)

Soup – 300ml per head

Stewing meat – 150-180g (5-6oz), raw, per portion

Sugar – 60g (2oz) per head per day

Tea (loose)

Tea (bags) – 2 cups

Vegetables – 120-180g (4-6oz) per portion (depending on how many veg. you are serving)

NB: Many of the above will need to be 'rounded-up' to full packets or tins per Patrol for ease of catering (particularly when Patrol cooking) but this extravagance will seldom be wasted!

Note down anything you haven't used so as not to buy it again.

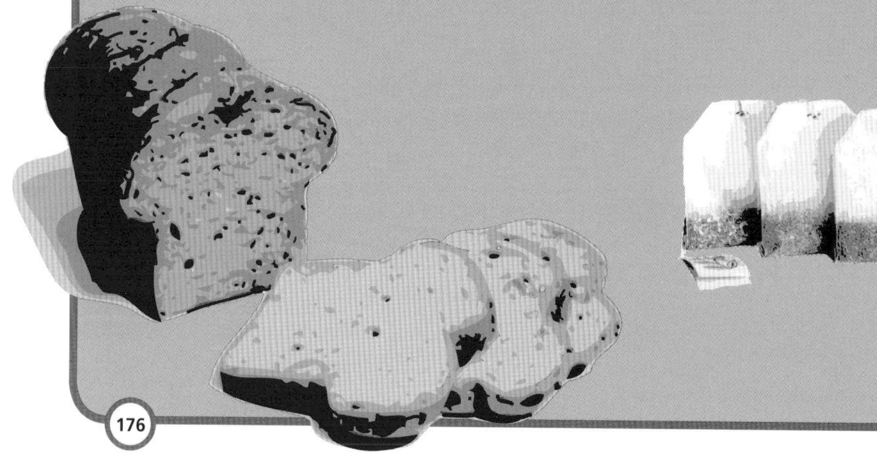

RELIGIOUS DIETARY REQUIREMENTS

When you are planning a menu, at camp or elsewhere you should take into account the dietary requirements of those you are catering for.

People may have different needs because they have a particular diet (eg vegetarians or vegans, have an allergy to a specific food or types of food), or they may belong to a religion which has dietary requirements.

You should always check with those you are catering for about their exact dietary needs but here is a list of the main principles for some of the main religions in the UK.

Food that Jewish people can eat is called kosher. The meat they eat must be killed in a prescribed Jewish manner. They cannot eat pork (or any meat with cloven hooves) or shell-fish (or any fish without fins and scales.) There are also certain poultry which they cannot eat. Meat and dairy products cannot be eaten in the same meal and different utensils (pots, crockery, cutlery and washing up equipment) are used for each. All the utensils which they use must also be kosher.

Food that Muslim people are allowed to eat is known as halal. The meat which they eat must be killed in a prescribed Islamic way. They cannot eat pork or seafood, except fish. The food they eat must not contain alcohol and they will abstain from all food and drink between dawn and sunset during the month of Ramadhan.

Sikh people do not believe in ritual killing and will refrain from eating meat which has been killed by such rites and so, for example, they will not eat halal and kosher meat. They will also abstain from alcohol. Some Sikhs will not eat beef and some will not eat pork. Because of the varieties of this, food which is served in a gurdwara (Sikh place of worship) is vegetarian.

Hindu people are forbidden from eating meat, fish, poultry or eggs. Some Hindus will occasionally eat meat although almost all of them will avoid beef. In addition, some Hindus will abstain from garlic, onions, mushrooms, alcohol, tea and coffee.

Many Christian people will avoid eating meat on Fridays and may observe fasting during the period before Easter which is called Lent.

Meat and fish are not eaten by many Buddhists and they may also abstain from 'pungent spices' such as garlic, onion and leek.

Bahai people will not take alcohol and during the festival of Ala, they will fast from sunrise to sunset.

'Within my Troop we have six different dietary requirements! When I planned the menu for camp, I had to learn culture with food first hand. I cooked with others for the dietary requirements, such as vegetarian, halal and kosher. As well as this, some Scouts had nut and dairy allergies. I learnt a lot about these ways of eating, and it gave me a lot more respect for people and how they eat!'

Rushil

SAFELY USE A HAND AXE

The axe is an important tool for all camps where open fires are used. The axe is a potentially dangerous tool. It must only be used by trained Scouts and the safety guidelines must always be followed.

Hand axe

For use with one hand, it is used to cut and trim small firewood, thin branches and twigs and should not be used on live wood. Any wood larger than five centimetres in diameter (about the size of your wrist) can be cut more easily using a bow saw.

All hand-axes should have an accompanying mask, which covers the blade and fits securely round the back of the head.

Safety guidelines

> Don't wear scarves, ties, lanyards or any loose clothing, to prevent the axe being snared in clothing.

> Wear strong leather shoes or boots, rather than trainers or soft shoes.

> Clear the ground nearby and make sure there are no overhanging branches, ropes, people or other obstructions within three axe lengths of you (one outstretched arm and the length of three axes). Never ask anyone to hold the wood you are cutting.

> Inspect the axe before use. Never use it if the head and haft do not line up straight, if the haft is split, chipped or otherwise damaged or broken, or if the head is loose.

> Never use a blunt axe - it can slip or bounce off wood yet can still penetrate flesh.

> Always use a chopping block below the wood to be chopped and don't let the axe go into the ground.

> Chop directly over the chopping block. The part to be cut should be resting on the block.

> Always stop when feeling tired. If you carry on, you are more likely to miss and cause a serious injury.

> Mask the axe when not in use.

> Carry the axe cradled upside down in your hand with your arm by your side. Make sure the axe bit is facing forward with your fingers out of the way so that if you fall the axe will go into the ground.

> Pass the axe to someone else by standing side by side, facing the same direction. Pass the head first. Alternatively, place the axe on the ground, leaving the other person to pick it up, head first.

Care of the axe

> Mask the axe when not in use, using a correctly fitting mask and not by sticking it in the ground. An axe may be masked temporarily in the chopping block but make sure that the blade follows the grain of the wood, is secure in the wood, and that the haft is not overhanging the block so that it can't trip anyone.

> In camp, keep all axes and saws dry. Never leave them out overnight. Fit the mask or sheath and keep them out of the way in a store tent (but not just inside where someone might kneel or step on them going into the tent!).

> Sharpen the axe with a round carborundum stone (available in different grades of coarseness). You should start with a coarse stone and then finish with a fine stone depending on how much sharpening the axe requires. It should be used with oil. Move the stone round in small circles on each side of the axe face. Keep your fingers away from the edge.

> Keep the axe head greased to prevent it rusting and oil a wooden handle regularly with linseed oil.

> Replace a damaged haft with a new one - never attempt to repair it.

Tricks of the trade

> Like any tool, if it is well looked after, it will do its job better and last longer!

> Always use an axe within the marked out chopping area. Don't take it along to the source of wood. A bow saw would be more effective here.

> Make your chopping area a 'no go' area for anyone not properly trained or clothed. Be especially careful of younger campers who might be particularly inquisitive.

> Chop enough wood to keep the fire wood pile stocked but do not over-stock the pile.

Procedure

1. Crouch or stand with your feet apart behind the chopping block.
2. Hold the wood to be chopped with one hand.
3. With the other hand grip the hand-axe on the lower part of the haft, on the 'grip'. Hold the axe firmly but not rigidly. Note: only hold the hand-axe with one hand.
4. Chop the wood by keeping the axe and the lower part of the arm straight and bending your arm at the elbow rather than the wrist or shoulder. Chop at 45 degree angles to the length of the wood making alternate left and right cuts to create a small 'V'. The 'V' will get wider as you cut through the wood, creating the chippings, until it is cut in half. Do not try to cut at right angles to the length of the wood; this will make the axe bounce.
5. Always watch the point at which you are aiming. Indeed, when practising, it is a good idea to put a chalk mark on the log and try to hit that.
6. Clear chippings away regularly and use them for kindling.

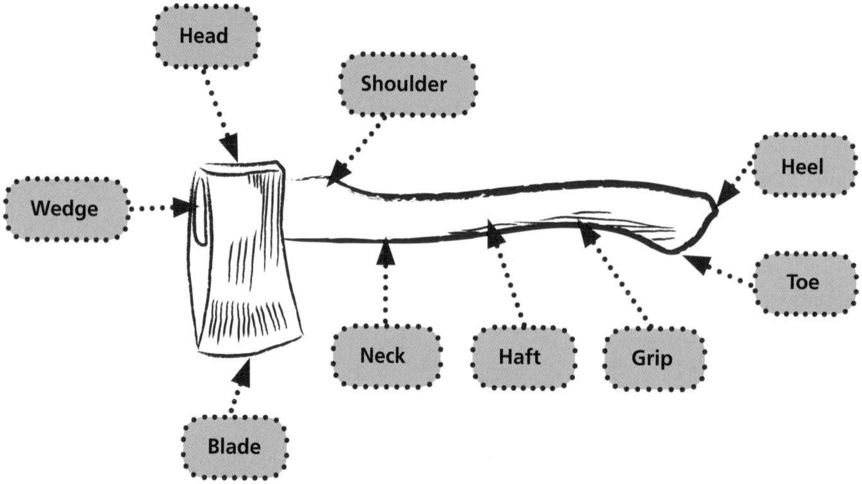

Head

Shoulder

Heel

Wedge

Toe

Neck

Haft

Grip

Blade

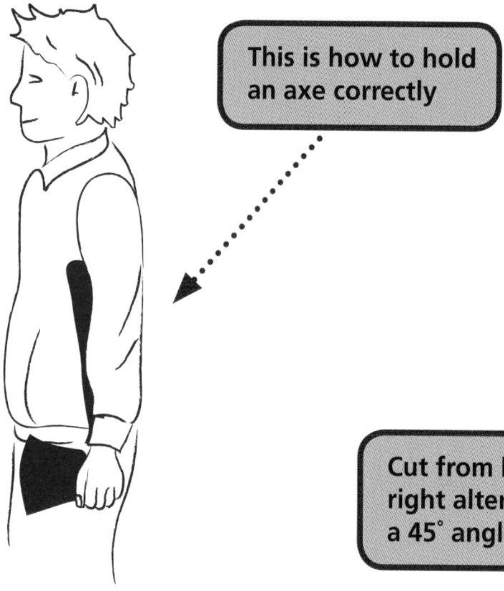

This is how to hold an axe correctly

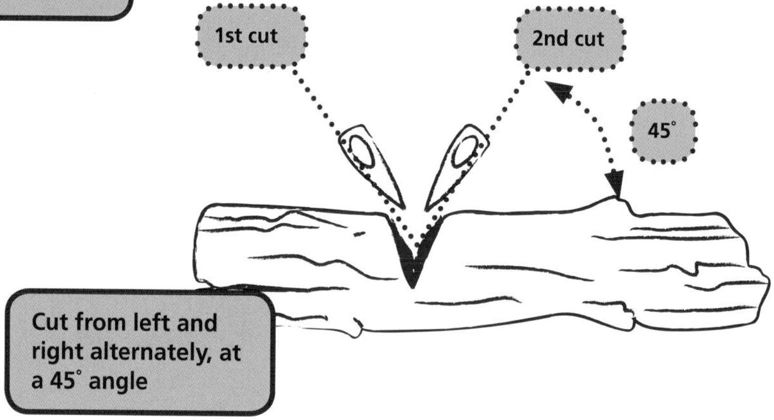

1st cut

2nd cut

45°

Cut from left and right alternately, at a 45° angle

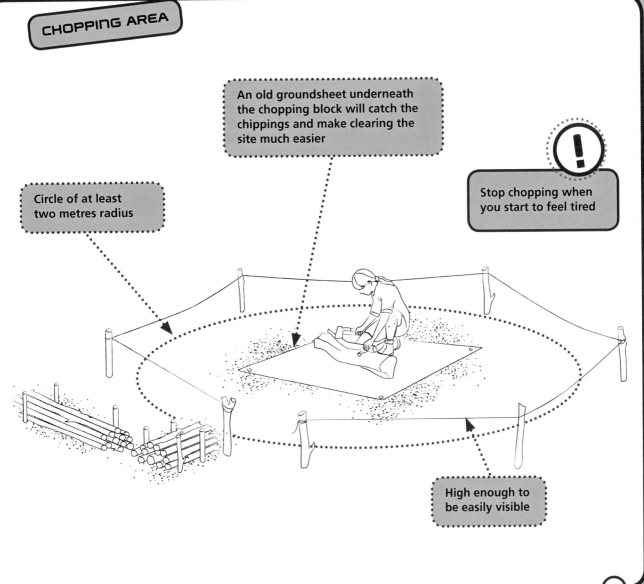

CHOPPING AREA

An old groundsheet underneath the chopping block will catch the chippings and make clearing the site much easier

Stop chopping when you start to feel tired

Circle of at least two metres radius

High enough to be easily visible

SAFELY USE A SAW

A bow saw is often used together with axes for preparing firewood and is essential for all camps where open fires are used. Bow saws are used to cut wood too large for a hand-axe and are safer and easier than the felling axe for cutting small timber. They should be greased to prevent them from rusting and, as blades are relatively cheap, they should never be sharpened but replaced regularly.

Using a bow saw

1. Make sure that the wood is held firmly. If you must use your hand for this, keep it well away from the blade.
2. Start slowly, pulling the blade backward towards you until the blade is well into the wood. Then push and pull in a steady rhythm using the whole length of the blade. Don't apply downward pressure; let the saw do the cutting. Trying to force it will often result in the blade jamming.
3. Always mask the saw after use. Either use a plastic 'clip-on' mask or tie a length of sacking around the blade.

LEAD THE COOKING OF A MEAL FOR A GROUP

Cooking at camp always goes more smoothly when someone takes the lead and organises the tasks. Here are some tips from two of the UK Patrol and a menu to try:

Dinner on wood fire

Minestrone soup with bread, sausage, mash and beans, steam pudding and custard, bread, butter , jam, biscuits, tea coffee and juice

3 tins of minestrone soup, sausages, potatoes (large bag), 2 tins of beans, 500g grated cheese, 3 steamed puddings, 2 pints of custard mix, milk, water, bread, butter/margarine, jam, tea, coffee, juice, milk, sugar, vegetable oil, salt and pepper

4.30pm Gather wood and light fire

4.50pm Wash hands and faces

5pm Start cooking

Stage 1

Peel potatoes, halve them put them onto boil, put soup on to boil and then leave to simmer gently. 45 mins to boil potatoes, 30mins for soup

Stage 2

Start sausages 15 mins into stage 1, beans 25mins into stage 1

Fry sausages until brown, put beans on to heat. As potatoes begin to soften then put water on for tea, coffee and washing-up

Stage 3

Take soup and boiled potatoes off the fire, drain then mash potatoes adding a little milk and butter to make them creamy. 15 mins

Stage 4

As dinner is served put water on and boil for steamed pudding being sure to pierce tins above the water line, make custard as required. 15mins

6pm Dinner is served

6.30pm Clean up dishes/ tidy site for evening

7pm Start evening activity

Serves 6

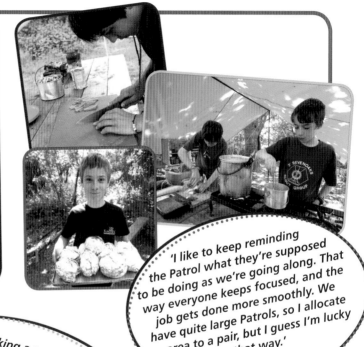

'I like to keep reminding the Patrol what they're supposed to be doing as we're going along. That way everyone keeps focused, and the job gets done more smoothly. We have quite large Patrols, so I allocate an area to a pair, but I guess I'm lucky in that way.'

Michael

'When cooking a meal with your Patrol, keep everyone busy, so the younger Scouts don't wander off and do their own thing. That way they will learn all the jobs that need doing so they can lead the cooking when they're a PL. Some jobs (like using sharp knives) should be done by an APL or I'll do them myself. Someone needs to keep an eye on the fire, feeding it with wood. Other jobs like washing up can be shared around when it's time for them to be done. The PL shouldn't try and do everything, because someone needs to stand back and organise the task. If cooking meat and potatoes, I'll always check that they are cooked through before serving up.'

Hannah

SAFETY PRECAUTIONS OF LAMPS

- Gas cylinder lamps. Lamps with fuel cylinders use either butane gas (blue cylinders) or propane gas (red cylinders). The fuel in the cylinder is a liquid which becomes a gas as it leaves the cylinder.
- Cylinder lamp safety. Most accidents occur when the fuel cylinder is changed. Safety rules are often printed on the gas cylinder or provided as separate instructions with a new lamp. When purchasing new gas lamps, it is strongly recommended to buy those with self-sealing cartridges. These are safer to use.
- Lighting the gas. All gas lanterns are easily lit – just apply a match and turn on the gas. Make sure you turn off the gas supply fully when the lamp is not in use.
- Sealed canisters. Sealed canisters of fuel are screwed to the burner holding the mantle. Screwing on the canister activates the valve which controls the gas flow.

How to tell if your cylinder is nearly empty

The liquid fuel turns to gaseous fuel as the pressure in the cylinder reduces. So a full cylinder contains a lot of liquid and feels heavier than one which is nearly empty.

Changing cylinders

These steps will make sure you change the cylinder safely.

1. Fully close the gas supply valve.
2. Allow the lamp to cool. There will be some escape of gas as you remove the empty cylinder because they are never completely empty.
3. Always change the cylinder outside in the open air. There is then less chance of filling a confined space, such as a tent, with highly flammable vapours.
4. Dispose of the empty cylinder carefully. Do not put a nearly empty container into a plastic bag or metal dustbin. Gas can build up during warm weather and can easily ignite.
5. Unscrew the top portion of the lamp. Any left over gas will escape as the unscrewing action breaks the seal between the lamp and the cylinder.
6. Separate the gas cylinder housing and the top portion of the lamp. On the bottom of the gas cylinder housing is a plate which, when turned, allows the empty gas cylinder to fall out.
7. Place the replacement gas cylinder in the housing and screw the base plate back into position.
8. Close the fuel supply valve and then screw the top portion of the lamp into place. This automatically punctures the gas cylinder seal and once tightened, the lamp is leak proof and ready for use.

Changing the mantle

1. Remove the top of the lamp, including the glass globe. Now is a good time to clean the globe with a solution of household detergent.
2. Remove the damaged mantle. The ash body can be brushed away with the fingers but make sure to remove the ties at the top and bottom of the mantle. These are usually located in grooves or behind ridges on the fuel supply column.
3. Unpack the replacement mantle, ensuring that you have the correct mantle for your type of lamp. The mantle looks like a multi-coloured 'tea bag' except that it has two holes. The larger hole is put on to the fuel supply column first, pulled down into position and tied securely. The upper hole is adjacent to the appropriate ridge.
4. With the gas supply turned off, apply a lighted match and allow the mantle to burn completely. It shrinks as it burns, usually turning a greyish-white colour.
5. Carefully reassemble the lamp.

Lighting cylinder lamps

1. Apply a lighted taper through one of the base plate holes and gently turn on the gas. As the globe fills with gas, it will ignite with a soft 'plopping' noise and the mantle will begin to glow. Do not attempt to touch the mantle with the burning taper or it will collapse.
2. Use the fuel supply valve to adjust the amount of light.

Winter expeditions:

Gas lamps are less efficient in very cold weather. In fact, butane (blue cylinder) does not light below a temperature of -1°C. On winter expeditions, propane should be used. Better still, use a torch.

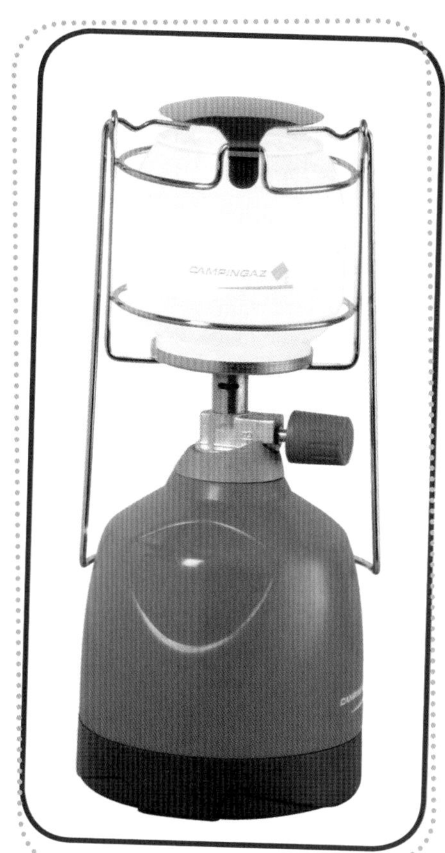

SAFETY PRECAUTIONS OF STOVES

Methylated spirit stoves

This is a simple-to-use stove ideally suited to mountaineering and camping trips where there are only a few of you. It comes in a self-contained set including pots, frying pan, windshield, support and burner unit. It uses meths (methylated spirits) so no priming is required and it is quite good in breezy conditions although it can also use up fuel quickly.

1. The air holes in the lower windshield should face into the wind. The stove operates efficiently and economically in a well-sheltered position.
2. As maximum burning time is about 25 minutes (half an hour using the slow burning device) and to refill a hot stove is very dangerous, it is worth buying a spare spirit burner, which may be filled while cold and exchanged for the empty hot burner whenever necessary.
3. The stove will boil 1 litre of water in eight minutes. For slow burning, swivel the brown lid to one side. To extinguish the flame, close the brown lid and place the device over the burner. Before transporting the stove, remove the slow burning device and twist the screw cap firmly into place.
4. The frying pan is designed to be inverted for use as a lid. When you fry in it, lift the three folding pot supports attached to the top of the windshield. Fold them down when supporting smaller pots or cans.

Warning

> Meths burns with a light blue flame almost invisible to the eye. Be sure when refilling that the burner is NOT ALIGHT! Allow the burner unit to cool down before refilling.

> Never cook in the tent, and even cooking in the entrance is dangerous if people try stepping over you. Tent fires can cause terrible burns when hot material sticks to the skin. Find the shelter of a tree or take a small tarpaulin to cook under.

> Read operating instructions and practice before heading on the trip.

COOK A BACKWOODS MEAL

Backwoods cooking

Backwoods cooking is the art of cooking without using traditional utensils, such as pots and pans but by using sticks, cabbage leaves and aluminium foil instead. It is an ideal activity for camp, where you have open fires and an abundance of wood to make natural utensils. Try some of the following popular backwoods recipes.

1. Spud eggs

Cut the top off a potato, hollow it out, crack an egg into it, replace the lid and wrap in two layers of foil. Put in hot embers for 40 minutes.

2. Sausage casserole

Wrap sausages, chopped onion and any choice of other vegetables in cabbage leaves, seal with one layer of foil and put into embers for around 30 minutes.

3. Orange eggs

Scoop out the flesh from half an orange and crack an egg into it. Cover the egg with the other half of the orange and place on hot embers for 15 minutes or so. Remove with care!

4. Kebabs

Peel the bark from a long 'green' (ie living) stick (not laurel or yew) and push a mixture of chopped chicken, onion, mushroom, peppers and tomato onto it. Cook over hot embers until the chicken is white. Tip: Pierce the food with a knife first so that it threads on without breaking.

5. Twists or dampers

Mix self-raising flour, water, milk and an egg (or just flour and water if you wish) to make a thick dough. Roll into a 'snake' and wrap it around a green stick (see above). Toast over embers until lightly browned and serve with butter and jam.

6. Baked apple

Cut out the core of an apple, place the apple on foil and fill the hole with raisins, sultanas, sugar and, if desired, chocolate. Wrap in two layers of foil and cook in hot embers for 20 minutes or so. Eat with care as the sugar is very hot!

7. Chocolate banana

Slit an unpeeled banana lengthways (but not all the way through) and push chocolate buttons inside. Close it up, wrap in two layers of foil and cook in hot embers for up to 15 minutes.

Cooking without utensils, called backwoods cooking, is not only great fun – it also cuts down on the washing up!

Hot embers

Begin by building up the fire with fairly large pieces of wood. Let them burn through to leave you with a bed of hot, glowing embers.

This is nearly always the best type of fire for backwoods cooking.

Try this method to cook:

> sausages
> twists
> chops
> apples
> toast
> bacon
> tomatoes
> onion
> kebabs (a bit of everything)

Skewers

Many types of food can be cooked on wooden skewers.

Find a thin, green stick – one that bends but does not snap. Any wood will do except yew, holly, elm and laurel which are poisonous.

Peel the bark off and make a point at one end. The skewer can then be pushed through the food and hung over the fire or laid with one end on the ground and the other on the back of a reflector fire. Or you could simply sit and hold it, turning the food as it cooks. You can use two 'y' shaped sticks to support the skewer.

Reflector fire

This type of fire is especially good for backwoods cooking because you can direct the heat straight at the food. Use logs or large stones (but not flints as they can explode) behind the fire, held up with wooden stakes drive into the ground.

Take care not to sit opposite the reflector or you will be baked as well!

Fiji Oven

Dig a hole in the ground and build a fire in the bottom. Get it going well and put several large stones (not flints) on top. When the stones are really hot, lay some large leaves (such as cabbage leaves) on them. Next, pile in the food – meat, potatoes and other vegetables – then cover with another layer of leaves. Finally cover well with earth and leave to cook about six hours.

'To stop food cooked in foil from burning, wrap in foil as normal. Then take wet newspaper, wrap again so that there are about two layers all round. Then wrap in foil again. Cook for slightly longer than normal. Check by peeling back the outer foil. When the paper is well charred, the food is probably cooked.'

Ben

LASHINGS

Diagonal Lashing:

> Begin with a timber hitch to draw the spars together

> Pull the knot at right angles and wrap the rope three times around the spars, keeping the rope tight all the time

> Wrap three more turns, this time over the timber hitch

> Apply two frapping turns to pull tight the rope turns

> Finish off with a clove hitch.

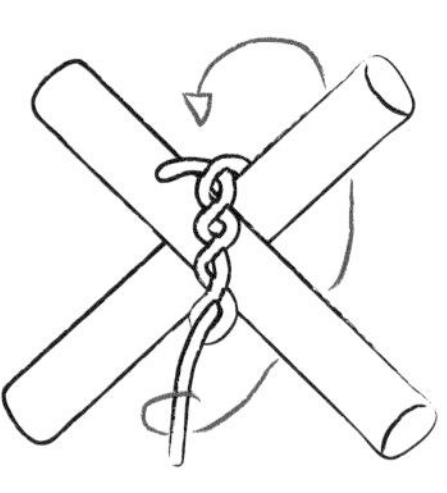

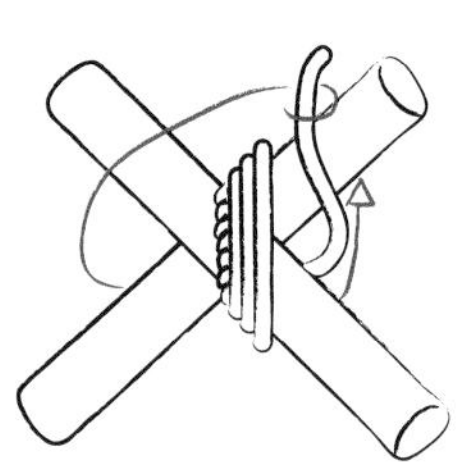

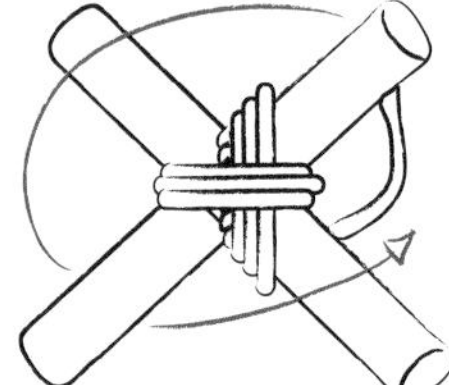

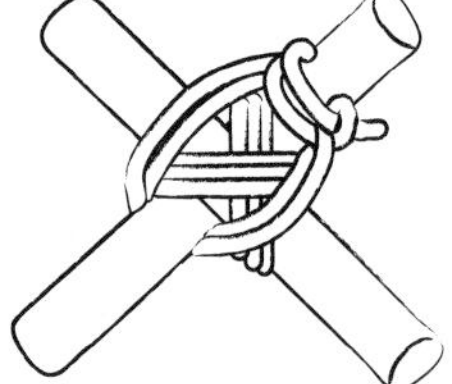

Japanese Square Lashing

This is used as an alternative to the square lashing for light spars and staves.

> Take the middle of the lashing rope round a spar (fig1)

> Using both ends together (rope doubled) lay 3 turns as in ordinary square lashing (fig2)

> Take one end across the diagonal and behind the crossed spar. The other rope doubles back in front of the vertical spar (fig3)

> The ends are now going in opposite directions to make frapping turns (fig3)

> Finish the lashing with a reef knot across a spar (fig4).

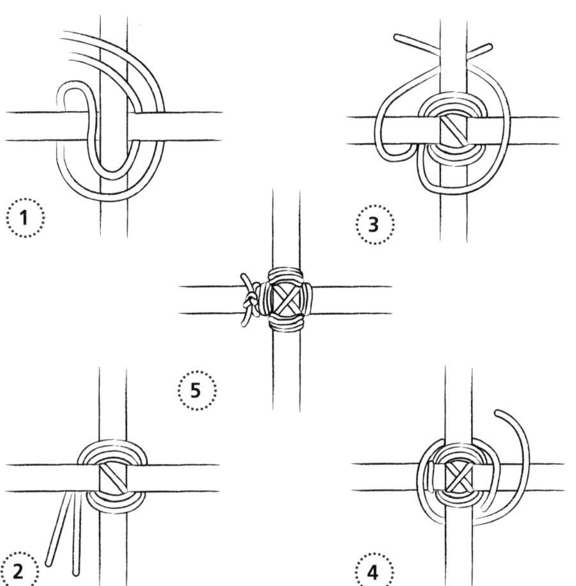

Filipino Diagonal Lashing

This is used as an alternative to the usual diagonal lashing for light spars and staves.

> Start with the middle of the rope and pass the ends through the loop (fig1)

> Lay three turns around both spars and then three more turns at right angles (fig2 + fig3)

> Split the two ends of the rope and make frapping turns between the spars (fig3)

> The two ends, now going in opposite directions, are pulled tight

> Finish off the lashing with a reef knot across one of the spars (fig4).

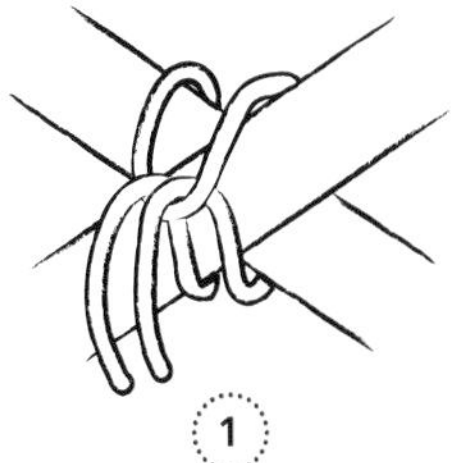

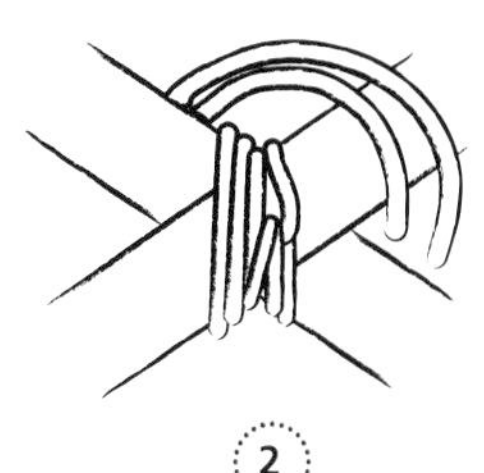

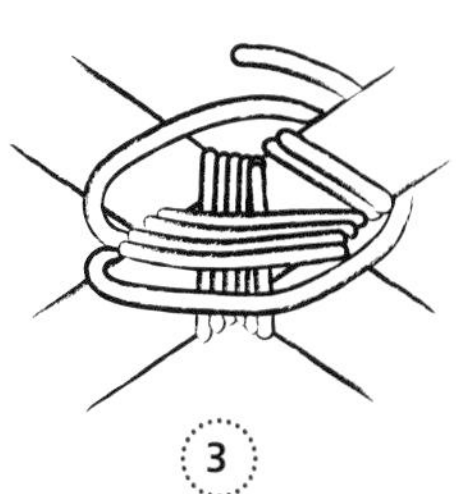

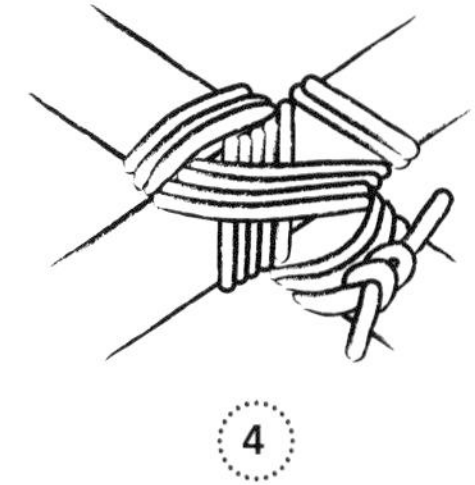

WHIPPING

The ends of a freshly-cut rope will rapidly fray and unlay if nothing is done to prevent it. Before using a rope, whip the two ends to keep them from unravelling.

There are various methods of whipping a rope, and here are three methods.

Plain Whipping

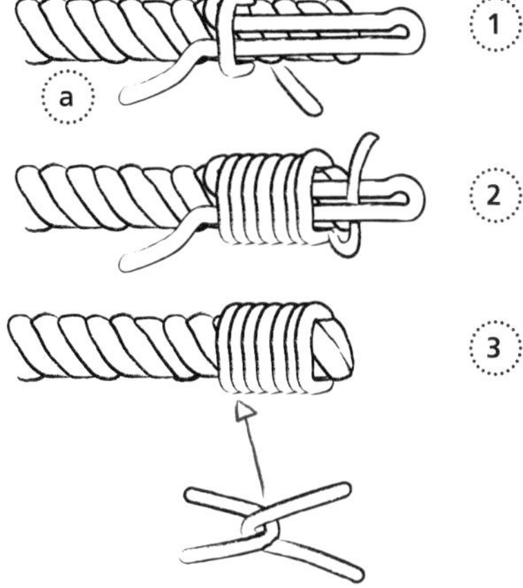

To whip a knotting rope, use a thin twine about 30 cm long. Make one end into a loop and place it at the end of the rope. End A should be fairly short. Wind the longer end of the twine around the rope and the loop, spiralling away and drawing each turn tight. When the whipping is as wide as the diameter of the rope, thread the twine through the end of the loop. Pull end A hard until the loop has disappeared under the whipping. Trim off the two ends. Then whip the other end of the ropes.

West country whipping

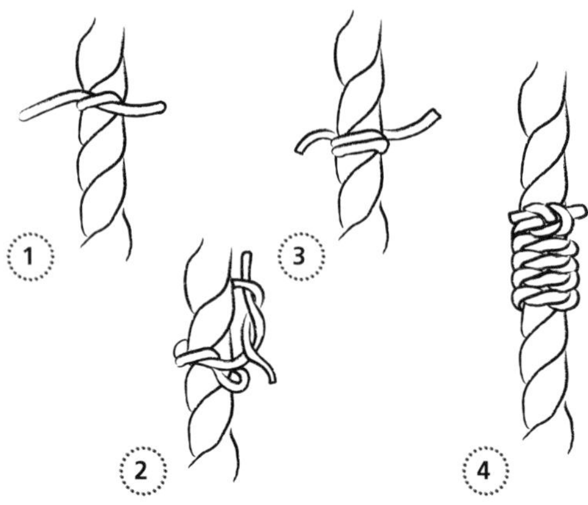

This is the easiest form of whipping. Tie a Thumb Knot a few centimetres from the end of the rope using thin, strong twine. Then tie another Thumb Knot at the back of the rope, and continue tying Thumb Knots on each side of the rope to within about a centimetre from the end. Finish off with a Reef Knot, and trim with a sharp knife.

For a more permanent type of whipping use the Sailmaker's whipping.

Sailmaker's whipping

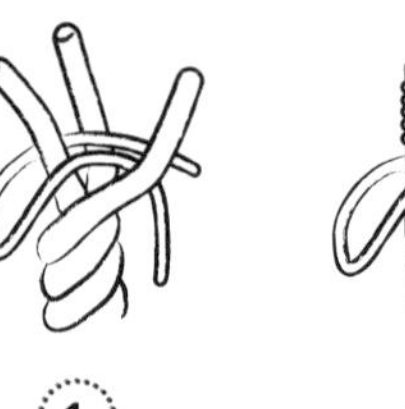

1. Open the lay of the rope and place a loop of twine around one strand. Relay the rope.
2. Hold the loop down with one hand, leaving the short end free. With the long end of the twine make tight turns around the rope, close together, towards the end of the rope.
3. Raise the loop and slip it over the end of the strand it is around. Pull the short end to tighten. Join the ends of the twine with a Reef Knot.
4. Trim the end with a sharp knife.

HOW TO MAKE A CAMP DRESSER

Instructions:

1. Drive four staves into ground, a basin width apart, and whatever length is needed
2. Tie square lashings to attach cross poles to dresser
3. Attach a series of shorter canes to form the drainer on the dresser
4. Add washing up bowl, and get washing!

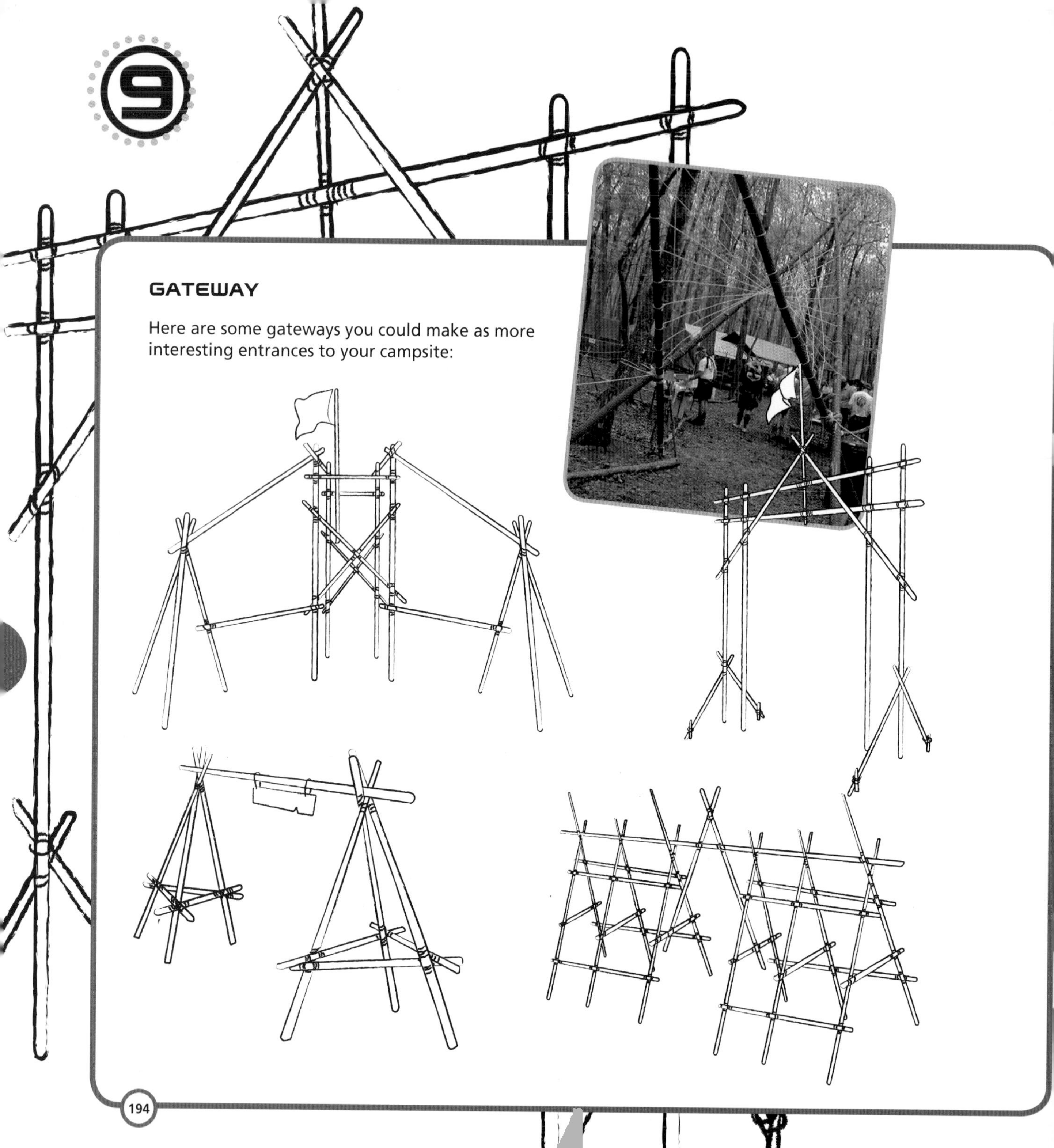

GATEWAY

Here are some gateways you could make as more interesting entrances to your campsite:

CAMP OVEN

Metal box oven

You will need:

- A well cleaned cake tin or oil drum
- Tall thin tins or metal/clay drainpipe
- A metal sheet
- A metal grill.

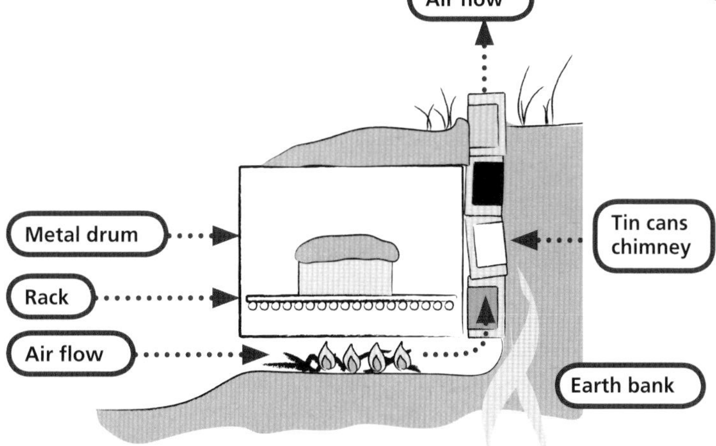

Make a chimney from tall thin tins, or metal/clay drainpipe at the back and pile the earth around it.

Find a bank and dig a hole or trench in it.

Rest the metal container in the top of the hole in the back or over the trench.

Use the lid of the container or a suitable metal sheet as the oven door.

A grid should be inserted into the oven to make a shelf, which will stop the food burning on the bottom.

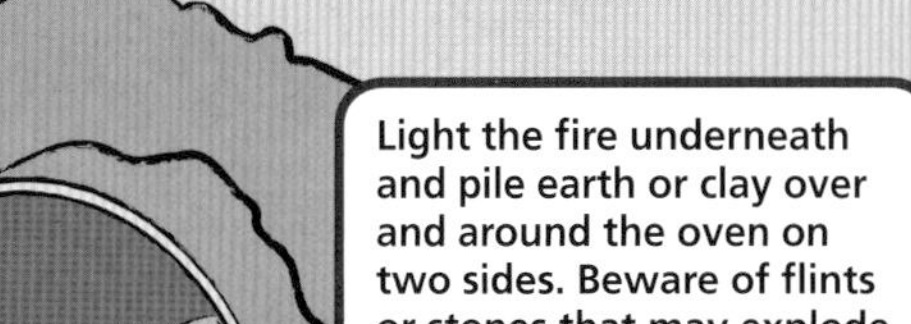

Light the fire underneath and pile earth or clay over and around the oven on two sides. Beware of flints or stones that may explode.

HAYBOX OVEN

The haybox oven works best for cooking casseroles, rice and porridge. The oven works by using insulation to continue cooking a meal that has been part-cooked on the fire. Make sure that you are not rushed for time as cooking takes roughly twice as long as normal.

How does the haybox oven work?

The principle of haybox cooking is very simple. Any heat applied to a pot after it reaches boiling point replaces the heat lost to the air. When the cooker is insulated, heat in the food is prevented from escaping. Therefore no additional energy is needed to complete the cooking process.

You will need:

> A solid wooden box, a tea chest or a hole in the ground. Any insulated container that can withstand cooking temperatures and fits relatively snugly around the pot.

> Cotton sheeting and a pillowcase.

> Insulating material, eg hay, polystyrene beads, newspaper torn into strips and rolled into small balls, straw, wool, cardboard. Ensure the material does not release any toxic fumes or fibres so be aware of fibreglass and foams.

Making the oven

> Line the bottom and the sides of the box with sheets of newspaper.

> Place thick layers of hay in the bottom of the box and fill up to halfway. Press down firmly.

> Select a pot with a tightly fitting lid and stand it in the centre of the box on top of the hay.

> Pack more hay or other insulating material around the pot (approximately two to four inches of thickness) and up to the rim. Make sure you can still lift the pot easily from the hay.

> Remove the pot and line the nest with old cotton sheeting to prevent bits of hay getting into the pot.

> Pack more of the hay into a cotton pillowcase and fit it snugly on top of the lid.

> Cover the box with a piece of wood or board to create a heat trap.

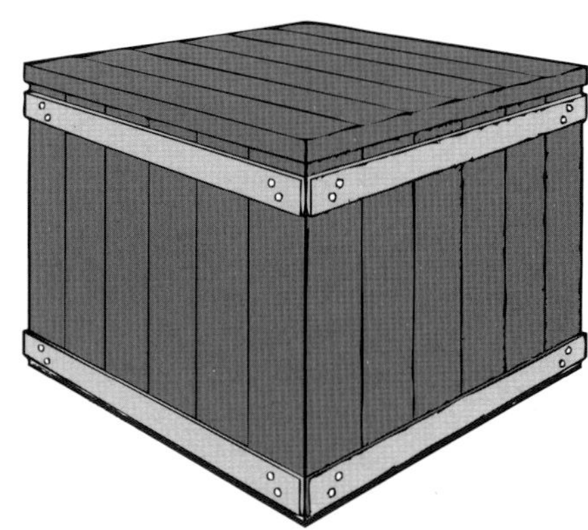

Preparing the food for the haybox oven:

> Prepare the stew or casserole, as you would usually do on a stove, but ensure that the pot is as full as possible.

> Bring the dish to the boil and simmer for a few minutes (five minutes for rice or other grains, 15 minutes for beans or potatoes). It is approximately a third of the overall cooking time.

> Quickly transfer the pot to the haybox while still boiling, for the remaining two-thirds of the cooking time.

> When ready to eat, remove the pot from the haybox and bring back to the boil, stirring occasionally to ensure the entire dish is heated through. Serve immediately.

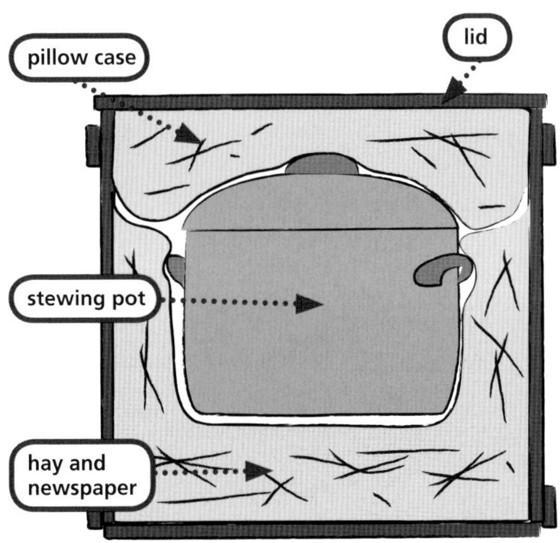

LEAD A PIONEERING PROJECT

Here are some ideas of pioneering projects you could lead. You may find some books with more ideas in your Scout meeting place.

The swing boat

Poles:

100mm x 4.5m	6	(sheer legs and base)
100mm x 3.0m	3	
75mm x 2.4m	3	(cross members-top)

Rope:

12mm x 6m	20	(main lashings)
12mm x 8m	2	(guylines)
12mm x 9m	2	(for supporting the seat)
15mm x 6m	2	(pulling ropes)

Sundries:

Spare tent pegs	4
Frapping mallets	
Serving mallets	
Mallet	
Pickets	8
Tape measure	
3m stout plank	
Chalk	
Pick and Spade	

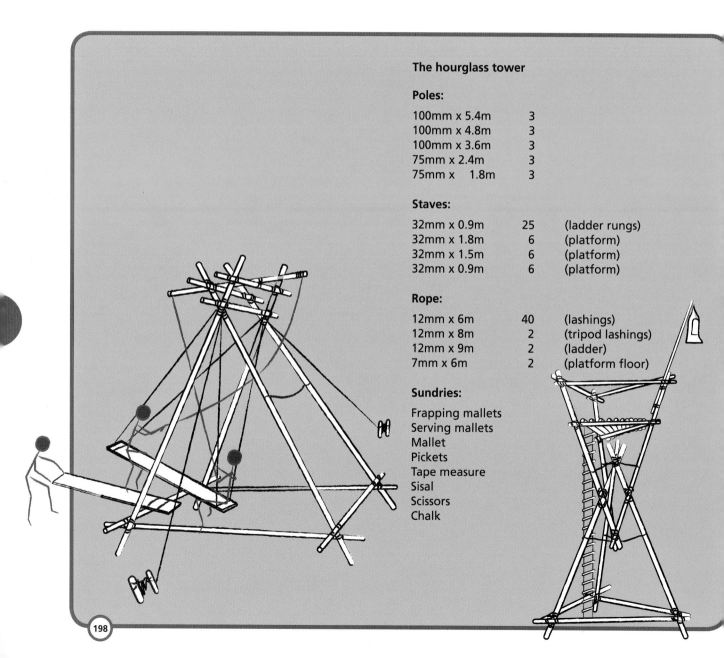

The hourglass tower

Poles:

100mm x 5.4m	3
100mm x 4.8m	3
100mm x 3.6m	3
75mm x 2.4m	3
75mm x 1.8m	3

Staves:

32mm x 0.9m	25	(ladder rungs)
32mm x 1.8m	6	(platform)
32mm x 1.5m	6	(platform)
32mm x 0.9m	6	(platform)

Rope:

12mm x 6m	40	(lashings)
12mm x 8m	2	(tripod lashings)
12mm x 9m	2	(ladder)
7mm x 6m	2	(platform floor)

Sundries:

Frapping mallets
Serving mallets
Mallet
Pickets
Tape measure
Sisal
Scissors
Chalk

BUILD A BIVOUAC AND SLEEP IN IT

> When building a bivouac, remember small is beautiful. The air inside will warm up more quickly than in a large space.

> Have insulation underneath you. Dry leaves, ferns, etc. will trap air.

> Keep out draughts. Have a small entrance hole and block with at least a log at the base.

> Design your shelter according to your surroundings and what materials you have around you. You need to build quickly in an emergency and not spend time and energy hunting for perfect materials to match a rigid plan. For example, you could use old plastic sheets or a tarpaulin strung between trees or supported against a wall.

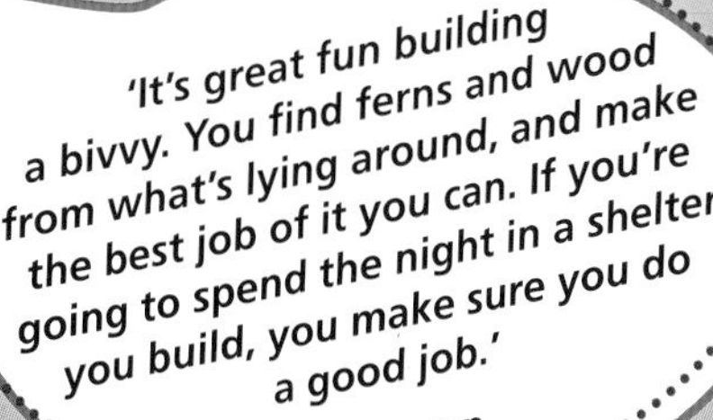

'It's great fun building a bivvy. You find ferns and wood from what's lying around, and make the best job of it you can. If you're going to spend the night in a shelter you build, you make sure you do a good job.'
Cameron

OPEN AN AIRWAY AND GIVE CPR

Oxygen is essential to support life. Without oxygen, the cells in the body start to die, and the cells in the brain start to die after just a few minutes. Oxygen is taken into the body when we breathe in air and is absorbed into our blood via our lungs. The oxygen rich blood is then pumped around our body, reaching all the body's tissues through the network of blood vessels. By the time the blood returns to the heart it has little or no oxygen left, but it is pumped via the pulmonary arteries, back to the lungs, where it is oxygenated and the carbon dioxide is removed.

Remember: If you encounter a casualty who may need CPR, get adult help if at all possible. However, the first person to arrive at an incident may be the only person who can save the casualty's life, so it is important to know how to open and airway and give CPR.

Opening an airway

The airway of an unconscious casualty may become blocked by the tongue slipping back in the throat. This is because muscular control is lost during unconsciousness. Simply lifting the chin and tilting back the head may be all that is required to start the casualty breathing again.

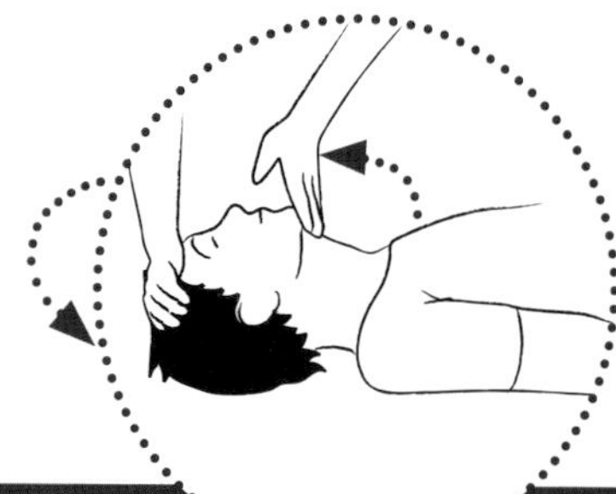

Breathing for a casualty

If your casualty has stopped breathing, you may need to breathe for them, and when the process is combined with the chest compressions – the process is known as CPR (cardiopulmonary resuscitation).

The air we expire still contains sufficient oxygen to satisfy the needs for a person who is not breathing on their own. By physically blowing into the mouth of your casualty and giving them rescue breaths, you force air into their lungs which can then oxygenate their blood. As you turn away to take another breath, the chest will fall and the stale air will be exhaled.

Chest compressions can then be used to push the blood around the body.

Maintaining circulation

If the casualty's heart has stopped, the blood stops moving in the blood vessels, cutting off the supply of fresh oxygen, vital for the survival of the millions of cells in the body.

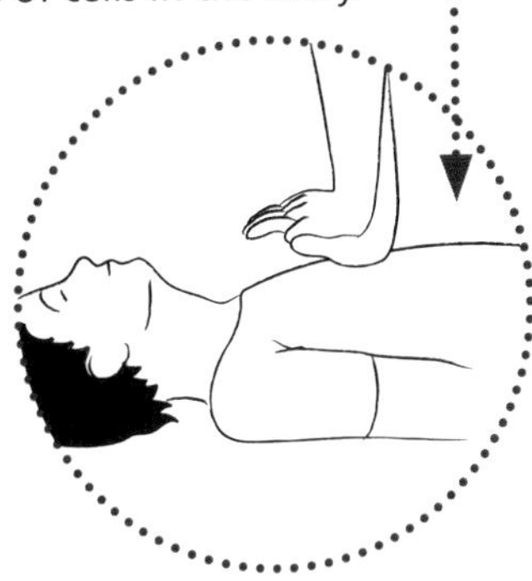

Some circulation can be maintained by pressing down with the heel of the hand on the casualty's chest at the base of the breast bone. By pumping on the chest for 30 compressions at a time, blood is expelled from the heart and pushed around the body.

The skill of doing CPR cannot be learned from a book, although you will find a more detailed explanation in the current First Aid Manual of the UK's leading first aid providers. Rescue breaths and chest compressions must not be practised on a breathing person – but in your training, you may have the opportunity to use a resuscitation dummy that will help you judge the required rhythm and pressure.

When rescue breaths and chest compressions are combined, they are done at the rate of two breaths to 30 compressions.

In films we have all seen the non-breathing casualty carried from the sea only to make a near miraculous recover after receiving only a few rescue breaths. In reality this rarely happens. The process of CPR may simply keep the casualty from dying until medical help arrives.

'By humming Nelly the Elephant twice in your head while giving chest compressions gives the beat of 30 compressions at the correct rate.'

Cameron

RECOVERY POSITION

The best way to learn how to move a casualty is to practise under supervision.

The recovery position is used when a casualty is unconscious but breathing. It allows the person to remain on their side, with their head supported. The advantage of this position is that should they be sick, they are unlikely to choke on their own vomit. Even a young child can manoeuvre a large adult into the recovery position, once the correct techniques are learnt and applied.

1. If the casualty is wearing glasses, remove them and put them somewhere safe, and remove any bulky objects from the pockets.
2. Move the arm nearest to you, so that it is at right angle to the body, elbow bent and palm facing upwards.

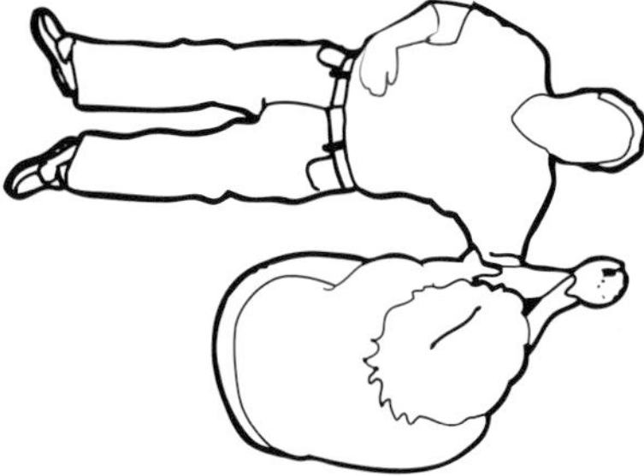

3. Bring the arm furthest away from you across the casualty and hold their palm outwards against the cheek nearest to you.
4. With your other hand, raise the knee of the leg furthest away from you until the foot is flat on the floor.

5. Whilst holding the casualty's hand against their cheek, pull the raised knee so that the casualty rolls towards you on to their side.

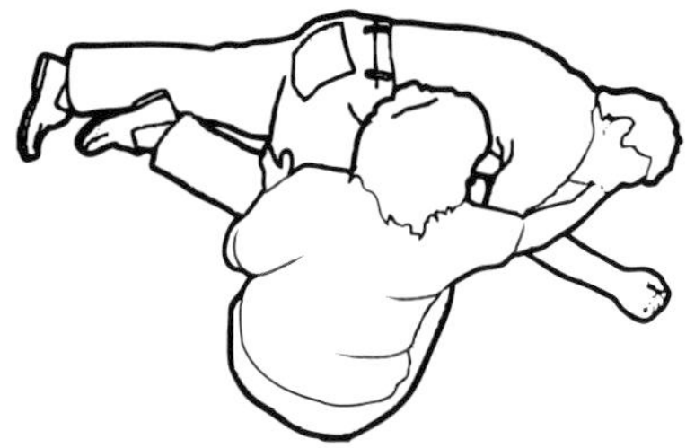

6. Pull their leg so that the top of the leg is at right angles to the body and the knee is at right angles.
7. Check that the airway is open, the hand under the cheek will help to keep the head at the right angle (see image below).
8. When the casualty is in the recovery position, check whether they are breathing again by listening and feeling for 10 seconds.

FRACTURES AND SEVERE BLEEDING

A fracture is a crack or a break in a bone. Bones are strong and considerable pressure is required to break the larger bones in the skeleton.

Stable and unstable fractures

A stable fracture is one where the broken ends do not move about. This may be because they are not completely broken or because they are already jammed together. Such stable breaks are most likely to happen in the wrist and ankle. While they are painful, they can, with care, be moved without danger of causing further injury to surrounding blood vessels or organs.

An unstable fracture is where the two ends of the bone are separated. Any movement of the injured area may result in the ends of the bone causing further damage in the surrounding area.

Unstable fractures can be 'closed fractures' where the skin is not broken, or open fractures where the bone breaks through the surface of the skin.

Recognising a fracture

As we have already seen, there are a variety of different fractures, so the signs and symptoms will vary. There may be:

- Swelling and bruising at the site of the fracture – and the limb may appear to be deformed
- The casualty is unlikely to be able to move the injured area and there will be pain
- If it is a limb it may appear shortened, bent or twisted
- The casualty may be showing signs of shock
- A section of bone may be protruding through the wound.

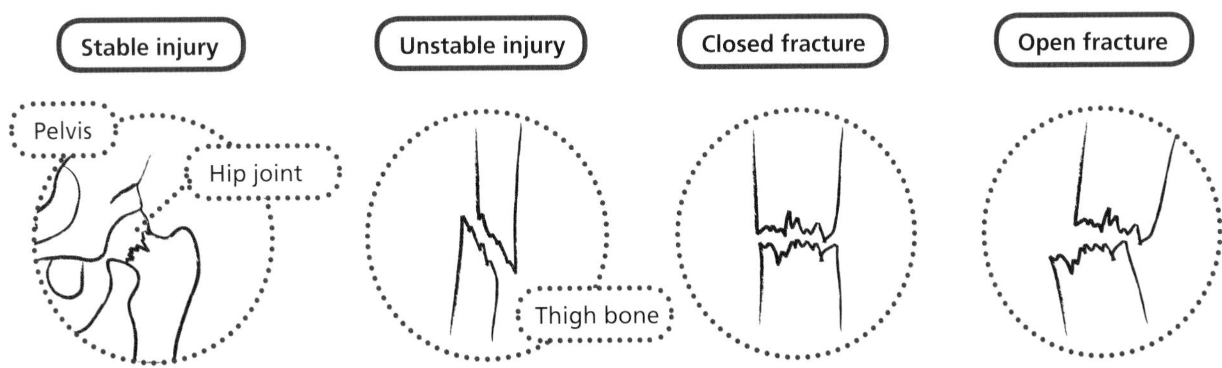

Action to take for a closed fracture

It is important to prevent movement of the injured area, and to get the casualty to hospital.

> Keep the casualty still and in a comfortable position.

> Support the injured area with whatever is to hand, such as a bandage or blanket.

> Phone for an ambulance.

> Don't allow the casualty to eat or drink, as a general anaesthetic may well be needed on arrival at the hospital.

Action to take for an open fracture

To prevent blood loss and limit the chance of infection, it is important to keep the injured area still. As before, the casualty will need to be taken to hospital as soon as possible

> Wearing disposable gloves if you have them, gently cover the wound with a non-fluffy pad or sterile dressing. If the wound is bleeding, apply direct pressure without pressing on the protruding bone.

> Build up pads of clean non-fluffy material around any protruding bone.

> Hold in place with a roller bandage and secure with a safety pin.

> Support the injured area with whatever is to hand, such as a bandage or blanket.

> Phone for an ambulance.

> Don't allow the casualty to eat or drink, as a general anaesthetic may be needed on arrival at the hospital.

BLEEDING

When a wound is bleeding badly, this can be both dramatic and distressing. If the bleeding continues and is not controlled, the casualty's heart may stop.

Action to take to control severe bleeding

> Put on disposable gloves and cut or remove clothing so you can see the wound.

> Apply direct pressure, ie push down on the wound with your fingers or the palm of your hand using a sterile dressing or non- fluffy clean pad. However, if a pad is not readily available it is important to apply direct pressure without it.

> If the injury is to an arm or leg, raise and support it above the level of the casualty's heart. Always handle with gentle care if you suspect that the bone may be broken.

> Help the casualty to lie down, on a blanket if possible.

> Secure a dressing with a bandage which is tight enough to maintain pressure.

> Support the injured part in a raised position using whatever is to hand.

> Phone for an ambulance.

TEMPERATURE EXTREMES

Unlike many of the injuries we have looked at that result from accidents that are sometimes difficult to avoid, this last section deals with injuries that with care and planning should be avoided.

Sunburn

Sunburn is caused by over exposure to the sun. Most sunburn is not serious but in several cases the skin becomes lobster-red and blistered. Sunburn can generally be avoided by applying a high factor sun lotion to all exposed areas of flesh on warm, sunny days. Even on some apparently overcast days the sun can still burn. When at camp or out in the open, don't be afraid to follow the Australian advice and Slip, Slap, Slop!

> Slip on a T-shirt and sunglasses

> Slap on a sun hat

> Slop on the sun lotion, so that your skin does not get over-exposed to the harmful effects of the sun.

A casualty who is sunburnt should be moved into the shade and the skin cooled with cold water. Encourage the casualty to drink water, and if the burns are quite mild, they can be soothed with calamine lotion or another aftersun lotion. For serious sunburn, seek medical aid.

Dehydration

About 70 per cent of the human body is made up of water. It is important for our digestion, the functioning of our joints, healthy skin and removal of waste products. We become dehydrated when more fluid is lost from the body than we take in, causing an imbalance in important minerals needed by our muscles and nervous system.

About two-thirds of the water we need comes from drinks while most of the remaining third should come from the food we eat. As the average adult loses around 2.5 litres of water every day through the normal processes of breathing, sweating and waste removal, you will see how important it is to take in sufficient liquids at regular points during the day. The water loss can increase considerable when you are active or the weather is hot so in turn you need to take in more liquids.

The main symptom of dehydration is feeling thirsty but other possible symptoms might include:

> Dry mouth, eyes and lips

> Headache

> Tiredness

> Dizziness or light-headedness

A short rest in a shaded area to take a drink of water or juice is usually sufficient to rehydrate someone who is thirsty.

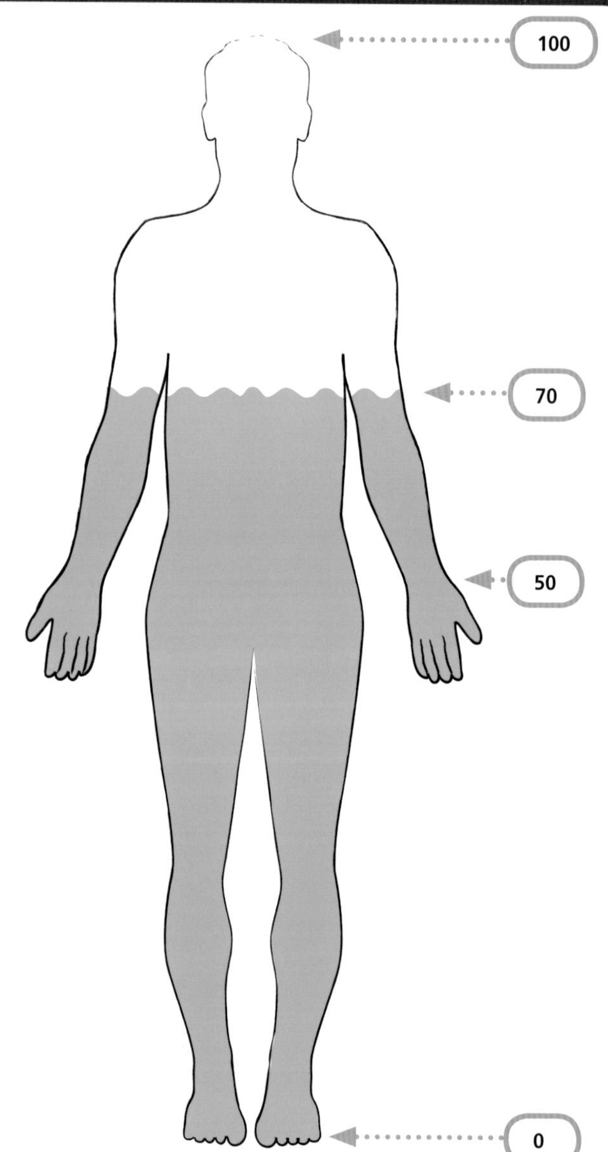

Heat Exhaustion

In many ways heat exhaustion is a more severe form of dehydration, caused by the loss of water and salt from the body through excessive sweating. It usually affects people who are not acclimatised to hot or humid conditions, but it can affect people who are already unwell and have been vomiting or have diarrhoea.

The symptoms may include:

> Headache, dizziness and confusion
> Loss of appetite and feeling sick
> Sweating, with pale clammy skin
> Cramps, particularly in the arms and legs
> Rapid shallow pulse and breathing.

The casualty will need to cool down, so find a shaded place for them to lie with their legs raised. Help them to drink plenty of cool liquids, preferably water, and if possible make up a mild salt solution of one teaspoon of salt to a litre of water. Even if the casualty recovers quickly, it is important they are checked over by a doctor.

Hypothermia

Our core body temperature is normally around 37°C, but when subjected to cold, the temperature can start to fall. When it drops by just 2°C, hypothermia will start to develop. Hypothermia can be brought on in a number of different ways. The elderly can die from hypothermia, resulting from long periods in poorly heated houses. Many alcoholics and drug addicts die from hypothermia in what is now referred to as 'urban hypothermia' No matter how it is caused, when the body is no longer able to keep itself warm, the core temperature will start to fall, and when it drops by 7°C to 30°C (86°F) the condition can frequently lead to death.

For those involved in outdoor activities, there are probably two sorts of hypothermia to watch for. The first is caused by 'rapid cooling', often associated with an activity such as sailing or canoeing in the colder months of the year. It is also possible to develop hypothermia gradually over a number of days.

When surrounded by cold water, the body cools 30 times faster than in still dry air. So following a capsize in a canoe or dinghy, where the individual has got cold very quickly, the best course of action is to get warm again quickly, under a hot shower. At most boating bases this would present no problem.

If the cooling process has taken place over a longer period, the warming process should also be slower.

Imagine this situation at camp…

A Scout has not slept well overnight and she then decides to skips breakfast. She is a bit disorganised in her tent, and although she knows she is with a party going hiking, forgets to pack her waterproof. It's a cold day – with a strong wind blowing and before long it starts to drizzle with rain. Without waterproofs, the Scout's clothes are soon wet and she starts to feel very cold and miserable. Her body is working hard, but with a poor night's sleep and no breakfast to provide energy for the day, it is soon running out of fuel and to make matters worse, all body heat is just escaping through trying to warm up her wet clothes. Before long she starts feeling the effects of hypothermia. She starts shivering and her skin is cold to the touch. She may become apathetic (lose interest is what is going on around her) or disorientated (not seeming to know where she is going) and her behaviour may become irrational and out of character. She may become lethargic and as the condition worsens, her breathing becomes slow and shallow, and her heart beat slows. If she gets really cold her body will not allow blood to flow to the extremities of her body and so it is impossible to find a pulse in the wrist.

Many suffering from serious hypothermia will attempt to remove their clothes, while others will just lie down and fall into a sleep from which they will not wake up.

The best treatment for hypothermia is prevention and that involves being properly prepared and equipped for the activity ahead. However if you suspect a member of your group is getting cold, the sooner you act, the sooner the situation can be remedied.

> Seek some shelter as quickly as possible

> While shielding the casualty from the wind, remove as many of any wet clothes as possible and replace with spare dry clothes, including a hat and gloves if available

> Insulate the casualty from the cold. Put them in a sleeping bag and cover with a space blanket or survival bag

> If the situation is serious, send for help, but don't leave the casualty alone if at all possible

> Help the casualty to warm up by giving them some 'fuel' to generate energy ie warm drinks and high energy food from your emergency rations

> Remember if one person is very cold, others may also be getting near the same condition. Use a buddy system, so members of the party look out for each other.

ASSOCIATED ACTIVITY BADGES

Nights Away (Staged)

Pioneer

Quartermaster

Survival Skills

'When I joined Scouts I wasn't sure if I was an adventurous person. Since then I've tried so many activities with my Troop that I can never wait for the next big adventure. I'd like to try flying, so I suppose the sky's the limit!'
Charlotte
Adventure
MAKE EVERY DAY
A BIG ADVENTURE

REQUIREMENTS

Take part in three different activities, ideally on separate occasions. Examples of various suitable activities are detailed below. This is a guideline rather than an exclusive list.

Adventure Activities

a. Climbing
b. Hill walking
c. Hiking
d. Explore a town or area you don't know
e. Orienteering
f. Plan and undertake a journey by public transport
g. Caving or Pot holing
h. Pony trekking or horse riding
i. Cycling
j. Sailing
k. Canoeing
l. Water-skiing
m. Surfing
n. Dragon boating
o. Bellboating
p. Sub-aqua
q. Canal boating
r. Rafting
s. Pulling
t. Gliding
u. Powered aircraft
v. Hovercrafting
w. Stunt kiting
x. Hot air ballooning
y. Paragliding

For each activity:

a. Have knowledge of the safety issues involved and the use of any equipment needed for the activity
b. Show an awareness of environmental issues around the activity (such as erosion at popular climbing areas)
c. Know about further opportunities to take part in the chosen activities.

EXAMPLE OF ACTIVITIES

Canyoning

Gorge walking

Waterskiing

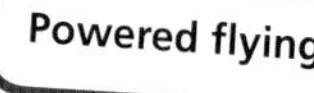

Sailing

Wind surfing

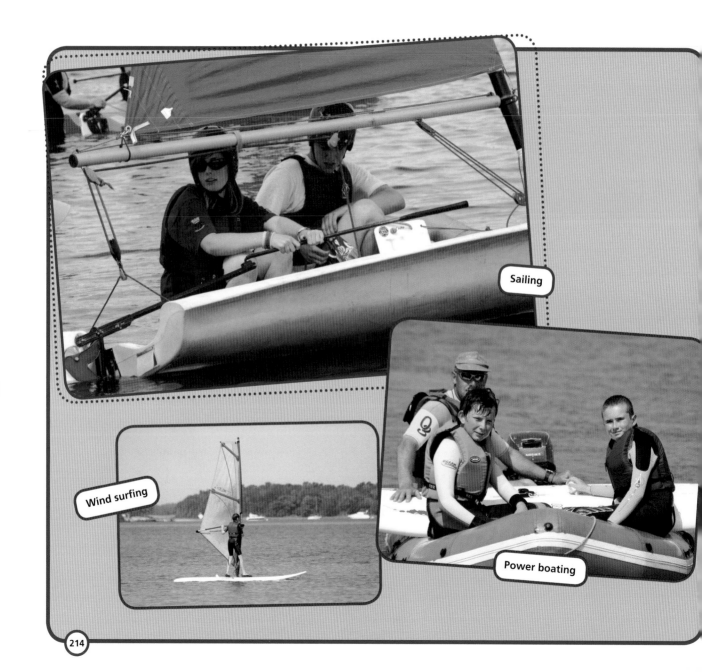

Power boating

Rafting

Sub-aqua

Horse riding

Karting

Cycling

Assault courses

High ropes

Climbing

Abseiling

SAFETY RULES

You will probably do many adventurous activities during your time in Scouts, some of which will count towards the Adventure Challenge. Lots of these activities will be delivered by trained instructors, who have the necessary qualifications and expertise to ensure your safety.

Often you will have a safety briefing from the instructor before the activity. Make sure you listen carefully to all the instructor says, and then follow the instruction given. The word adventure implies that there is some risk in what you are doing, so safety is of great importance.

Some of the safety rules, like wearing harnesses and helmets at heights, are obvious, but there may be other rules that are more subtle. There is probably a good reason for this, and the instructor will normally be happy to tell you why things are done a certain way.

Remember, lots of the adventure activities you will do have Activity Badges linked to them, which are there to recognise your achievement and skill in an activity. If you gain a badge, there is also the option of going on to become a Scout instructor in the activity, and you will wear a gold ring around the activity badge. See page 279 for more information on this.

ENVIRONMENTAL ISSUES

As thrilling as it is to climb a rockface or power a jet ski, every activity we do has an effect on our surroundings, and it is important that as a Scout you are conscious of the environmental impact of your activity.

Get into the habit of asking yourself questions about your adventure, so that you can limit any damage you do, and improve the activity for future adventurers. Here are a few examples:

> If climbing on natural rock, are you eroding the rock at an unacceptable rate? Could you use a less frequently visited location to reduce the impact? Is it more responsible to use an artificial or indoor climb?

> If you are trying a motor sport, such as karting, powerboating or flying in powered aircraft, what is the effect of the fuel on the environment? Could you use a cleaner or more efficient fuel? Is there a way of driving or flying that uses fuel more sparingly?

> When hill walking or orienteering through rural areas, are you leaving evidence behind that you have visited? Remember the saying – Leave No Trace. Take all litter with you, do not tamper with wildlife or tree lines, and observe the Countryside Code (see page 250).

It may not be possible to have zero impact on the environment through your adventures, but a good Scout does their best to protect the planet and use the Earth's resources responsibly.

FURTHER OPPORTUNITIES

The Adventure Challenge will whet your appetite for the outdoor life, and challenge you to go beyond your boundaries. You'll start to pick up new skills, but this is not the end. For activities that really spark an interest, why not aim to get the relevant Activity Badge? Once you've got that, you can take your achievement even further by doing and Activity PLUS. See 280 for more details. Besides that, there are also award schemes for external agencies and National Governing Bodies that you could attempt. You may be able to develop your ability within Scouting, or you could join a local club to share your interest with other young people. Scouting is about helping you find out what you're good at, and then encouraging you to go as far as you can.

Take your activity passion further. Visit the A to Z Directory of Activites at www.scouts.org.uk/activities

Fact:
11 out of the 12 men who have walked on the Moon were Scouts.

ASSOCIATED ACTIVITY BADGES

Aeronautics

Caver

Air Spotter

Climber

Angler

Dinghy Sailor

Aviation Skills (1-3)

Dragon Boating

Canoeist

Emergency Aid (Staged)

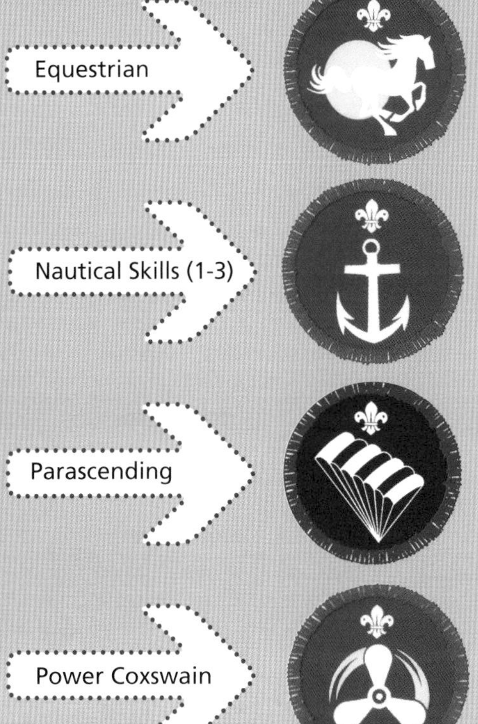
Equestrian
Nautical Skills (1-3)
Parascending
Power Coxswain

Pulling
Snowsports
Street Sports
Water Sports

'Planning my own expedition helped me to develop my leadership skills. When you're faced with a 20km hike, a map, compass and patrol of six, you're forced to be independent. The sense of achievement when you get to your destination is terrific!'

Ben

AN EXPEDITION IS A JOURNEY WITH A PURPOSE.

REQUIREMENTS

Complete the activities in one of the following two areas:

Area 1 - Expedition – 'A Journey with a Purpose'

Take part in an expedition over two days (including a night away) with at least three friends. Be involved in the planning of the expedition, complete relevant training and be properly prepared.

During the expedition:

a. Play a full part in the team
b. Journey for at least four hours each day
c. Use a map to keep track of where you are
d. Stay overnight at a hostel or other suitable venue, or camp overnight at a suitable site
e. Cook the evening meal and breakfast
f. Achieve at least one goal, agreed with your leader before the expedition.

The expedition may be on foot, canoe, cycle or sailing boat. Other options may be appropriate, and should be agreed with the Scouts involved.

Area 2 - Exploration – 'A Purpose with a Journey'

Take part in an exploration over two days (including a night away) with at least three friends, and report or present your findings. You must be involved in the planning of the exploration, complete relevant training and be properly prepared. You must have completed some initial research into the subject to be investigated. The challenge should take place somewhere you have never been before or don't know well.

!

During the exploration:

- Play a full part in the team
- Travel for at least 90 minutes to a hostel, campsite or other suitable venue
- Use a map to keep track of where you are
- Conduct the exploration within an agreed area (discussed in advance with the Scout) collecting evidence and information for the report or presentation
- Stay overnight at the venue and cook the evening meal and breakfast
- Complete the exploration before returning home
- Have the report or presentation ready within 4 weeks of the exploration.

The journey may be on foot, or by public transport, canoe, cycle, aircraft, wheelchair or boat. Other options may be appropriate, and should be agreed with the Scouts involved.

The 'exploration' element should last 4 – 5 hours over the two days and could vary from an investigation into bird life in a wood to visiting museums in a town.

PLANNING AND PREPARATION

Expeditions

An expedition is 'a journey with a purpose' and for your Expedition Challenge Award you are expected to have a 'goal' - something you will find out at a particular place, or as you travel on your journey.

Your journey should:

> Be Planned
> Be Safe
> Be Fun
> Be Challenging
> Have an Aim
> Involve Teamwork
> Have a Result – something you have all discovered.

Ellen MacArthur, the fastest ever sailor to complete a solo non-stop circumnavigation of the globe in 2005.

Your Expedition

Expeditions can be:

> An afternoon exploring a country or suburban or city area new to you
> A late night hike or an all night hike
> Walk in a Country Park or country ramble on footpaths through woods and fields
> Walking a tow-path along a river or canal
> A cycle ride
> Canoeing or Pulling on Rivers or Canals
> Walking part of a 'Long Distance Footpath' near to you
> Discuss with your parents taking a bus or train at the start or end of your journey. This can be an adventure too
> Taking a tent and having a 2 day Expedition
> Staying in a Youth Hostel.

These can all be great fun and equally challenging.

'How much further is it?'

Once you have learned to pack all you need in a light backpack, have the right equipment and training, and become strong enough, you should aim to hike between 10-15 kilometres a day. An overnight hike carrying your tent, food and sleeping bag could cover 20- 25 kilometres. An expedition should be difficult and challenging, but if your Scout Leader thinks you are ready for it, you should find it enjoyable too. Remember, it is not the distance that matters, it's the discovery!

Planning and Preparation

The success and enjoyment of any expedition is all in the planning and preparation. If you attempt something that is too far or too difficult, if you have the wrong clothing or equipment, or if your pack is too heavy you will have a bad experience. This is sad, because most Scouts find backpacking to be one of the best experiences they have ever had. They remember the friends they walked with, the enjoyment of the countryside, being without adults, cooking and camping on their own, even in the rain, as a great adventure.

You need to learn:

> How to read a map

> To use a compass all the time

> To wear the right clothes

> To pack the right things and nothing else

> To learn to choose and cook the right foods

> To pitch your tent quickly in the dark

> To make the right decisions as a team

> To stay safe at all times

> What is needed in a first aid kit for expeditions

> First Aid for dealing with blisters, sprains, cuts and hypothermia.

Your expedition could involve lightweight camping or staying in a hostel or bunkhouse

General Planning

On your first hikes and expeditions you will probably be going along with an older and more experienced Scout, maybe your PL, who will have the main responsibility for the activity. Do all you can to help and learn, especially by keeping an eye on the map, checking compass bearings yourself and learning what to do when it's your turn to be a hike group leader.

Always keep your parents and those at home informed of everything you are doing, but don't let them pack your rucksack, they don't have to carry the nine pairs of trousers they will want you to take!

Your expedition will probably take place during the summer or early autumn but be prepared for the weather to change from sunshine to rain and back, so have sun-cream and also all your kit kept dry in double plastic bags.

Personal Preparation

Firstly, you need to be FIT, not super-fit, but in the two weeks before the hike it is good to get some extra walking, football, swimming or cycling into your routine. Make sure you take any medication or sanitary requirements with you. Girls would probably feel more comfortable wearing a sports bra. Don't promise to ring your parents or friends at particular times as mobile phone coverage is not always good outside of urban areas.

EQUIPMENT PLANNING

Rucksack. This should be around 65l in size. Any smaller and you won't be able to keep everything inside and dry. If you're buying a rucksack, ask the retailer for advice on what size is suitable for you. Cheap rucksacks are often as good as expensive ones for basic Scout hiking.

Sleeping Bag. You should get one with a hood, at least 3 season, packs to about the size of a football and that weighs no more than 1.5 Kilos. The sleeping bag with the wide opening top that packed into a big roll that you used as a Cub is not suitable for hike camping.

Raincoats and over-trousers should be totally waterproof, a simple one layer zip jacket with no quilting as these soak-up water, become useless and cannot be dried out.

Boots. Boots are essential for supporting your ankles on uneven ground. You are at a fast-growing stage, so spend as little on boots as possible. Soft boots can be cheap, comfortable and reasonably waterproof.

Keeping weight of your pack down.

No-one enjoys carrying a heavy pack. The basic rule for everything you have to carry is:

Some people even cut the handle off an old toothbrush to save weight. The idea is that if you can cut everything in half, your pack will weigh half as much, so take:

> A tiny torch
> A tiny piece of soap, or just wet-wipes
> One tiny squeeze of toothpaste, or share with the group
> Take a very small towel
> The lightest pair of spare trainers
> One very light plastic bowl and just a spoon.

Full Kit List with a few ideas and suggestions.

Rucksack. Start by lining your rucksack with a large plastic sack. Get a leader to adjust straps properly.

Tent. 2 – 3 kg. If it's a tight squeeze for three, wrap your rucksacks in plastic bags and store outside the tent, under a tree.

Sleeping bag. Double wrap it in plastic, inside your pack.

Roll Mat. This insulates you from the cold ground - carry outside your pack and wipe dry.

Sleeping things. Always have a t-shirt and bottoms to wear at night to change out of the damp clothes you hiked in. Pack your pyjamas inside your sleeping bag where you can find them in the dark.

Spare Clothes. Make a small pack of very light spare clothes and trainers, hopefully you won't need them.

Wash Kit. Only take enough soap and toothpaste for one use.

Towel. Take a very small hand towel. Old worn ones are lighter.

Torch. A small torch with spare batteries is all you need.

Eating Things. A light plastic bowl and mug, spoon, sharp knife.

Cooker. Gas or a Trangia™ - with pots and fuel.

Small tin opener. If you need it.

Lighter. Have two or three in the group, so you can always find one quickly.

Water bottles. About 2 litres each. Old lemonade bottles are fine. Don't drink it all, save some for cooking. Village church yards usually have taps, but run some water-off first.

Compass. One each, and get into a routine of checking every road and path all the time.

First Aid Kit. Per group. Plasters, elastic bandage for sprains, tweezers for thorns.

Fluorescent Jacket/ bands. You will almost certainly walk on, or cross, a road - So be seen!

Emergency Chocolate. It is always good to have something for when you are totally wet, cold and lost, if only to cheer the others up.

Mobile Phone. A really useful thing to have, but you may not always get a good signal. Agree with your leader if you are to take one.

Whistle. For emergencies. Learn the emergency signal code.

Some more items to take if you have space....

- A washing-up sponge with soap on it wrapped in a small bag.
- A fire-lighter block... you might like to sit around a small fire at night.
- A book, game or small radio.
- Insect repellent.
- Sun cream – essential in the summer.
- Camera
- Pen and pad.

FOOD

Food and cooking

On a hike or expedition looking forward to cooking a meal is one of the things that keeps you going! However, too many Scouts are so tired when they arrive at the camp site, they can't be bothered to cook. This can be very dangerous as energy needs to be replaced and it is the group leader's job to maintain the discipline of keeping everyone doing their jobs and getting a meal cooked. You may only have one pot, or two cookers at the most, so meals need to be carefully planned. You will not be carrying a lot of fuel, so meals need to cook quickly and efficiently. You may even want to sit around and all eat a meal straight out of the pot - it saves washing up!

Boiled rice, instant potato or pasta are good hot filling foods when eaten with a sauce, cheese, sausages or thin strips of meat. Have fruit, cake, instant custard or chocolate for afters. Or mix them all together! Hike food can still be fun. Look around your supermarket for new things to take hiking.

NEVER cook in the tent, and even cooking in the entrance is dangerous if people try stepping over you. Tent fires can cause terrible burns when hot material sticks to the skin. Find the shelter of a tree or take a small tarpaulin to cook under.

Selecting and carrying food

Rather than give you ready made menus, here are about 40 ingredients.

What hike meals can you make out of them?

> Dry foods need to be taken out of boxes (extra weight) and put into plastic bags. But keep the instructions! Instant porridge, sugar, pasta, flour, rice, flavoured noodles, cereals, instant potato, popping corn, soups, trail-mix.

> Soft food can be kept in plastic boxes. Bread, ready prepared salad, fruit, cake, margarine, crisp bread, rolls, cream cheese.

> Save small medicine containers for small amounts of salt, cooking oil, sugar, ketchup, curry powder, spices, chocolate spread, marmite. What ever you fancy to make a meal more enjoyable.

> Eggs can be broken into a plastic bottle and taken as an 'instant omelette.'

> Meat can be frozen to allow it to be carried on hot days. Sausages, burgers, ham, bacon, mince.

> Tins should be kept to a minimum but in cold weather a quick hot meal of tinned stew, beans and sausages or spaghetti bolognaise might be a life saver.

> Drinks like instant soups, chocolate, coffee, tea, fruit powder.

Remember to take into account the dietary requirements of your group.

PACK A RUCKSACK

The way a rucksack is packed is important because it can affect your balance, your posture, and your breathing. Therefore, it is important to think about where you put things. The main rule is to pack the light things in the lower part and the heavier things in the upper part. This means that the centre of gravity is high on your back and the rucksack is much more comfortable to carry. The total weight will be the same however you pack it, but it is much less tiring when the rucksack is packed in such a way that it helps your posture and stresses the muscles that you use a lot in everyday life.

Items that you might need to lay your hands on quickly should be in the side pockets or just under the top for easy access. When you pack a rucksack it is easiest to pack everything in plastic bags. This keeps all your things dry even if the rucksack leaks in heavy rain and it also helps to keep order in the rucksack. You can even pack using plastic bags of different colours to help with identification. For instance, your wash kit in a yellow bag, your cutlery in a red bag and so on. This makes it much easier to find a specific item. The sketch on the next page shows how your rucksack should be packed.

Tricks of the trade

There is a huge range of rucksacks on the market and when you are buying your own, it can be a confusing business. The important thing, apart from price, is to choose a rucksack that fits you and is not too big or too small. If your rucksack is too big for your back, it will be very uncomfortable to carry and might damage your back for life.

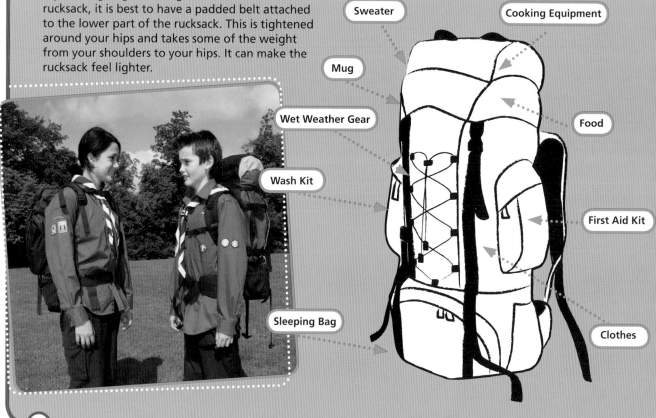

If you are going on a long walk or hike with a rucksack, it is best to have a padded belt attached to the lower part of the rucksack. This is tightened around your hips and takes some of the weight from your shoulders to your hips. It can make the rucksack feel lighter.

When you go away, always take extra straps and buckles as you never know when some will get lost or broken.

SIX FIGURE GRID REFERENCES

Grid references are a way of clearly describing any point on an Ordnance Survey map.

1. Look at a local Ordnance Survey map and pick a point on it like a fork in a path you have been to before. It is covered with a grid of blue lines each covering 1km by 1km. Each box in the grid is 2cm x 2cm for a 1:50000 map and is 4cm x 4cm for a 1:25000 map.
2. Along the bottom of your map there are two-digit numbers (like 46 or 04 or 75) attached to every vertical line of the grid and similarly there are two-digit numbers attached to every horizontal line of the grid.
3. Now, put your finger on the point in Stage 1. We are going to label the box it is in now. Move your finger to the bottom left hand corner of the box where the grid lines cross over. Write down the number attached to that vertical line, say 32 (it's the same at the top and bottom), then next to it write down the number attached to that horizontal line, say 45 (again it's the same at left or right side of the map). Put it all together and you have a grid reference of 3245. This is the four figure grid reference that is unique to that box on that map.

We need to be a little more accurate when walking, after all a four figure grid reference covers an area of 1000 metres by 1000 metres, not much you might think but perhaps there is more than one fork in a path in that square. To really be accurate we need to use a six figure grid reference.

4. Same as before but this time imagine that the grid box is split up with 10 equal spaced vertical and horizontal lines making 10 x 10 = 100 small boxes within the original box! If we numbered from the bottom left each new line from 0 to 9 then we can uniquely identify each small box this time
5. Try this out. Which small 'imaginary' box is your point from Stage 1 in? We have the 32 from last time - what's the extra number for the vertical lines (7)? Write it all down, 327. What about the horizontal lines (5)? Write all them down, 455. Put it altogether and its 327455. That's all there is to it.

Some thoughts for you

- With six figure grid references you uniquely identify an area on the map 100 metres by 100 metres
- It's not pinpoint accurate, although it is good enough for us
- The order is important. You must give the 3 digits along the bottom first then the 3 digits up the side.

COMPASS

A compass is an instrument with a magnetised needle which points to (magnetic) north and is therefore used for determining direction. They come in different shapes and sizes and indeed, the use of a suspended magnet (which always comes to rest in a north-south direction) was used many centuries ago as a primitive form of compass. Today, in one form or another, compasses are used on land, at sea or in the air, to help people specify direction.

Silva type compass – This compass is the one you are most likely to use for your expedition. It consists of a magnetised needle suspended in an alcohol-filled housing. The liquid helps to 'dampen' movement of the needle enabling it to be read more quickly. The compass housing has etched orienting lines and an orienting arrow, while the baseplate (on which the housing is mounted) has the direction of travel arrow and map scales etched onto it. This compass allows for bearings (an accurate method of determining direction) to be worked out simply.

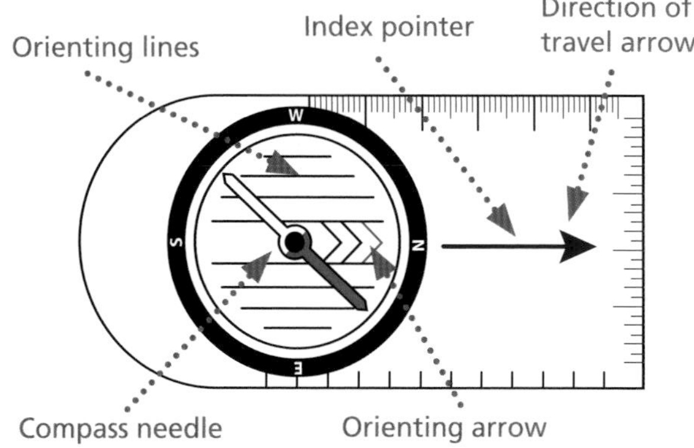

Get your bearings!

A bearing is the angle measured in the number of degrees between 0 and 360 that tells you the direction from one place to another. North is called 0 and therefore it follows that east is 90 degrees, south west is 225 degrees and so on. If we just used the points of the compass, (north, south, east, west and so on) we would only get eight different directions (or possibly 16 or 32 at most if we further divided the compass points, for example, south-southwest or north by northeast and so on). By using bearings, we can have 360, which enables us to be much more accurate.

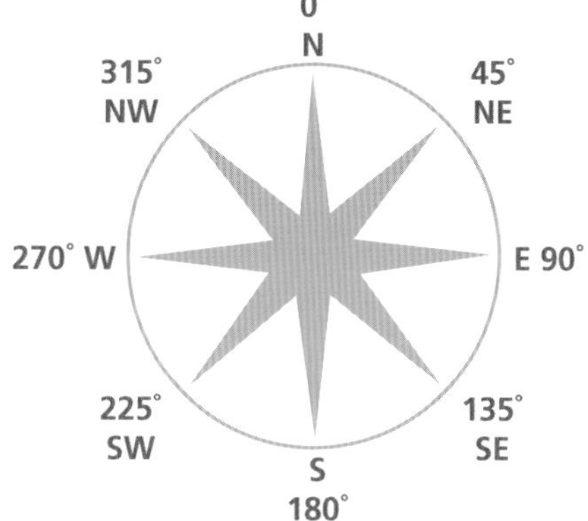

Once you have determined a direction (and bearing) in which to travel, it can then be checked at regular intervals to confirm that you're still going in the right direction, whether or not your destination can be seen. When using a compass proficiently, you need to be able to:

> Take a bearing - determine the angle between north and the direction of an object in terms of degrees

- > Walk on a bearing - use a bearing to get to a destination without necessarily using a map
- > Set a map - use a compass to correctly position a map in order to represent what can actually be seen.

The three norths

When working with a map and compass, there are three different norths to be considered! Fortunately, in the UK, we only have to consider and work with two of them in practical situations.

True north - Each day the Earth rotates about its axis once. The ends of the axis are the true North and true South poles.

Grid north - The grid lines, pointing to grid north, on Ordnance Survey maps divide Great Britain into 100 kilometre sections. They are then further sub-divided into one kilometre squares, which originate from an imaginary zero point to the South West of the United Kingdom, east of an imaginary zero point in the Atlantic Ocean, west of Cornwall. The majority of grid lines are 1.5 degrees west of true north and are therefore useful lines to refer to when taking bearings.

Grid North
True North
Magnetic North
1.5°
6.0°

Magnetic north - A compass needle points to the magnetic north pole. Unfortunately, it is not in the same position as the true North pole. The magnetic north pole is currently located in the Baffin Island region of Canada, and from the United Kingdom, it is west of true north. The difference between grid north and magnetic north is known as the magnetic variation and its value can be found in the orientation panel or margin of an Ordnance Survey map.

As true north is only about 1.5 degrees off grid north, it is so small that it is normally disregarded and only grid north and magnetic north are used.

Magnetic variation

The magnetic variation, (the difference between magnetic north and true north), is caused by the North and South poles not being directly 'opposite' one another. The lines of the Earth's magnetic field do not run in a regular pattern as they are affected by other local magnetic forces and the magnetic pole is always on the move. Some of these lines of magnetic variation are east of true north and others west of true north. Between the east and west lines there is a line of zero magnetic variation where the compass does point to true north - this line is known as the agonic line currently running through eastern Canada, United States of America and South America.

However, not only does the magnetic variation change as you move across the Earth's surface, it also changes with time. In 2008, the magnetic variation in the UK varied between two and five degrees. It is important to check the magnetic variation regularly, and this can be found on a map's orientation panel or margin. Remember also to check the year the map was printed, as a map that is 20 years or so old, could be up to 3 or 4 degrees out! In fact, the magnetic variation also varies from side to side and top to bottom on each and every map but these details can also be found on the map. This magnetic variation is important when combining a map and compass as you need to convert bearings from 'map to field'. To convert grid bearings (which are indicated by a map) to magnetic bearings (as per the compass pointing to magnetic north), add the current variation by turning the compass housing anti-clockwise. For example, if the current variation was 6 degrees, a grid bearing of 122 degrees would become 128 degrees. This is what the dial should be set at. The reverse is true for converting a magnetic bearing to a grid bearing; that is, subtract the current variation.

Remember:

From Grid to Mag you ADD

From Mag to Grid you GET RID

Taking a bearing

1. Hold the compass flat in your hand with the direction of travel arrow pointing towards your destination or objective.
2. Turn the compass housing until the compass needle lines up over the orienting arrow. Ensure the north pole of the needle, usually red, is used.
3. Read off the magnetic bearing (that is, the number of degrees) from the mark on the compass housing indicated by the index pointer.
4. Keep the housing in that position and check your bearing at regular intervals by lining up the needle with the orienting arrow and walking in the direction indicated by the direction of travel arrow.

Walking on a bearing

This is used when you can initially see your objective or destination and don't need a map. It is important to work out a compass bearing before the situation changes. This might be due to the weather (rain, fog and so on), the terrain you are in (valley, hills and so on) or a delay resulting in darkness. Any of these factors may mean you can no longer see where you are aiming for and, therefore, you will need to rely on the compass bearing.

1. Turn the housing of the compass until the bearing you require is against the index pointer.
2. Turn the compass until the needle lies over the orienting arrow.
3. Pick out a landmark along your direction of travel line and walk towards it.
4. Check your bearing and your objective at regular intervals.

Setting a map with a compass

This is for when you are using a map and compass together to reach a given destination, probably in unfamiliar territory.

1. Turn the compass housing until the magnetic variation for the area is shown against the index pointer.
2. Place the direction of travel arrow pointing along the vertical grid line with the direction of travel arrow pointing to the top of the map.
3. Turn the map with the compass in this position until the compass needle points to the north mark on the compass housing.
4. Your map is now 'set' and you should be able to recognise actual features from your map in front of you.

Combining map and compass

1. Place the compass on the map so that one long edge joins the start point and your destination, with the direction of travel arrow pointing towards the direction you wish to travel. (The direction of the map does not matter for this exercise).
2. Turn the compass housing until the orienting arrow points to the top of the map and the orienting lines are parallel to the grid lines.
3. Take the compass off the map and read off the bearing at the index pointer and add (or subtract) the local magnetic variation.
4. Turn the whole compass so that the needle comes to rest over the orienting arrow, with the red part to the north.
5. Hold the compass in front of you, pick out a landmark along your line of travel and walk towards it.

Common errors

When first learning how to use a compass, there seem to be many things to take into consideration … here are a few things which often 'go wrong':

> Failing to add on the magnetic variation. If the magnetic variation is, for example, 6 degrees, and you forget to add it on, you will be 105 metres off course for every kilometre travelled in a straight line. This gets proportionally bigger over greater distances.

> Not having the direction of travel arrow pointing from your start to finish. If you make this mistake you will walk 180 degrees out from your intended route!

> Orienting arrow pointing to the bottom of the map. Again, you will walk (180 degrees out) in the opposite direction.

> Not taking account of the magnetic effects of iron and steel around you. For example, watches, steel buckles, cars, buried pipes, reinforced concrete, wire fences, railway lines and other compasses (and even magnetic rocks!) can influence your compass. That is, these items might attract the compass needle in preference to the magnetic north pole therefore giving you an inaccurate reading. If in doubt, try to move away from such objects.

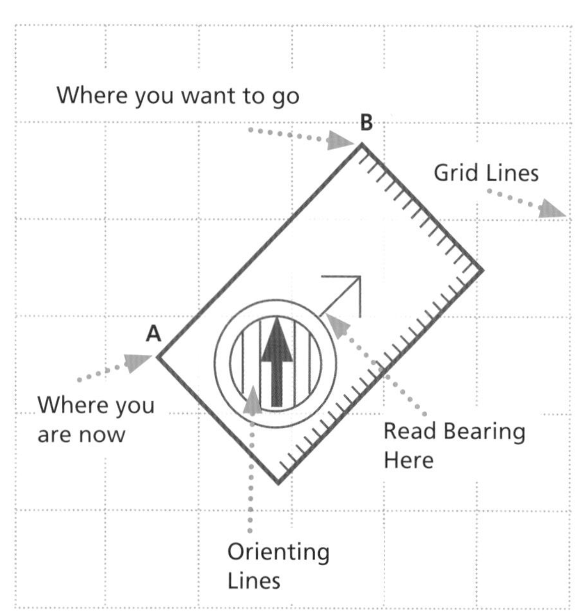

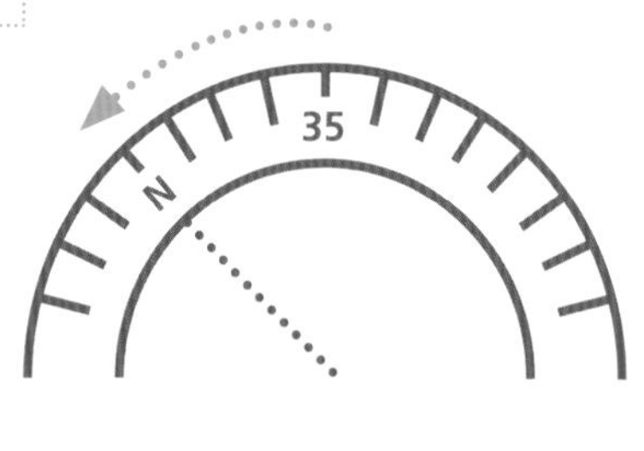

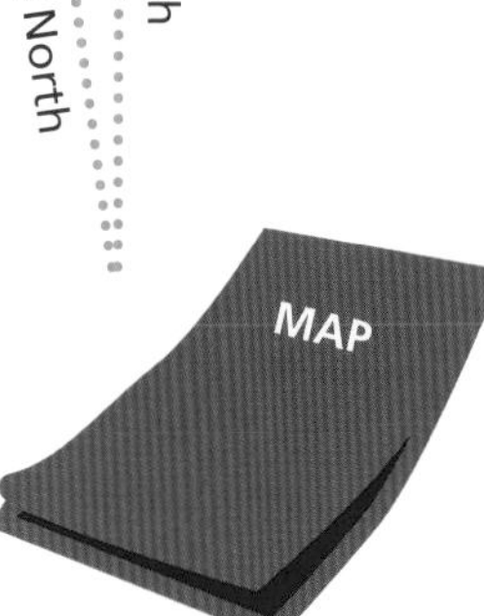

From Map to Compass
(add)

Compass to Map
subtract

NAISMITH'S RULE

This is a rule to help you to calculate the time you will take to walk a part of a journey so that you can estimate when you will arrive at a given point – your destination for example.

When you are carrying a rucksack full of food, clothes and equipment, you should always walk at the speed of the slowest member of the group.

You should aim to walk at about 3 kilometres per hour – that is one kilometre every twenty minutes. However, it is obviously harder to walk uphill than to walk on flat ground or to walk downhill. To take this into account, you should also add an extra minute for every 10 metres climbed.

So, to calculate how long you expect to take to walk for part of your journey, you should measure the distance of each part of your journey accurately and the height you climb.

Time taken = 20 minutes for every kilometre plus 1 minute for every 10 metres climbed.

Remember, you should also allow time for breaks every so often and also an hour for lunch.

ROUTE CARD

Route planning

You may be given a route to follow, or you may have to plan it all yourself. The important thing is to spend time looking at the map, reading it like a book, examining at all the footpaths, roads and hills, the names of farms and villages. If you get caught in the dark or bad weather you will benefit from remembering some of the places around you. Never draw on a map, it will ruin it for the next time it is used, but make a copy of the area you will cover and mark suggested routes in pencil.

Always plan to stay off roads as there is no enjoyment with noise and fumes for hours on end and you could easily stumble when you are tired and be hit by a vehicle. Look for footpaths that link together into an interesting route between the start and end of your journey.

When you have agreed on your route make yourself a set of laminated A4 size maps with the route highlighted. Every member should have one so all the team members can be aware of where they are all the time and take a full part in decision making. A copy of the full map should be stored safely in your pack in case you need to refer to it together with a copy of all instructions, phone numbers, camp site addresses.

Weather

Just before you go, always get a weather forecast from the television, radio or internet so that you can be prepared for the conditions you are likely to encounter.

Where to camp or stay

The most obvious place to camp would be at one of the many Scout campsites - your Leaders will know of some or you can use the internet to find one.

If you know of another site make sure your Leaders have checked it out and give their permission.

Many Youth Hostels allow you to camp and use their indoor facilities. Or maybe you would like to stay at a hostel: www.yha.org.uk

Choosing a camp site

Seeking shelter from the wind of bushes and small trees is a good idea especially when cooking. Ask the camp warden or landowner for advice, especially of areas that might become waterlogged in heavy rain.

If you are by a river, make sure it is not likely to flood your site, ask the landowner and look for signs of straw and twigs that mark a flood level.

ROUTE PLAN

(FS120409)

> To be completed in accordance with Policy, Organisation and Rules.

> Take a copy with you **and** leave a copy with a responsible local person - **cancel on return**.

Date: 3rd August			Day 1 of 2	or ~~One day~~	Map(s) Used: OL5732		
Objective: The Practical Expedition Guide					Magnetic Variation: 3° West		
Place or Grid Reference	Magnetic Bearing	Distance (km)	Height Gained (m)	Description of Route	Est. Time for Leg	Time (start)	Escape Routes
To: Jim's Farm 343 174	South 168	3.6	300	Take left path. Pass Mill Head. Ben's Mouth on right. Elgan Hill on left. Straight across at Steve's Pass at saddle. Up hill to Raise	2:30	9:00	(1) From Raise at Steve's Pass Take left hand path at Steve's Pass and descend to Millertown and follow valley path
To: Cairn 338 167	SW 212	0.9	50	Over saddle to peak	0:30	11:30	
To: Cairn at peak 343 151	South 164	1.8	150	Stick to LHS Path. Pile of stones on left. Cairn on left. Climb to peak	1:00	12:00	
				Lunch	1:00	13:00	
To: Cairn at path junction 343 144	South 176	0.8	downhill	Downhill. Ridge on left	0:20	14:00	(2) From Cairn at 343 151 Take LHS path at cairn and descend to valley path
To: Footpath / post junction 346 128	South 172	1.7	30	Pass cairn. Ridge on left. Pass Magna Pike on left	0:50	14:20	Use Naithsmith's Rule - adjusted to suit the abilities of your particular party - to calculate the estimated timings for each leg. It is usual practice to add 10 minutes per hour for a 'rest'; again adjust timings to suit your party.
To: Trundle Tarn 352 123	SE 124	1.2	downhill	Descend to Trundle Tarn. Winding path	0:50	15:10	
Totals		10	530		7:00	8:30	
Add 10 minutes per hour for safety				**...... thus estimated total journey time**		8:00	
Start Time	09:00		**Finish Time or reach Camp Site**	17:00	**Dark at**	21:30	

SCOUTS	Weather Forecast	Emergency
Scout Group	**Wind:**	**Note:**
UK Patrol	Speed/force .... becoming .... knots/mph at .... metres Direction	These notes are for those in the local area who have been handed a copy of this Route Plan. If the party fails to return by the agreed time please contact the first two listed below. If the Home Contact cannot be raised please telephone the appropriate Scout Headquarters' office.
Vehicle Registration No	**Temperature:**	
UK08 DFE	Sea level .... °C becoming .... °C at .... metres Cloud base .... metres	
Party Leader	**Outlook:** Bright and sunny, with slight chance of showers late afternoon	

	Equipment in Party	
Hannah (PL)		**Home Contact** Name Mr A McBay Address The Old Post Office, Littleton Telephone 020 1234 5678
Deputy Leader	THIS LIST IS NOT INTENDED TO BE A COMPLETE ONE OF ALL THE EQUIPMENT (BOTH PERSONAL AND COMMUNAL) BUT MORE TO GIVE OTHERS AN INDICATION OF HOW THE PARTY IS EQUIPPED SHOULD THERE BE AN EMERGENCY. ITEMS MARKED * SHOULD BE CARRIED BY EACH MEMBER OF THE PARTY [BUT REMEMBER THAT THE EXACT DETAILS OF THE EQUIPMENT WILL BE DEPENDENT UPON YOUR OBJECTIVE AND THE DURATION OF THE JOURNEY].	
Rushil (APL)		
Other Party Members	Insert numbers if appropriate:	Police – 999
Ben	..... Maps [minimum of 2] ..... Torch	**Scout Headquarters**
Hannah	..... Compasses [minimum of 2] ..... *Emergency Rations	**Duty Public Relations Officer:** Office Hours: 0845 300 1818
Charlotte	..... *Waterproofs ..... Survival Bag(s) or Tent ..... *Spare Clothing	Outside Office Hours: 020 7584 7031 **or if in Scotland:**
Cameron	..... *Whistle .... *Food/Drink [for journey]	Office Hours: 01383 419073 Outside Office Hours: 01383 412704
Darren	..... First Aid Kit ..... Sleeping Bag or Duvet ..... Watch ..... Small Stove and Utensils	**or if in Northern Ireland:** Office Hours: 028 9049 2829
Michael	..... *Emergency Card and Pencil ..... Matches [waterproof container]	Outside Office Hours: 028 9336 7302

EMERGENCY PROCEDURES

In general, the first thing you should do in most emergencies is to send for adult help. You should know before you set off on your expedition where you are going to get help at any time. You should include this information on your route card beside your escape route procedures.

Make sure that each member of the expedition is carrying their first aid kit. As part of your training, you should also know how to carry out simple first aid procedures – How to treat cuts, burns and blisters and be able to identify and treat exhaustion and hypothermia.

Cadet Direct Ltd

ESCAPE ROUTES

If something happened to someone in your group or your plans changed, for example because of bad weather, and you wanted to get help then you would just look at your map and choose a safe, quick way to get to safety. This is called an escape route.

This could simply be to return the way you came or a quick way of getting help by a different path to the nearest house or phone box. Look at your planned route, break it into sections and choose an escape route for each part.

You should also record the mobile phone number of your Leader or whoever is the agreed emergency contact for your expedition. Of course, if you have an incident that requires the assistance of the emergency services, they should be your first call.

By doing this now you can act fast if you need to when something goes wrong and it ensures that other people will know where to look for you if something goes wrong.

TREATMENT OF BLISTERS

Blisters are the number one foot ailment in hiking and they can turn the greatest hike into the most painful one. Blisters can be avoided having the correct hiking boots and hiking socks, and by early detection of possible problems.

What causes blisters?

> Heat: is the number one reason for getting blisters. The heat responsible for causing blisters is mostly caused by the friction between your skin and the inner of your boot. Sand and gravel in your boot can increase friction which is why they also cause blisters.

> Moisture: moist or wet feet from sweat or water are more susceptible to blisters as moisture softens your skin.

How to prevent blisters

Preventing blisters boils down to countering the factors that cause them. In general, keeping your feet cool, dry, and free of sand will do the trick. Here are some tips:

> First of all, select Hiking Boots with a good fit that do not chafe your feet or have painful pressure points. Choose watertight but breathable boots that give the proper ventilation that will get rid of excess moisture. Look for fully gusseted tongues that keep sand and gravel outside your boots.

> Give your feet ample rest. If you feel that your feet might be moist or overheated, it might be wise to take a longer rest where you take off your boots and socks. If you do so, you might want to change socks and dry the ones you had on. Having two pairs of socks used alternately is always a good idea to prevent blisters.

> If you decide to cool your feet in a stream or pool then make sure to dry them off well before you put on your socks and boots.

> When conditions allow it, take off your boots and socks and walk with sandals.

Early treatment of blisters

Blisters develop over a period of time and often you can already feel one coming up. Early detection and treatment is the key to preventing full grown blisters. If you feel a sore place or irritation on your foot, do the following:

> Take off your boots and socks immediately and remove any sand or gravel from your feet.

> Let your feet dry and cool down.

> Cover the sore area with surgical tape, band-aid, or even better, special blister coverings, which are an artificial skin that you can cut to shape and stick to your own skin. You can buy these in most chemists in a variety of brands and features.

> Remove the covering once you stop hiking and let the skin recover during the night. The next morning, you can judge for yourself to apply a new cover or not. In general, take precautions and apply it even if the area is only moderately irritated.

CYCLING EXPEDITIONS

As part of the expedition challenge why not choose to do your expedition by bike and also you could work towards the Cyclist Activity Badge on the way?

Most bikes nowadays are mountain bikes which are great for cycling in different terrains. The main thing that you need to consider is how to carry your equipment. The best way to do this is by panniers; these are like a rucksack but for your bike. You must not ride your bike and carry a rucksack on your back!

Remember:

> Helmets must always be worn when riding your bike, except where exemptions apply for those wearing turbans

> All bikes must be fully equipped with lights

> Cycling on footpaths and pavements is illegal

> Cyclists do have a legal right to use bridle ways but they must give way to horse riders and pedestrians

> The requirements for cycling adventures are the same as those for all other ventures; the expedition must involve travelling for a minimum of four hours on each of the two days in addition to other planned activity

> Expeditions should take place in normal rural country which is unfamiliar

> Routes may involve minor roads only and should include lanes, bridleways or unsurfaced tracks or any combination of these.

Various codes of conduct which must be looked at before you start your challenge are the Countryside Code, Highway Code, Mountain Bike Code and if you are in or cycling through Forestry Commission land a copy of their code.

You will need to learn general maintenance and repairs for your bike as all cycles must be in sound condition before beginning the expedition.

Some equipment which you will need to take with you :

> A good repair kit to carry out repairs, this should include puncture outfit, spare valve, spare inner tube, tyre levers and pump

> Spare brake blocks and brake cables

> Spare gear cables

> Spare chain links and chain tool

> Two or three spare spokes and a nipple tool

> Spanners, Allen keys, pliers and screwdrivers necessary for the above

> Some rag and a very small plastic container of 'swarfega' or liquid detergent.

A lock and chain would be useful to prevent your bike being stolen.

Front and rear lights are essential.

Footwear: there are specialist biking shoes which are available which have hard stiff narrow soles with shoe clips but these can be expensive and hiking boots or trainers with substantial soles would suffice, but must be worn in, if blisters are to be avoided!

Gloves are another useful bit of equipment, their purpose is to keep your hands warm, provide grip, prevent blisters and protect your hands if you fall.

Clothing: brightly coloured clothing should be worn which is highly visible in traffic with reflective strips.

Dressing for riding a bike is not too different from expeditions on foot and some of the same principles apply, eg layers of clothing which can be removed or added. It is essential to avoid clothing which is loose as it may cause an accident. Traditional materials such as wool or cotton will keep you cool or warm as circumstances demand. Alternatively use modern synthetics which do not absorb much water. Don't forget that your clothing will have to also be suitable around the camp in the evening or the morning when it may be chilly. Waterproof overclothing is essential.

Other personal and emergency equipment is the same as foot expeditions.

Achieving the Cyclist Activity Badge should be good training and give you good knowledge before undertaking your expedition. If you are able to, take part in a cycle training scheme offered by your school or local authority. To find out what's on offer, go to www.direct.gov.uk.

It is essential to have a good knowledge of maintenance because many things can go wrong with your bike during the expedition. Between the members of your group you should be able to do the following:

- Keep the bike clean and oiled
- Mend a puncture including removing and replacing the rear wheel
- Adjust and replace brake blocks and a worn brake cable
- Adjust the chain tension and repair a broken chain
- Adjust derailleur gears which have been knocked out of alignment and replace a snapped gear cable
- Remove and replace a broken spoke.

If you travel to school by bike that is a good start to practice for your expedition but you will need to build on that before undertaking the challenge; build up your fitness in the run up to the challenge and get used to carrying equipment as your bike is heavier and difficult to handle when fully loaded.

Packing panniers is the opposite to the principles when packing a rucksack, heavy items are placed in the bottom of the panniers so centre of gravity is kept low. Weight is also a crucial factor and must be balanced on either side of the bike. Spare clothing, sleeping bags and food must be waterproofed in plastic or polythene bags as panniers are no more water proof than rucksacks. Snacks, maps and waterproofs should be kept on top so they are accessible during breaks. Carrying a rucksack on your back will only make you unstable due to the high centre of gravity and will increase the likelihood of falling off the bike in an emergency stop. A small bum bag is useful for items needed on the route.

HORSEBACK EXPEDITIONS

These expeditions are definitely a challenge and doing your challenge by horse is not to be taken as an easy option.

Firstly to undertake a riding challenge you will need to have experience of horse riding, be able to ensure the wellbeing of the horse for the duration of the challenge and know what action to be taken if there is an accident with the horse.

Riding expeditions are the same as others and they should take place in rural country which is unfamiliar with route involving lanes, tracks and bridleways with approximately 4 hours of travelling each day.

Things to take into consideration

> The expense to hire suitable horses for your challenge.

> Horses must be familiar with the other horses in the group, as this may cause problems when they are being stabled or turned out at the end of the day.

> Horses are creatures of habit and have their own personalities, they do not take kindly to different surroundings and are capable of expressing their disapproval in a forceful way.

> Horses and ponies must be prepared and conditioned for expeditions, just as much as their riders.

For horseback expeditions camping equipment, food and items associated with the needs and care of the horses such as grooming tools and buckets may be left at the campsite but there is no reason why emergency equipment, sleeping bags and food should not be carried.

All Scouts must know the countryside and highway code - especially the elements related to riding. There is also a riding and road safety test published by the British Horse Society that contains useful information.

When planning your route in addition to the normal route an itinerary should be prepared which can be used to follow the route without the need to dismount. Using a map in the saddle can be difficult and if the map flaps around and is seen in the horse's vision, it may cause the horse to be startled.

Items and equipment needing to be carried during the day:

> Head collar and rope

> Hoof pick

> First aid equipment for the horse which should include antiseptic cream or powder, gamgee and a leg bandage

> Fly repellent

> Bailer twine to tie up gates, repair bridle, etc.

> A penknife is standard equipment.

Items which should be left at the campsite:

> Feed
> Grooming tools
> Water and feeding buckets.

All participants must wear an approved protective riding hat with safety strap which must be well fitting and securely attached so it will give protection in the event of a fall. Gloves are also recommended wear. Dress for horse riding must be suitable as for any horse riding activities, jodhpurs, boots, etc. Also choose clothing appropriate for any expedition, using layers which can be removed or added according to weather conditions and body warmth. Waterproofs must be packed, but be careful as these should not block vision, hearing or control of the horse and should not flap in the wind as this may possibly startle the horse.

Emergency equipment is the same as in any other expeditions.

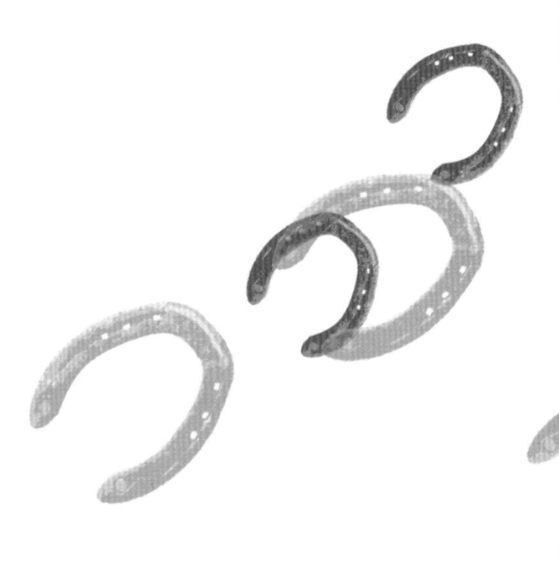

EXPEDITIONS BY WATER

An alternative for the Expedition Challenge could be to travel on the water, by canoe, pulling boat or sailing dinghy. That would also count towards one of the Nautical Skills Awards, and obviously depends on your boating skills, access to suitable waters and craft. The primary requirements of land-based expeditions still apply, as well as some extra points.

Choice of Craft - Whilst it would be possible to use single-handed boats, they are not always practical for carrying kit. Also, being on your own for a long period of time or being cramped up would probably not be much fun. Open canoes will be more suitable than kayaks, and larger sailing dinghies more suitable than small ones. If you only have access to very small craft, maybe some of your camping kit could be delivered to your campsite without reducing your feeling of independence and achievement, but that is very much a second best.

Personal Clothing - The weather makes a huge difference, and you need to plan for the worst. Many like wearing wetsuits, but for at least four hours on two days that would be rather uncomfortable. So too would wet feet, so the right footwear is important. Avoid wearing denim, as jeans are really uncomfortable when wet. Choose more suitable clothing.

Remember:

> Check with your leader the safety rules that apply

> Buoyancy aids or lifejackets are essential

> If you are paddling on moving water, canoe helmets may be suitable

> Hopefully you will not get soaked, but you are highly likely to get a little wet, so a change into dry clothes is essential at the end of each day on the water

> Hypothermia is serious, and the combination of wind and wet can speed up the onset of this substantially. A windproof top is essential and much more protection if the weather may be poor

> The fleet of craft in your expedition must stay close together, to give mutual cover, and help if necessary.

Route choice and planning

Planning your own route on unfamiliar water is all part of the challenge.

> Check charts, maps, and other publications. You may need to be briefed by someone who is a little more familiar with the waters in question, and you certainly need to have been boating on waters which are similar, to have developed your skills.

> Tides and currents are critical, making a huge difference to the distance you can travel.

> Boating with a load – your overnight kit – is normally slower. And if you are sailing, plan what you will do if the wind drops, or if it becomes too strong. You will probably need a good contingency plan, which may include some external support.

> Some experimenting in advance to see what type of speed you can average before making your final plans could be of great value.

Share the burden! By rotating round the various positions in the boat you can increase enjoyment, and possibly give everyone a bit of a break.

Access rules

Part of your training in whatever type of craft you are using will have included learning about how you usually need to get permission, or even a licence, to go afloat, or to launch craft. Do not forget this in your planning.

Capsize or falling overboard

Yes, it happens to all of us from time to time, so you must be prepared. You need an exposure bag or bivvy bag just in case things get really serious. And if your craft capsizes, not only does a group of people get wet, so does your personal and camping kit. Worse still, it might sink or float away.

> Secure all your kit in the vessel, so it will not get lost if the boat capsizes.

> Waterproof everything which must stay dry. Dry sacks are excellent for this (if a little pricey), or if there is room in your boat you can use large plastic canisters. But you can also improvise quite effectively with heavy duty plastic bags. Tie the neck securely (but with a knot which you can undo!), and then fold the neck back over itself and tie is again below the original tie, this time therefore round the doubled neck.

> You want easy access to things like drinking water, waterproof clothes, and snacks. Pack accordingly.

> You may need help, and a mobile phone might be the answer, if you have any reception. This will need packing where it will not get wet if you capsize. With appropriate training VHF radio and flares could be considered as extra safety features.

> Help or rescue could take a good while to get to some waterways, so you must have sufficient resources to look after yourselves while waiting.

Camping options

The obvious choice for most is to use normal lightweight tents, but with boats there are other options. With an open canoe you can prop it up at about 45° on one side, and use a tarpaulin to complete the shelter. In sailing craft you can improvise an awning, or even use a specially made boat tent. Camping this way can solve the problem of finding a suitable camping spot.

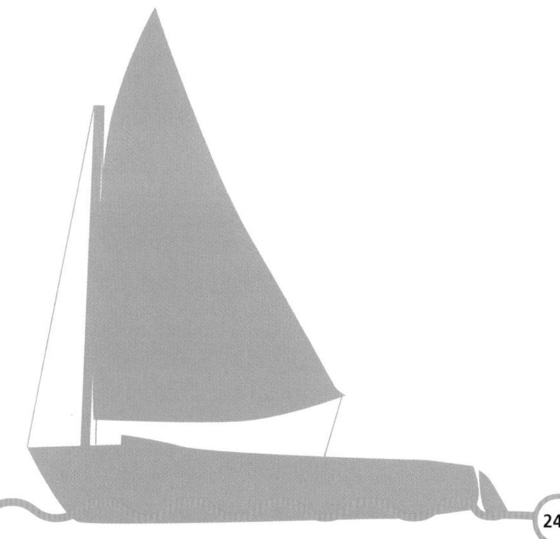

IDEAS OF PURPOSES

A journey with a purpose

All expeditions must have a clearly defined and pre-conceived purpose. A report related to the purpose of the challenge should also be produced.

> The route must be drawn around whatever the purpose is.

> The group should try and choose a purpose which is of interest to all members of the group.

> The purpose could be one of the following:

Nature: Wildlife, flowers, trees, birds, mammals

Buildings: Churches, pubs, farms, villages, houses

Environment: Footpaths, litter, pollution

Local: History, ghosts, legends, famous people, historic buildings, prehistoric standing stones, stone circles, burial grounds, battle grounds

The ideas are endless – choose one of these or think of one of your own.

You should try and prepare before you go – maybe do some research or make up some forms to fill out on your way.

It would also be useful to keep a diary of your expedition.

Present your diary and your purpose work to your Scout Leader or do a presentation at your Troop meeting or Group AGM.

You could do this as a:

> project

> tape recording

> performance (song, dance or drama)

> video

> oral presentation

> blog or website.

On your exploration you may need:

Note pad, pencil, camera, dictaphone.

BE IMAGINATIVE

IT'S YOUR EXPEDITION!

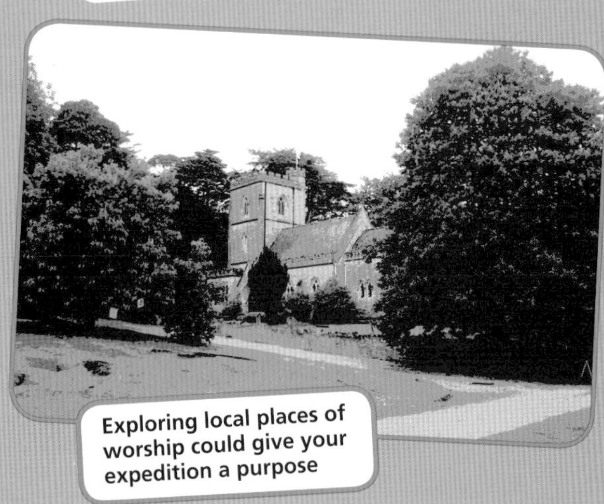

Exploring local places of worship could give your expedition a purpose

KEEPING A RECORD

It's a good idea to produce a diary, log or account of your expedition. This will help you with the presentation.

In your diary you could include your daily menu, kit list, route map and route card.

Make the diary as humorous as possible while still being factual – make your Leader laugh when they read it!

Weather reports or observations can also be included: did the heat or rain cause your group any problems?

Include group morale during the expedition – were there any low points, did the group get lost, were there any arguments? Did something funny happen along the way? What were the group's high points, like the view from the top of a hill or swimming in a stream en route?

Photographs or sketches and drawings could be included.

Also make notes of what equipment you wish you had taken and what equipment should have been left behind. Was the menu OK or would you take any different food?

Presentation

The project can be presented:

- verbally
- written
- exhibited
- taped
- online.

The form of presentation should be agreed with your leader before the expedition.

A suggested form of presentation is as follows:

- **Introduction** – explain purpose, introduce team members, dates of expedition.
- **The diary / log** – extracts can be read with copies of routes and routecards displayed.
- **The menu** – what the group ate, whether it was liked. Maybe have sample food available in the background.
- **The equipment list** – individual and group equipment to be displayed.
- **Conclusion** – did you achieve your purpose, did you enjoy it, and thank those that helped you.

Get all members of the group involved with the different sections of the presentation.

The Scout Leader will place equal importance on the diary/log and purpose as the expedition itself, so a successful walk is only half the challenge.

And don't forget plenty of photographs and use your imagination.

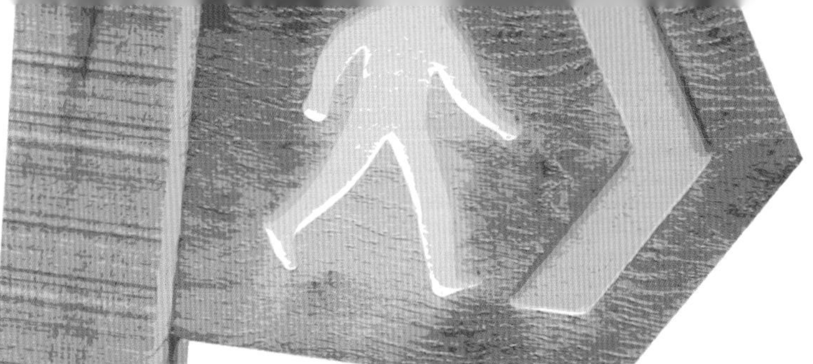

COUNTRYSIDE CODE

There are five points to the Countryside Code which you must follow when you are visiting the country.

1. Be safe - Plan ahead and follow any signs

Even when going out locally, it's best to get the latest information about where and when you can go; for example, your rights to go onto some areas of open land may be restricted while work is carried out, for safety reasons or during breeding seasons. Follow advice and local signs, and be prepared for the unexpected.

> You're responsible for your own safety. You may not see anyone for hours and there are many places without clear mobile-phone signals so as an added precaution, let someone know where you're going and when you're likely to be back.

> Check weather conditions before you leave, and don't be afraid to turn back

2. Leave gates and property as you find them

Please respect the working life of the countryside, as our actions can affect people's livelihoods, our heritage, and the safety and welfare of animals and ourselves.

> A farmer will normally leave a gate closed to keep livestock in, but may sometimes leave it open so they can reach food and water. Leave gates as you find them or follow instructions on signs. If walking in a group, make sure the last person knows how to leave the gates.

> In fields where crops are growing, follow the paths wherever possible.

> Use gates and stiles wherever possible - climbing over walls, hedges and fences can damage them and increase the risk of farm animals escaping.

> Our heritage belongs to all of us - be careful not to disturb ruins and historic sites.

> Leave machinery and livestock alone - don't interfere with animals even if you think they're in distress. Try to alert the farmer instead.

3. Protect plants and animals and take your litter home

We have a responsibility to protect our countryside now and for future generations, so make sure you don't harm animals, birds, plants or trees.

> Litter and leftover food doesn't just spoil the beauty of the countryside, it can be dangerous to wildlife and farm animals and can spread disease - so take your litter home with you. Dropping litter and dumping rubbish are criminal offences.

> Discover the beauty of the natural environment and take special care not to damage, destroy or remove features such as rocks, plants and trees. They provide homes and food for wildlife, and add to everybody's enjoyment of the countryside.

> Wild animals and farm animals can behave unpredictably if you get too close, especially if they're with their young - so give them plenty of space.

> Fires can be as devastating to wildlife and habitats as they are to people and property - so be careful not to drop a match or smouldering cigarette at any time of the year. Sometimes, controlled fires are used to manage vegetation, particularly on heaths and moors between October and early April, so please check that a fire is not supervised before calling 999.

4. Keep dogs under close control

The countryside is a great place to exercise dogs, but it's every owner's duty to make sure their dog is not a danger or nuisance to farm animals, wildlife or other people.

> By law, you must control your dog so that it does not disturb or scare farm animals or wildlife. You must keep your dog on a short lead on most areas of open country and common land between 1 March and 31 July, and at all times near farm animals.

> You do not have to put your dog on a lead on public paths as long as it is under close control. But as a general rule, keep your dog on a lead if you cannot rely on its obedience. By law, farmers are entitled to destroy a dog that injures or worries their animals.

> If a farm animal chases you and your dog, it is safer to let your dog off the lead – don't risk getting hurt by trying to protect it.

> Take particular care that your dog doesn't scare sheep and lambs or wander where it might disturb birds that nest on the ground and other wildlife – eggs and young will soon die without protection from their parents.

> Everyone knows how unpleasant dog mess is and it can cause infections – so always clean up after your dog and get rid of the mess responsibly. Also make sure your dog is wormed regularly.

5. Consider other people

Showing consideration and respect for other people makes the countryside a pleasant environment for everyone - at home, at work and at leisure.

Whether you're walking on your own or with a large group, you'll have an impact on the local environment. Follow these brief rules to make it more pleasant for visitors and locals alike.

> Busy traffic on small country roads can be unpleasant and dangerous to local people, visitors and wildlife - so slow down and, where possible, leave your vehicle at home, consider sharing lifts and use alternatives such as public transport or cycling.

> Respect the needs of local people - for example, don't block gateways, driveways or other entry points with your vehicle.

- By law, cyclists must give way to walkers and horse riders on bridleways.
- Keep out of the way when farm animals are being gathered or moved and follow directions from the farmer.
- Support the rural economy - for example, buy your supplies from local shops.

This code applies in England and is operated by Countryside Access. Variations of the code exist in Wales, Scotland and Northern Ireland, but the key principles of this code are relevant everywhere in the UK countryside.

More info:

Wales - **www.countrysidecodewales.org.uk**

Scottish Outdoor Access Code
www.outdooraccess-scotland.com

Northern Ireland - **www.countrysiderecreation.com**

ASSOCIATED ACTIVITY BADGES

Hillwalker

Meteorologist

Hikes Away (Staged)

SEA SCOUTS
SEA SCOUTS
SEA SCOUTS

12 AIR AND SEA SCOUTING

SEA SCOUTS AND AIR SCOUTS FOLLOW THE SAME PROGRAMME AND GO FOR GOLD JUST THE SAME AS ALL MEMBERS OF THE SCOUT SECTION.

They wear a different uniform, and may flavour what they do with more nautical or aviation activities. If you are an Air or Sea Scout, the following pages will explore some of the activities, skills and badges on offer, but these are all available to all Scouts, so read on!

TAKE THE PLUNGE

AND REACH NEW HEIGHTS.

AIR SCOUTS

Air Scouts is a branch of Scouting, not a separate organisation, following the same programme with an added aeronautical twist to the programme and many aviation related activities that you can undertake and participate in.

An Air Scout is recognisable by the colour of their uniform shirt of light blue and a grey beret, with an Air Scout Identification Badge to supplement the normal insignia.

Within the Balanced Programme, the Air Activity Badges cater for those with an aviation interest, especially Air Scouts, but they can be achieved by any Scout in any Troop with an active air activities-based programme.

Air Scouts start with the Scout section as part of an Air Scout Group, or sometimes as an Air Scout Patrol in a 'standard' Scout Group. Just under 60 of these Air Scout Troops are recognised by the Royal Air Force, which entitles the Air Scouts in the Group to wear an RAF Recognition badge and when opportunities allow, camp on RAF Stations and fly in service aircraft. When it's time for you as an Air Scout to move up to Explorer Scouts, you can continue as an Air Explorer Scout within the Explorer Unit.

Air Scouts officially started in 1941 although many Scout Troops near to airfields and gliding clubs started to include air activities in their programmes in the 1930's. 2006 was the 65th Anniversary of Air Scouting.

Participating in air activities as a Scout can range from high adventure gliding or powered flights, parascending and ballooning, model aircraft and rocketry to kite making and flying as well as visits to airfields. Such a wide variety of air activities and sports can be undertaken by all Scouts, although if you are an Air Scout your Troop's programme may have a higher proportion of them.

A number of Counties have made local arrangements, either with flying, gliding or parascending clubs, for you to participate in an exhilarating aviation experience of some sort. In addition, the governing bodies of the sports can give you more information. For some aviation sports (not included here), such as parachuting and hang gliding you will have to wait to be in Explorer Scouts before being allowed to undertaking them due to their rules or the law.

Ballooning

Who can fail to be excited by the sight of a majestic hot-air balloon drifting over the countryside on a balmy summer evening? There is a great feeling of peace and tranquillity around.

Balloon flying can be quite expensive when provided by a commercial operator.

However some private balloon owners are often happy to introduce groups of Scouts to their hobby and hopefully give a practical demonstration.

Preparing the balloon for flight is a lengthy operation and there is plenty of opportunity for enthusiastic Scouts to make themselves useful as part of the ballooning ground crew, especially at the increasing balloon festivals around the UK. There is equipment to move about and vast amounts of balloon fabric to hold. Also in the latter stages of inflation, ballast is needed for the basket. Post flight activity also lends itself to assistance from Scouts, which could even lead to you rescuing the balloon from a local farmer's field!

Because of the vast bulk and weight of an inflated balloon, this activity is only practical when the air is very still. This would be at first light or in the evening. A cross-country flight would last an hour or two, but obviously this is restricted by the passenger capacity of the basket. This is usually three or more, up to a vast 24 in one case. A way of flying more Scouts is for the balloon to be tethered and rise to 100 feet or so, then back down to change over passengers.

Gliding

Quietly whistling around the clouds and with the potential to fly for several hours, gliding is an exhilarating and affordable way to learn to fly. There are many gliding clubs around the UK who can offer a gliding experience flight.

The main forms of launching a glider are by winch or aero-tow. The former is generally cheaper but unless the weather is providing plenty of lift, it may be a very quick flight. Also the launch is quite dramatic and could be a little frightening if you are a nervous person.

An aero-tow will take the glider to far higher altitude, which generally gives a long flight, with the chance for you to try the controls and get a first real flying lesson.

Some gliding clubs additionally use a powered glider. This has a small motor, which is used to gain altitude and then switched off in order to fly as a glider. This glider type can also be used to extend the range on cross-country flights.

There is always a job for enthusiastic and well-disciplined Scouts to do, such as helping to retrieve gliders after landing. However there is an amount of time to be spent awaiting your turn, and airfields can be very exposed to the weather. Some gliding providers specialise in providing a Scout package, linking the Aeronautics Activity Badge with a half-day gliding experience.

Hovercrafting

Hovercrafting is the activity of riding on a small powered craft which is lifted off and flying centimetres above the ground powered and steered by large fans. Hovercrafting can take place on land or water. Sport hovercraft come in different shapes and sizes from single-seaters to being able to carry up to a whole patrol and are great fun both as a passenger experience or learning to fly!

A number of Scout Groups have built and operate their own 2-3 seater hovercraft as part of their regular Troop activities. Hovercraft plans are easily found and it is a great project activity.

For more info see **www.hovercraft.org.uk**

Parascending

Parascending is the basic tow form of Paragliding, the sport of flying canopies, originally based on parachutes – known as either 'rounds' or 'squares' – where you are towed into the air by a Land Rover or winch before gliding back down to land.

Parascending is a great team activity that gets you outdoors - and high above the earth to enjoy some marvellous views. Apart from just enjoying the flying experience, Parascenders can take part in target accuracy competitions. It is normally carried out on very large fields or airfields.

Parascending offers great scope for an air experience flight for you. First flights can be carried out towed on 100 or so metres of rope behind a Land Rover. These flights are usually with a basic round canopy and are controlled entirely by the vehicle driver.

After being towed across the field, the canopy and pilot are brought gently back to the ground. These flights will generally only be a few minutes long. Pilots may then be taught to release from a longer rope and land on their own. Flying square canopies means more forward speed and comes with more experience.

There are a number of Scout parascending teams around the UK, who as well as offering weekend courses also often attend County and International Camps providing flights to give young people their first taste of the air.

By becoming involved at a Scout Parascending Club, you can also learn to help with the launching and perhaps progressing on to be a tow 'operator' or even an instructor as you move up to Explorer Scouts.

Powered flying

Flying in a light aircraft or in a microlight is an entirely different experience from being an airline passenger. Many Scouts enjoy being in the centre of the action, often next to the pilot, during take off, flying at relatively low altitude over land and coastlines, and landing. You are briefed before take off on what to expect, the sensations of flight and safety matters, and you will likely get to see how it all works before taking off. Flying offers good opportunities for using your map reading and compass skills from a different perspective.

Most air experience flights last about 20 minutes and a number of flying organisations in the UK may be able to offer an Aero Camp Experience or a low cost or even a free 'Young Aviator' air experience flight. For Scouts with a real yearning to becoming a pilot, a number of flying scholarships are available on an annual basis from various flying organisations.

Many Scout Troops also get involved with their local flying clubs, doing various service aspects, including helping as marshals and stewards at local fly-ins and air shows.

Model flying a rocketry

Making aircraft or glider models or even rockets and flying or launching them is just as much an air activity for you as a Scout. It requires many practical and creative skills at all levels, from making and flying a simple chuck glider to launching a high-powered rocket reaching heights of thousands of meters.

For more info see **www.bmfa.org**

One of the easiest ways to learn how to fly model aircraft is to use electric Round-The-Pole (RTP) models, which is a great Troop meeting or camp activity as you can fly the models indoors or outside. This is where a model aircraft is connected by wires to a central pole and the skill is to take off, fly and land the plane using remote control skills.

If you are thinking of heading for the stars, then why not try your hand at model rocketry? Either making your own model or from kits, you can reach heights of hundreds of metres, and have fun retrieving the rocket after it has deployed its recovery chute. With a lightweight disposable camera on board you can even take your own aerial pictures!

Projects

It may be that your Troop may wish to consider being involved in air activities in some other way, such as being an active on a project with an aircraft restoration group, helping to rebuild an old aircraft or aviation facility.

Kite flying

Kite flying is a fun air activity that can be undertaken by you, your patrol or troop just about anywhere and by anyone. Kiting is an ever-growing sport with Recreational Kiting and Traction Kiting to try! Kiting can even be done with a mountain board or in a buggy for extra thrills (and spills)!

Kites can be designed with many different shapes, forms, and sizes. They can take the form of historic flat geometric designs, box kites and other aerodynamic forms, or modern sparless inflatable designs known as parafoils.

Kites were invented in Asia a long time ago for both spectacular and military purposes. Creative aerial displays at religious festivals wowed the crowds, and kites were used in battle for the delivery of messages and munitions, and for observation. By lifting an observer above the field of battle, and by using aerial photography from kites, the army could spy on their enemies.

Kites were the precursors to aircraft, and were instrumental in the development of early flying craft. Alexander Graham Bell experimented with very large man-carrying kites, as did the Wright brothers. In fact even Lord Baden-Powell was one of the first people to design and build his own man carrying kite in 1894 and eventually also obtained his pilot's licence.

Asian kite designs often emulate flying insects, birds, and other beasts, both real and mythical. The finest Chinese kites are made from split bamboo, covered with silk or other lightweight material such as polyester, and hand painted.

Modern acrobatic kites use more than one line to allow fine control of the kite's angle to the wind. This multi-line kite flying has in modern times developed into a sport, with local competitions for precision flying and for the artistic interpretation of music. For a local kite flying event near to you visit www.kitefliers.co.uk and search the calendar or visit www.thekitesociety.org.uk for some simple Kite plans for you to build.

Para-karting

Like sand yachting, para-karting is fast, fun, green and clean. An air activity sport that harnesses the power of the wind to propel you as a 'pilot' in a three-wheeled buggy using powerful 'traction' kites. Para-karting is gaining in popularity in many places around the UK and is easy to participate in.

Any large open area of ground can be used. Large fields are okay, airfields better, but the best para-karting is done on beaches where the surface is usually flatter, smoother and the wind is stronger and more consistent.

Speeds of double the speed of the wind are fairly easy to achieve so having the right safety protection is important.

Inland buggy sites are more suitable for smaller kart (buggies) which are very manoeuvrable. Beaches are more suitable for high-speed cruising (and racing) as the larger, heavier buggies require greater distances to get up to speed.

With other members of your troop you might even like to consider building your own Buggy, with designs being freely available on the Internet.

© Chris Barker

The Beaufort Scale

The internationally recognised Beaufort Scale is a general guide for kitefliers and kite surfers:

Although the Beaufort Scale extends to Force 12, flying in winds stronger than those described above are not recommended and care should be taken regarding possible changes to prevailing conditions, gusts etc. If in doubt, select a kite on the small side and cautiously test the wind at higher altitudes where it is likely to be stronger and possibly blowing in a different direction.

Beaufort Number & Description	Wind speed (mph)	Wind speed (kph)	Knots	Visual signs to look for - on land	General effect on kites and flying	Visual signs to look for - at sea
0 Calm	<1	<1	0-1	Smoke rises vertically	Kites only fly with assistance	Sea like a mirror
1 Light Air	1-3	2-5	1-3	Smoke drifts	Only suitable for light-weight kites	Ripples
2 Light Breeze	4-7	6-12	4-6	Leaves rustle, wind felt on face	Good wind for experienced fliers	Small wavelets with glassy crests
3 Gentle Breeze	8-12	13-20	7-10	Small twigs move constantly, flags flap	Excellent wind for beginners	Large wavelets, crests begin to break
4 Moderate Breeze	13-18	21-30	11-16	Dust and loose paper move. Branches move	Better for medium sized kites	Small waves, some white horses
5 Fresh Breeze	19-24	31-40	17-21	Small trees and large branches sway	Breakages can occur to larger kites	Moderate waves, many white horses
6 Strong Breeze	25-31	41-50	22-27	Large branches move. Wind whistles around wires	Limit for most fixed wing kites	Large waves, some spray
7 Near Gale	32-38	51-61	28-33	Whole trees move	Power kites only with experience	Sea mounts, foam blown in streaks

SEA SCOUTING AND WATER ACTIVITIES

Sea Scouts are first and foremost Scouts like any others, wearing the same badges, following the same programme, and with the same Promise and Law. But as a distinct branch of Scouting there are some key differences:

Sea Scouts wear a different uniform, specifically a blue jersey or a blue shirt, and in most cases, a hat.

Water activities feature strongly in their programme. Activities such as sailing, canoeing and kayaking are likely to be extended to the more traditional rowing and stern sculling.

Some nautical traditions feature in their meetings, such as hoisting an ensign to a gaff, rather than breaking a flag, and piping the 'still' and 'carry on' on the bosun's call.

The three nautical awards (Basic Nautical Skills, Nautical Skills and Advanced Nautical Skills) run concurrently within the balanced programme, and lots of other activity badges for water activities are available (see page 275).

More on features specific primarily to Sea Scouts is given later in this chapter.

WHY WATER ACTIVITIES?

The early experiences of Baden-Powell himself included many adventures on the water, in particular with his older brother Warington. Those early experiences played a major role in the value he placed on adventure.

It is easy for Scouts to get afloat, in all sorts of different boats. From early beginnings in small craft on still, sheltered water, you can progress to exciting waters, demanding boats, and challenging activities. Boating provides great opportunities for adventure in the great outdoors, for teamwork, for taking responsibility, and for developing resourcefulness and leadership skills.

Water activities information

Sea Scouts do not have a monopoly on water activities of course; all these activities are available for Scout Groups. Most Sea Scout groups will participate in more than one of these activities, and some in a great many of them.

Personal clothing and equipment

As with all adventurous activities, it is essential that you wear suitable clothing and safety equipment. Your instructors can give you more detailed guidance appropriate to your waters, expected weather and water temperature, but here is some general guidance.

Hypothermia (see the Outdoor Plus Challenge) is a serious threat outdoors, especially whenever you might get wet, and even more so where there is a combination of wind and wet, even when it does not seem a particularly cold day when you start.

Buoyancy aids or lifejackets are essential.

Canoe helmets may be suitable whenever you paddle on moving water, or where there is a risk of banging your head. This would also apply with bat polo in a swimming pools, where paddles tend to fly around wildly.

In colder weather, wet feet can change a great day into misery; wear suitable small waterproof boots – your local chandlery can advise you.

A windproof top is likely to be required for most boating in the UK climate. Do not forget the dangers of the chill factor.

Wetsuits can effectively extend the boating season by increasing the time you can manage when in the water, and indeed when back in your boat again. You may well want to wear a waterproof (windproof) over the top. Dry suits are better still, but very much more expensive.

Dinghy sailing

Capturing the power of the wind to move about the water can be very exhilarating. There is huge variety in the type of boats you can use, the types of water you sail on, and the activity you do on the water. A sheltered stretch of inland water can make an excellent starting place, but you are likely to want to progress into sailing in stronger winds, perhaps in river estuaries. You may enjoy simply sailing around, passage making, or even sailing overnight journeys.

There are hazards in all adventurous activities, so you must receive proper guidance, training and supervision to progress safely, and Scouts must of course follow Scouting's activity rules.

A traditional way of learning to sail is to go out in a fairly large sailing dinghy with an experienced helm. Lots of enjoyment can be had, and lots of good practice learnt. Wayfarers and Bosuns in particular are used by many Scout Troops for two-handed sailing. The Sea Scout Dinghy (Coypu) can also be rigged for sailing, and the Home Counties gig – a Scout-designed open boat of about 6 metres – makes for great experiences.

The more recent trend has been for formal teaching based on the training schemes of the Royal Yachting Association (RYA), the national governing body for dinghy sailing. This is probably more likely to start in smaller dinghies, such as Toppers or Picos. Scouts who like lots of action are probably more likely to prefer this way. A mixture of formal and informal training, and of sailing in large and small craft can be great fun.

If your Group does not have its own facilities, there are many Scout centres, local authorities, sailing clubs and commercial establishments offering great opportunities.

Kayaking and canoeing

The simple difference between a kayak and a canoe is that kayaks are normally for one paddler with a covered deck, whereas canoes seat more than one paddler and have an open deck. Kayaks require a double-bladed paddle, and canoes use a single blade.

Most start their paddling on calm waters, and then progress to gently moving water, and then for those who want, on to wilder waters. The sport embraces slalom and playboat activity, where you test yourself around obstacle courses or through turbulent waters, journeying and boatpacking, and sprint paddling.

Whilst kayaking is an individual sport, these activities are always done in groups of at least three, and teamwork is an important feature, from launching to recovery, including rescue and mutual help.

The Canoeist Activity Badge allows you to master the basic strokes, and you can then progress to with a PLUS badge and become a proficient paddler in wild waters. The British Canoe Union (BCU) is the governing body for the sport, and has its own award scheme.

Rowing, pulling and stern sculling

These activities are common, and greatly valued in Scouting, but rather unusual in other walks of life. Some clubs use very different types of craft, with sliding seats, and two, four or eight oars. Fewer Scout Groups are involved in this form of rowing.

Pulling is great for having fun on the water, for gaining an understanding of the behaviour of small craft, for fitness training and teamwork, just like the other water activities.

Basic dinghy rowing is sometimes used by yachtsmen for handling tenders, small boats used for getting from moorings to the shore.

Offshore sailing

In this activity you live on a larger sailing vessel, from six metres up to the great tall ships. The essential sailing skills and teamwork are complemented by living aboard, coping sometimes with tough conditions, and making exciting, overseas passages. To experience offshore sailing, you are most likely to get access through one of the Scout offshore sailing providers, eg The Discovery Sailing Project (www.dsp.uk.com) and Adventures Offshore (www.adventuresoffshore.co.uk)

If you have the services of qualified and approved adults to run such activities, chartering vessels is always an option, albeit rather expensive. Many young people make up the crews of tall ships and other nationally and internationally run opportunities. You can find loads of opportunities through the Association of Sea Training Organisations (ASTO). You will find the gateway to masses of opportunities at www.asto.org.uk

Powerboating

Without doubt, Scouts who get opportunities to handle powerboats get a real buzz from doing so, whether it is helming a workboat on sheltered waters, or a high speed rib. The RYA is the national governing body for this activity, responsible for the national award schemes.

Windsurfing

Modern boards designed for basic training have come on in leaps and bounds making this activity easy to start, but beginners are bound to find themselves swimming rather more than zooming along on their boards to start with! It takes a little more perseverance to get the basics than with most other small boat handling, but with good equipment and instruction you should quickly find yourself getting some real thrills.

Again, the RYA is the NGB for this activity, and offer an excellent award scheme. Of interest too could be the T15 regional windsurfing championships, a great, all-comers' competition for under-15s.

Boatpacking

You will not find the word in the dictionary, but you will find Scouts doing this. Just as you can load your back with the survival equipment for a night, away camping, so you can do the same in all sorts of boats.

This could be in a fleet of kayaks, although the trend towards short playboats may make this challenging. But open canoes are great, so too pulling boats and larger sailing craft such as Wayfarers. You might take tents with you, or shelter in the boats, or possibly under them. The feeling of independence and self-sufficiency, achievement and fellowship, make the effort most worthwhile.

All the obvious requirements as for backpacking are essential – training, equipment, route planning, tide and weather checks, appropriate supervision, and the activity rules of The Scout Association.

Dragon boating

A great fun activity, popular at some activity centres as you can get lots of people afloat simultaneously.

Model boat building

Many young people really enjoy model making, some enhancing their models with radio controls. Build model powerboats or sailing craft and just like all the other activities, achievement here can count towards other Scout awards.

Radio communications

The use of PMRs (Private Mobile Radios) can be very useful for group activities afloat, although you need to practise using them to gain the necessary proficiency in their use to avoid confusion. Scout Groups can obtain the necessary licence from Scout Headquarters for a small charge.

You need a proper operator's licence to use marine radio afloat other than under the direct supervision of a suitably qualified adult.

Other water activities

This list is not exhaustive, but it does include the more popular water activities in Scouting. Scouts may include other water activities, just occasionally or quite regularly, such as sub aqua, water skiing, jet skiing, or water polo.

There are many water activities to learn more about on the A to Z Directory of Activities at www.scouts.org.uk/activities

ON THE WATER, IN THE WATER

A full boating programme can usefully be complemented by personal training in swimming, lifesaving, survival skills, marine radio procedures, and emergency aid.

Swimming pool activities

Defeat the winter blues and develop your water confidence in swimming pools! It is not always easy, or cheap, to get access to swimming pools, but there is a lot more than basic swimming you can do if it can be set up. Such activities are great fun, great for confidence building, and great for specific skills training. But don't forget, swimming pool practice is preparation for doing the real thing outdoors.

Kayaking skills

But it need not stop there; introductory kayak paddling skills and games can be practised very effectively in swimming pools, when the outdoor conditions may not be suitable or pleasant for the less experienced.

The more advanced skills of kayak rolling are also most effectively learnt in a swimming pool, where the instructor can teach you the hip flick, and be in the water to work the paddle with you as you develop the technique.

Staying afloat

It is also a good idea to practice being in the water wearing a buoyancy aid or lifejacket. This activity can be developed to practising the HELP and HUDDLE positions.

Access to water

Regular access to water, be it a river, canal, estuary, lake, or the sea, is a primary requirement for any Sea Scout Group. Some lucky Groups have a headquarters building adjacent to suitable water. Others make use of places with public access, sailing clubs, canoeing clubs, campsites, local authority facilities, and activity centres.

Local waters are unlikely to be suitable for the full range of water activities you might want to do, so you may have to look further.

National directory of waters

The Scout Association classifies all waters in the UK, and your Leaders will need to check what qualifications are needed to run Scouting activities on any particular stretch of water. You can find details at www.scouts.org.uk/waterways

RYA recognition and BCU certification

Some Sea Scout Groups, Districts, Counties, and Scout Activity Centres are recognised by the RYA as training centres, and can issue the national certificates. Likewise, lots are also able to issue BCU certificates. Search out your local facilities.

SPECIAL FEATURES OF SEA SCOUT GROUPS

The activities above can be included in the programme of any Scout Group, although Sea Scouts will probably include lots of them in their regular programmes. But there are some features beyond including lots of water activities in their programmes which really do apply more specifically just to Sea Scouts.

Ceremonial

The colours ceremony at the start of meetings and events, and the sunset ceremony at the end, are conducted using a red ensign rather than a Union Jack. You never break an ensign, you simply hoist it with dignity, and not to the masthead, but to a gaff (which may not always be practical in a small Scout meeting place).

There are slight variations in the details of proceedings, but this is typical, and good practice. When the Duty Patrol Leader is ready the hoist the ensign, the still is sounded on a bosun's call, and the Troop salutes. When the ensign is secured, the PL salutes, the carry on is piped, and the salute is ended.

Sea Scout Salute

By convention, most Sea Scout groups adjust the Scout salute just a little, to make it more consistent with naval tradition. The hand is kept horizontal, shortest way up, shortest way down.

Bosun's Call

Piping the call looks, and sounds easy, but you will need to practise. For the most part just two notes are made, a high one, and a low one.

Tying a cap tally band

The tally bands for Sea Scouts caps come separately, so they have to be tied on. You may need to practice with some old ribbon before using your expensive tally band.

Centre the cap tally with the first 'S' of Scouts directly below the front seam of the cap. At the left hand seam of the cap, tie an overhand knot making sure that the tally does not move.

Form a bight by bending over the upper tail and folding it back on itself

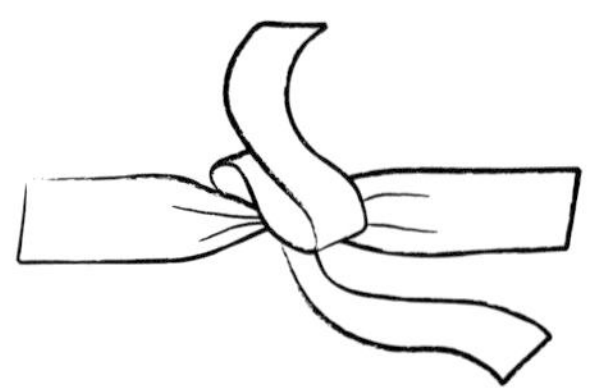

Take the lower tail and pass it under and then over this bight such that the tails end up next to each other.

A bight is now formed in the right hand tail and should be tucked behind the first bight just before the centre of the bow.

Carefully tighten the knot, being careful to ensure that the bows are of the same length and are not too long.

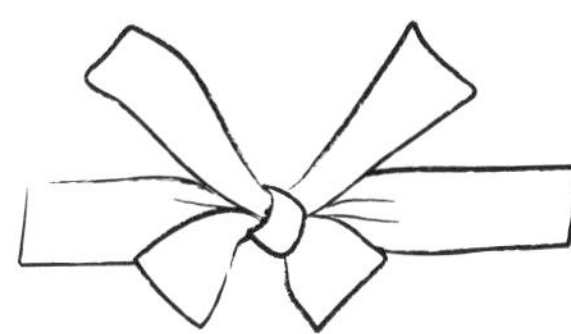

The tails can now be cut to the same length as the bows with the ends being trimmed at an angle.

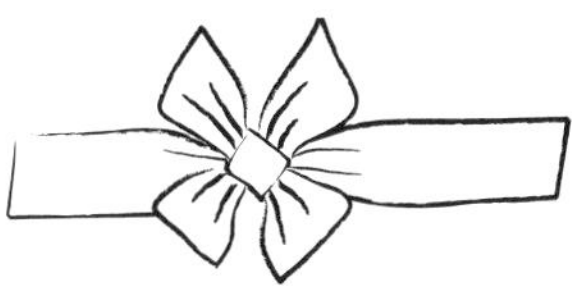

RN Recognition

There are nearly 400 Sea Scout Groups, and 101 of these are recognised by the Royal Navy. They have a formal inspection by the Navy about once every eighteen months. These groups also enjoy a number of privileges: Leaders, Explorer Scouts, Scouts and Cubs wear the Royal Navy Recognition Badge, Groups fly a special defaced Red Ensign, and they are eligible to attend three annual events for Scouts: a Summer Camp, Soccer Sixes and a Swimming Gala. All of these take place at Royal Navy premises, and the Scouts get to sleep onboard a Naval ship.

They are also eligible to use the Navy's facilities, to visit Portsmouth Heritage area attractions at heavily discounted rates, and apply for funding to purchase boats or go through training for activity qualifications.

Glossary

Colours opening ceremony

Gaff part of a ship's mast to which the flag is hoisted

Ensign flag used on ships. The Red Ensign is used by Sea Scout Groups

Bosun's call a pipe used on ships to pass commands

Still alert

Carry on at ease

Tally band band tied to a cap, bearing the words Sea Scouts

ASSOCIATED ACTIVITY BADGES (AIR ACTIVITIES)

Basic Aviation Skill

Air Spotter

Aviation Skills

Astronautics

Advanced Aviation Skills

Astronomer

Aeronautics

Meteorologist

Air Researcher

Parascending

ASSOCIATED ACTIVITY BADGES (WATER ACTIVITIES)

Basic Nautical Skills

Dragon Boating

Nautical Skills

Lifesaver

Advanced Nautical Skills

Power Coxswain

Canoeist

Pulling

Dinghy Sailor

Water Sports

JESSOPS
PHOENIX

'Although the Chief Scout's Gold Award is got by doing Challenges, it doesn't stop there. If you want, you can show your skills in loads of activities, from astronomy to yachting and gain activity badges for these.'

Michael

'I enjoyed the Photographer Activity Badge so much, I'm now working towards the Photographer PLUS.'

Hannah

- Participation Awards
- Partnership Awards
- Activity Instructor
- Activity PLUS
- Position of badges on uniform

FIND OUT ABOUT OTHER AWARDS...

PARTICIPATION AWARDS

These badges are awarded to celebrate a young person's commitment to Scouting and for taking an active part in the Programme. If the young person has already been a Member, the badges will continue from the previous Sections. For those Scouts who have been a Beaver Scout or Cub Scout, you will need to liaise with their Leaders to check the date of the last award. The Participation Badges are numbered. You can award a Participation Badge every twelve months from the time the Scout joins your Troop, up to a maximum of four badges.

PARTNERSHIP AWARDS

These awards encourage your Troop to link up with another Section within your Scout Group, or a Troop in another Group, or another youth group or organisation, to work on a project that will help other people.

There are three awards:

> Faith
> Environment
> International Friendship

The criteria for the awards can be found in your *Scout Badge Book*.

ACTIVITY INSTRUCTOR

Instructor Badges can be achieved for almost all Activity Badges in the Scout Section.

The requirements are as follows:

1. Hold the Activity Badges
2. Have knowledge of the Activity Badge requirements, sufficient to enable them to instruct a Scout in that Subject.
3. Attend a training course covering the technical skills involved in the Activity Badge and the use of appropriate training methods.
4. Assist with the training of Scouts in the subject over a period of at least three months.

Notes

1. Requirements 1, 2 and 3 must be completed before a Scout can begin requirement 4.
2. For those subjects that do not have a recognised technical skill course, an individual training programme can be arranged with a suitable qualified instructor.
3. The gaining of certain external instructor awards eg St John Ambulance, Royal Lifesaving Society, National Cycling Proficiency Scheme automatically qualifies the Scout for the appropriate Instructor Badge.
4. A Scout who has already gained an Instructor Badge may be exempt from the training methods section of the third requirement.
5. It may not be possible to gain an Instructor Badge in some areas such as paragliding, where there are clear age restrictions.

'When you get good at an activity, it's great. But when you're able to show other Scouts how to do it, that's something else.'

Darren

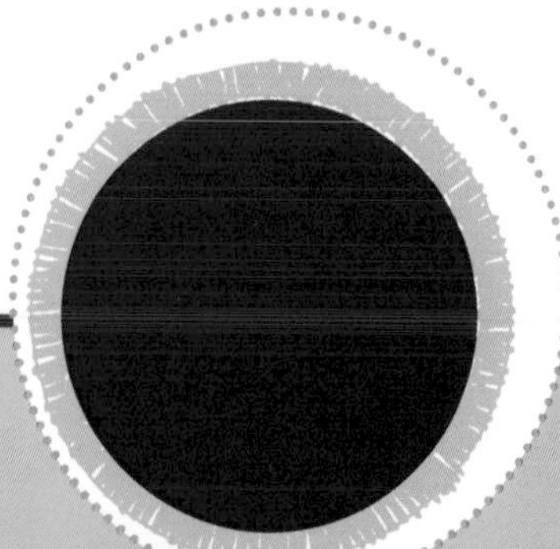

ACTIVITY PLUS

Activity PLUS badges can be awarded if you develop your skills or knowledge to a higher level than the Activity Badge. It should represent a significant achievement, taking into account your abilities and the nature of the activity, as well as local facilities.

Complete the requirements below:

1. Hold the relevant Activity Badge.
2. Take part in further training in the activity, in order to develop the your skills.
3. Agree a target with the Troop Leadership Team before seeking to gain a PLUS badge. The target should develop your skills further.

Examples of appropriate targets are:

a. For the Canoeist PLUS, achieve the BCU Two Star Award

b. For the Cyclist PLUS service the bikes of all the members of your Patrol, and carry out a longer cycle ride

c. For the Meteorologist PLUS, keep a weather diary for an agreed number of months

d. For the Dragon Boating PLUS, train for a month as part of a team to compete in a National Dragon Boat Competition

4. Achieve the target to the satisfaction of the Troop Leadership Team.

Note: POR and relevant Activity Factsheets should be referred to where appropriate.

A PLUS badge can be awarded for any Activity Badge, apart from the following:

Any Staged Activity Badge

Basic Aviation skills

Aviation Skills

Advanced Aviation Skills

Basic Nautical skills

Nautical Skills

Advanced Nautical Skills

13
OTHER AWARDS

POSITION OF BADGES ON UNIFORM

Group Badge
(if worn on back of scarf)
Occasional Badges
Union Flag
Moving-On Award
Gallantry/Meritorious Conduct Awards
Participation Awards
Scouts logo
Group Name Tape
Activity Badges
County/Area Badge
The Membership Badge
District Badge
Group Badge
(if not worn on back of scarf)
Challenge Badges
Patrol
Chief Scout's Award
Leadership Stripe
Partnership Awards

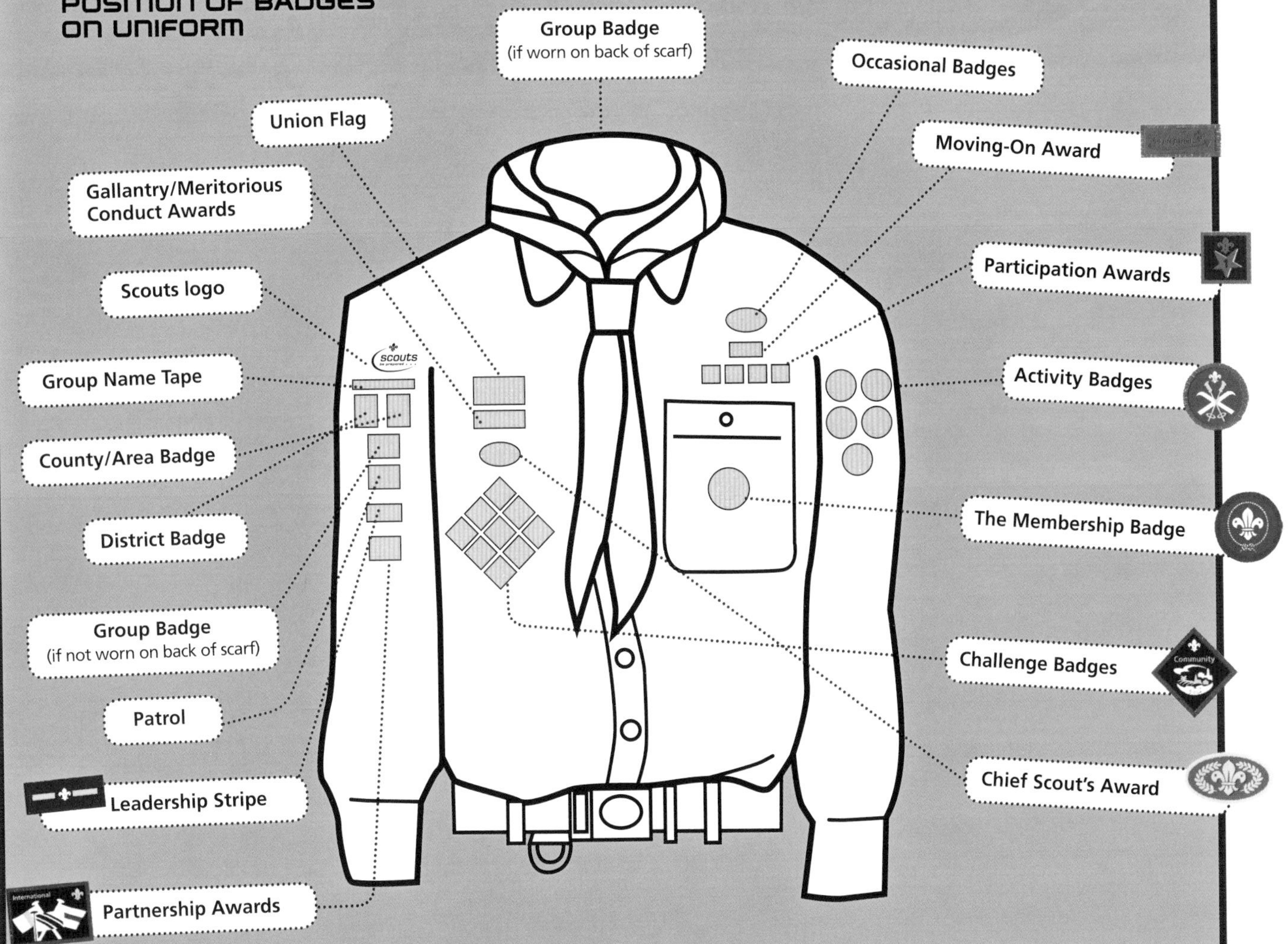

'Scouts has empowered me to make decisions and be more independent. When adults say young people can't be trusted, I can point to ten examples when I've been given the chance to take the lead, and succeeded.'
Rushil

14 LEADERSHIP

'It's not just Patrol Leaders and Young Leaders who get the chance to learn leadership skills in Scouts. Any Scout of any age will learn the practical skills to lead a team, whether that's in a game or on the leg of a hike.'

Hannah

TAKE THE OPPORTUNITY AND DEVELOP YOUR LEADERSHIP SKILLS!

INTRODUCTION TO LEADERSHIP

The word leader is used in many different places in Scouting.

> There's the adult leader (or leaders) who run the Scout Troop.

> There may be Young Leaders, who are Explorer Scouts undertaking a period of service with your Scout Troop.

> You may have Patrol Leaders and Assistant Patrol Leaders in your Troop (and possibly a Senior Patrol Leader too!).

One of the biggest opportunities in Scouting is being able to develop your leadership skills. You don't have to be one of the leaders mentioned above to be able to do this. From time to time there will be opportunities for you to lead others both within and outside of Scouting.

You might have already had experience of being a leader. If you were a Cub Scout you could have led your Six as a Sixer. If you take part in competitive sports you may have been selected as the team captain.

In the Scout Troop there are often opportunities that occur and need someone to take the lead. In many situations these opportunities will be undertaken by older Scouts who may already be Patrol Leaders. But opportunities for developing leadership potential are available to all Scouts.

The term 'leadership' can be used at different times to mean different things to different people. It could mean leading an activity during a Troop meeting or leading a group of Scouts on a hike or camp. These activities could be led by adults, Explorer Scouts or Scouts.

Whoever leads an activity needs to consider three main things:

> The individuals

> The team

> The task.

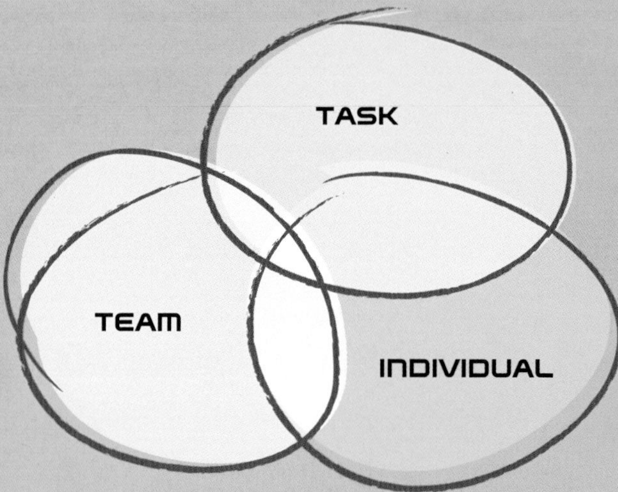

As the leader of an activity, you will need to make sure that every individual is involved and making use of their strengths. There may be one person who has difficulty with a particular task. It will be the leader's job to try and help this person.

You will also want to encourage the team to work together. There is a really good acronym to help us remember the importance of teamwork – T.E.A.M.

TOGETHER EVERYONE ACHIEVES MORE

Imagine a football team in which everyone was running about doing their own thing. They wouldn't score many goals!

This leads us to consider the task and the goals that we are trying to achieve. That task might be to put up a tent or to carry out a conservation project. We should make sure that we are clear about our objectives and our success criteria (how will we know that we have achieved our task?).

The leader's job is to make sure that the needs of all individuals are taken into account, the team works together and the task is achieved. Ignoring one of the areas or focussing too much on another will affect the end result. It's a balancing act and this can sometimes be quite a challenge – but you do get better at it the more opportunities you have of leading.

So what should we expect of our leaders – and what would other people expect of you when you are given the opportunity of leading?

A leader should:

> Set an example

> Be able to work with others

> Listen to other people's ideas

> Help people solve problems

> Accept responsibility

> Delegate and share tasks

> Have good self-control.

There may be other qualities that you think a leader should possess. Developing your leadership potential within Scouting will also help you to apply these skills outside of Scouting too.

Can you think of a leader that you admire in your local, national or international community? What makes them a good leader?

Styles of leadership

Leaders have different ways of leading – we call them styles of leadership.

Sometimes a leader needs to be directive. A leader may have to be directive when there is an important task to be completed, perhaps a matter of safety for the leader and his or her team.

A democratic leader offers advice and support to the team, but the team members share in the planning and decide what to do.

At other times a leader may lead in a very quiet way. Sometimes this is called 'leading from the back' and is an informal style of leadership. This might be to make a decision to let someone else, who has the experience and expertise, to do the leading.

There is no 'right' or 'wrong' style of leadership. There may be times when one style is more appropriate than another, and a good leader will decide which style to adopt for any specific purpose.

'Never doubt that a small group of thoughtful, committed citizens can change the world. Indeed, it's the only thing that ever has.'

Margaret Mead

LEADERSHIP STRIPES

There are three badges in the Scout Section to recognise leadership.

A Scout who takes on a leadership role in the Troop can be awarded one of these badges.

One Leadership Stripe

This is usually awarded to Assistant Patrol Leaders, or Scouts who have taken on responsibility for a particular aspect of Troop life.

Two Leadership Stripes

This badge is usually awarded to Patrol Leaders, or Scouts who have significant responsibility for an aspect of Troop life, such as chairing a Forum.

Three Leadership Stripes

This is usually awarded to Senior Patrol Leaders who provide direct support to the leadership team. They may or may not be responsible for a Patrol, but they will be making a significant contribution to the life of the Troop, perhaps through the Troop Leadership Forum.

Finding out more about leadership

There is a resource available from the Scout Information Centre called 'Scouts...Taking the Lead'. It is primarily a resource for Adult Leaders to use in developing the knowledge, skills and attitudes of young people as they take on additional responsibility in the Troop.

As you get towards the end of your time in Scouts, you may like to consider whether you would like to become a Young Leader when you move on to Explorer Scouts. You can discuss this with your Scout Leader who will put you in contact with your District Young Leaders' Unit.

TAKING THE LEAD!

be prepared...

15 Moving On

'There's a bit more freedom at Explorer meetings. Now I'm at the end of Scouts I feel like I can do more, and Explorers gives you the opportunities to make more decisions. I was at a meeting recently where the Explorers were asked what they wanted to do in the programme. We came up with ideas, and the Leaders can just say yes or no. Then we try to organise the events we've come up with. It's a challenge, but that's exactly what I joined for… it's good.'

Hannah

REQUIREMENTS

The requirements for the Moving-On Award are:

- Check that you are registered with your District Explorer Scout Administrator.
- Talk with your Scout Leader about the options available in Scouting.
- Take part in three activities that are of interest to you with the Unit or Units.
- Talk to the Leaders of the Units that are of interest to you.

EXPLORER SCOUTING – YOUR NEW ADVENTURE

All through your time as a member of the Scout Troop you will probably have seen Explorer Scouts taking part in various activities – international expeditions, karting, climbing as well as joining in with Troop activities from time to time.

Once you are about the age of 14 (and definitely before you are fourteen and a half) you have come to the end of the Scout section and it is time for you to have a go at new things and take the skills that you have learned in the Troop to the next level. The core age for the Explorer Scout Section is 14 to 18 years old and it is based around the same building blocks as the Scout programme. Although some of the things that you will do in the Unit will be similar to Troop activities, you will have the chance to take things you have enjoyed even further and have new experiences.

When you join the Explorer Scout Unit you will also notice that you will be able to have a bigger say in the activities you do and the chance to lead many of them. If there is something that you can organise, perhaps something you have already enjoyed doing, why not offer to run it? Of course – you can offer to run something you have never done before and have always wanted to do!!

You will find that because there are more people who have had a variety of different Scouting experiences, there will be a greater range of activities on offer and there will be more freedom of choice in what you can take part in and who you do these activities with. Explorer Scouts is your chance to meet new people and make more friends.

As you have come up through the Scout Group, you may have met a few Explorer Scouts who are Young Leaders. If it interests you, you too will have the chance to help with a Beaver Colony, Cub Pack or a Scout Troop through the Young Leaders' Scheme.

The top award in Explorer Scout section is the Queen's Scout Award, which is also the highest award anyone can achieve through any of the five sections in Scouting. There is also the opportunity to gain the Chief Scout's Platinum and Diamond Awards. The Duke of Edinburgh's Award will also be available to you.

THE MOVING-ON AWARD

To help you to move on to Explorer Scouts successfully, the Moving-On Award has a few steps.

The requirements for the Moving-On Award are:

- Check that you are registered with your District Explorer Scout Administrator.
- Talk with your Scout Leader about the options available in Scouting.
- Take part in three activities that are of interest to you with the Unit or Units.
- Talk to the Leaders of the Units that are of interest to you.

In principle, your first step should be to talk to your Scout Leader to find out where and when your District Explorer Scout Units meet. Another good source of information about local Explorer Scouting would be a Young Leader in your Troop if there is one. It is an excellent idea to move up to Explorer Scouts with some friends of the same age if you can. Your Scout Leader will be able to help you to make contact with the Explorer Scout Leader of your local Unit, who will be able to give you an idea of the Unit's programme of activities for the next few weeks.

Take part, have fun, make friends and enjoy!

INDEX

Acknowledgements

Edited by Alasdair McBay and Elis Matthews

Contributors:

The UK Patrol, Gillian Barratt, Catherine Cooper, Andrew Corrie, Simon Corrigan, Dave Griffiths, Dean Harding, Dave Hopley, Jonathan Jones, Eddie Langdown, Chris McCann, Chris Nagle, Kenneth Robertson, Charlie Roper, Chris Shaw, Louise Slee, Alec Stanworth, David Sturdee, Linda Thelwell, Stuart Walton

Thanks to:

3rd Sevenoaks Scouts, 4th Harrow Scouts, 12th Warrington East Scouts, 22nd Southgate Scouts, Blair Atholl International Jamborette

Sue Burton, Juultje Holla, John Kennedy, Katie McCreadie, Bob Simpson, Mark Tuddenham, Andrew Wright

And the many other staff and volunteers who have contributed to this resource.

Photography by:

Allan Baxter
Norman West
Patrick West
Simon Corrigan
Bertie Downard

Designed by:

Julia Weiss for Cavendish Design & Advertising